SCENE DESIGN
FOR STAGE
AND SCREEN

Scene Design
for Stage
and Screen

Readings on the Aesthetics and Methodology of
Scene Design for Drama, Opera, Musical
Comedy, Ballet, Motion Pictures,
Television and Arena Theatre

Edited and Introduced by
ORVILLE K. LARSON
Department of Speech
University of Massachusetts

GREENWOOD PRESS, PUBLISHERS
WESTPORT, CONNECTICUT

Library of Congress Cataloging in Publication Data

Larson, Orville Kurth, 1914-   ed.
    Scene design for stage and screen.

    Reprint of the ed. published by Michigan State
University Press, East Lansing.
      1.   Theaters--Stage-setting and scenery.   I.   Ti-
tle.
[PN2091.S8L29   1976]   792'.025   76-10460
ISBN 0-8371-8320-0

To My Mother

Originally published in 1961 by Michigan State University
Press, East Lansing

Reprinted with the permission of Michigan State University Press

Reprinted in 1976 by Greenwood Press,
a division of Williamhouse-Regency Inc.

Library of Congress Catalog Card Number 76-10460

ISBN 0-8371-8320-0

Printed in the United States of America

Table of Contents

Table of Contents

ACKNOWLEDGEMENTS

I am indebted to the authors of these readings who wrote articles especially for this anthology.

I am grateful to Cecil Palmer and Company, Duell, Sloane and Pearce, The University of California Press, and Theatre Arts Books, the periodicals AMERICAN ARTIST, THE HOLLYWOOD QUARTERLY, SATURDAY REVIEW OF LITERATURE, and THEATRE ARTS, and the NEW YORK TIMES for permission to reprint selections.

Mr. Gil Odun, Curator of Theatrical Art, Detroit Institute of Art, the Italian architects, Guido Frette and Carlo Emilo Rava, G. G. Gorlich, publisher of PROSPETTIVE, and Mrs. Mary Hall Furber and the Robert Edmond Jones estate have my thanks for helping me gather materials.

A portion of a grant from the All-University Research Council of Michigan State University assisted in preparing the manuscript.

And finally, I wish to thank all the designers who helped, in one way or another, in the preparation of this anthology.

ORVILLE K. LARSON

INTRODUCTION

Until fifty years ago, a theatre scene designer was an architect or painter. Scene design was a side line. A setting was not integrated with the other elements of the production; it was a thing apart, a handsome or startling background for action, something to be admired for its own sake. Not until he adopted the organic theory of production did the scene designer become an artist in his own right, devoting himself exclusively to the theatre.

The organic theory of production, developed in Europe just prior to World War I, fuses all elements of production into an artistic whole in accordance with the demands of the script to bring the play to its greatest realization. The theory had a strong impact on America. Books and articles by Gordon Craig and Adolphe Appia, the importations of Granville-Barker's productions of Shakespeare and Shaw and Max Reinhardt's oriental pantomime, *Sumurun,* Samuel J. Hume's exhibition of scene design in Cambridge, and Joseph Urban's settings for the Boston Opera, all reflected its influence.

The first organizations to adopt the theory in this country were the non-professional art theatres, The Washington Square Players, Provincetown Players, the Toy Theatre of Boston, and The Little Theatre of Chicago. Theatre critics have honored the artists who designed the settings for these groups, crediting them with establishing the new stagecraft in America, but the facts are otherwise. No designer for art theatres, except Lee Simonson, significantly influenced the American theatre, and Simonson did so only after he began to work for the professional Theatre Guild.

Introduction

It was Robert Edmond Jones[1] who, with his designs for *The Man Who Married A Dumb Wife* (1915), *The Devil's Garden* (1915),[2] *Redemption* (1918), *The Jest* (1919), and *Richard III* (1920), did the most toward founding the new stagecraft in America. No one has written more eloquently about his craft; in his lucid way, Jones reveals the kind of thinking imperative for scene design. He declares that "scenery isn't there to be looked at, it's really there to be forgotten,"[3] now a fundamental principle of American scene design. Moreover, he says, a good setting is not a picture, but an image. "Everything that is actual must undergo a strange metamorphosis, a kind of sea-change before it can become truth in the theatre. . . . It is something seen but it is something conveyed as well, a feeling, *an evocation.* . . . It is a presence, a mood, a warm wind fanning the drama to flame."[4] He censors the producers who tried to perpetuate the European practice of commissioning fine artists to design scenery, painter-decorators who use "masses of color to hold the eye and dazzle the brain but which were not in keeping with the playwright's vision."[5] Criticism that American scene designers are wholly eclectic and that there are no "schools of design" attest to the degree to which American designers have embraced Jones' ideas; indictments of the plight of the easel painter in America, such as Eugene Berman's, indicate his influence.

When the Washington Square Players reorganized into The Theatre Guild in 1919, Lee Simonson, who had occasionally designed settings for the Players, became its chief designer. The fullest explanation of Simonson's theory of

[1] Who worked only in the professional theatre.

[2] In collaboration with director-producer Arthur Hopkins.

[3] "The Future Decorative Art of the Theatre," *The Theatre*, May, 1917, 266.

[4] "Art in the Theatre," *The Dramatic Imagination*, New York, 1941, 29.

[5] "The Future Decorative Art . . . ," *op. cit.*

scene design appeared in 1932 in *The Stage Is Set.* Like Jones, Simonson declares that a setting is only as important as the play. Scene design cannot be divorced from the production it serves. Simonson also explains that the successful designer must be a technician as well as an artist. A paramount problem is the shifting of scenery. The way that scenes are shifted can affect the direction and ultimately the interpretation of the play because it can control the size and shape of the ground plan of the setting. The ground plan forces the actor into certain patterns of movement, and inasmuch as movement has meaning on the stage, the setting can thus reveal and intensify the meaning of the play. [Thus, "a setting can establish a dynamic relationship between the immobile setting," and "a stage setting may best be defined as a plan of action."[6]]

Norman Bel Geddes made his debut on Broadway almost at the same time as Lee Simonson. Like Robert Edmond Jones, Bel Geddes was an independent designer. Until he retired from the theatre to work exclusively in industrial design, he created many scenic tour-de-forces, such as those for *The Miracle* and *The Eternal Road.* Bel Geddes never wrote on scene design. Fortunately, however, before he left the theatre, Norris Houghton[7] elicited his ideas.[8] Bel Geddes, like Simonson, believed that a stage setting is "the organic

[6] *The Stage Is Set,* New York, 1932, 284.

[7] Norris Houghton's interviews, though written in 1936, are the best summary of the aesthetic principles and methodology of the first and second generations of American designers whose ideas still dominate American scene design.

[8] Norris Houghton, "The Designer Sets the Stage," *Theatre Arts Monthly,* Oct., Nov., Dec., 1936, and Feb., 1937. In addition to the visit with Bel Geddes, this series of interviews includes talks with Robert Edmond Jones, Lee Simonson, Jo Mielziner, Vincente Minnelli, Mordecai Gorelik, Donald Oenslager, and Aline Bernstein. The Jones, Simonson, Gorelik, and Oenslager interviews are included in this anthology.

outgrowth of the action of the play."[9] Scene design and play direction were inextricably a part of a single pattern to Bel Geddes, who always thought of design in terms of the movement of the actors, light, three-dimensional space, and the playwright's ideas. For the majority of the plays on which he worked, Bel Geddes also worked out the action for the director. In fact, he himself directed many plays. According to Houghton, Norman Bel Geddes stands as close to the image of Edward Gordon Craig's ideal man of the theatre as anyone the American theatre has produced.

Robert Edmond Jones, Lee Simsonson, and Norman Bel Geddes, then, were the titans of the first generation of American scene designers, and they dominated scene design well into the thirties. The craft unions, particularly that of the scene painters, quickly recognizing the growing status of scene designers, forced designers to join the United Scenic Artists in 1923. In the middle twenties, a second generation of scene designers, led by Aline Bernstein, Cleon Throckmorton, Raymond Sovey, Jo Mielziner, Donald Oenslager, and Mordecai Gorelik, emerged. Of them, Mielziner, Oenslager, and Gorelik have wielded the greatest influence.

Jo Mielziner, perhaps the most prolific scene designer, has turned out hundreds of settings since his debut in 1924. He has often expressed his ideas in interviews,[10] but he has written little on scene design.[11] His ideas resemble those of

[9] "The Designer Sets the Stage," *Theatre Arts Monthly*, Oct., 1936, 781.

[10] Aline Louchheim, "From Script to Stage: Case History of a Set," *The New York Times Magazine*, Dec. 9, 1951, 7.

[11] He says he's too busy. Several seasons ago, this editor beseeched him to publish the lectures on scene design he delivered at Fordham University the summer of 1947. Mielziner replied that he would write about scene design when he was too old to be actively engaged in the theatre. However, the happy news is that he is presently working on a book on scene design, even to the extent of committing himself to a publisher.

Jones' and Simonson's, to both of whom he was once apprenticed. In a *New Yorker* profile, Mielziner called himself an "aider and abbettor" of the director.[12] In an article, "Death of a Painter,"[13] he also suggested that the scene designer had better be part dramatist too.

Donald Oenslager has combined academic and professional careers. He made his debut on Broadway and began teaching stage design at Yale University in 1925, and he has remained active in both fields. At Yale he taught many successful designers, including the recent Broadway arrivals, Peter Larkin, Charles Elson, and William and Jean Eckart. Oenslager has frequently written on theatre and scene design, notably in *Scenery Then and Now* (1936), but perhaps nowhere more effectively than in the catalogue of an exhibition held in 1956 which commemorated his career as a scene designer and as a teacher.[14] "Good designing," he said, "is good thinking, with freedom of imagination supplanted by reasonable performance in execution." Again, "The designer is an eclectic and mannerist who works within the limitations of the stage, script, and production." Finally, as revealed in Houghton's interview, he declares the designer to be an artist-craftsman.

Mordecai Gorelik is the only American scene designer to propose a theory of design. Influenced by Robert Edmond Jones, under whom he once worked and whom he deeply reveres, Gorelik evolved the principle of the dramatic metaphor. Believing that "a good setting is not a picture but an image," Gorelik defines the dramatic metaphor as "the central image of each setting which sums up and notifies the

[12] "Jo Mielziner, Aider and Abbettor," *The New Yorker*, April, 1948, 37ff.

[13] *The American Artist*, Nov., 1948, 32ff.

[14] "Design in the Theatre Today," *Donald Oenslager, Stage Designer and Teacher*, A Retrospective Exhibition, Detroit Institute of Art, 1956, 11.

audience of all the creative thought the designer has [put] on each setting.[15]

Gorelik has been the designer most concerned with the sociological implications of design, especially earlier in his career, when, as Houghton's interview reveals, his first questions about any play he was going to design were, "For whom is this play being produced?" and "What kind of an audience is going to see this play?" Social consciousness has also led Gorelik to become a strong advocate in this country of Epic theatre, an intellectual form of theatre which he sees as eventually supplanting the realistic and symbolistic theatre of today. He has written about the relationship of Epic theatre to scene design and of its influence upon the theatre in general, notably in *New Theatres for Old* (1940).

During the thirties, American scene design came of age. Boris Aronson, Albert Johnson, Stewart Chaney, Howard Bay, Lemuel Ayers, Raoul Pene du Bois, Syrjala, and Harry Horner consolidated the position of the scene designer on Broadway. This third generation of designers also crystallized the maturity and technical proficiency that has since characterized American scene design.

Few of these designers however concern themselves with the aesthetics of scene design, though Harry Horner, in "The Designer in Action," gives an excellent account of the methodology of design.[16] Howard Bay has on several occasions analyzed the ills of present-day trends, among them a trend that since World War II is related to a queer and twisted kind of economics "having nothing to do with anything except somebody's determination to have an over-dressed stage and to hell with the play." The key questions, he maintains, are not artistic but economic: "How many

[15] "Metaphorically Speaking," *Theatre Arts*, Nov., 1954, 79.
[16] *Theatre Arts Monthly*, April, 1941, 265ff.

men will it take to shift the scenery and how many box cars are needed to move it?"[17]

A fourth generation of designers came to Broadway during the Second World War, including Oliver Smith, Rolf Gérard, Frederick Fox, Horace Armistead, Leo Kerz, Wolfgang Roth, Eugene Berman, and Ralph Alswang, several of whom have written on design, usually in *Theatre Arts*. Some are little more than publicity spreads announcing the opening of their latest commission. Others have written about the relation of the designer to the producer, or about his position relative to that of his colleagues in other fields of art. Leo Kerz complains that a great deal of present-day design is still more dependent upon the caprice than upon the understanding of the producer. Oliver Smith believes that the scene designer is far behind the architect in the dramatic use of space, color, and form. Eugene Berman, bitterly indicting the American theatre, charges that there is an invisible but very definite cultural iron curtain which separates Broadway from the rest of American art. Broadway directors and producers are "insular" in their thinking. "Hardly anyone of them," he says, "really know what is going on in the rest of the intellectual and artistic world." Berman is also dissatisfied with the working conditions the economics of Broadway forces upon designers, particularly easel painters who wish to design.

Since World War II, the sphere of activity of the American designer has enlarged. Previously, the designer was rarely called upon to design for anything but the legitimate and musical comedy theatre. Today, he wins commissions in all the arts: for example, Harry Horner has won an Academy

[17] "Settings by . . . Howard Bay," *Theatre Arts*, Feb., 1953, 66ff. A few seasons ago, Jo Mielziner told me that he never entertained a solution to a scene design problem on Broadway that required a full crew of more than thirty-two men. A larger crew would be a financial hardship to the producer.

Award for his work in the movies, as has Jo Mielziner; Donald Oenslager designs for the opera, Mielziner for the ballet; Fredrick Fox for theatre, opera, and television; Oliver Smith, who first designed for ballet, is today most sought after in all areas; Syrjala is equally acclaimed for his television and stage settings, as are William and Jean Eckart; Rolf Gérard's and Horace Armistead's activities extend from ballet to opera to theatre. Thus, the American designer is steadily growing in stature as in all the theatrical arts.

In the past decade, the Broadway theatre has been enriched by the talents of Peter Larkin, Ben Edwards, Charles Elson, Elden Elder, Jean and William Eckart, Lester Polakov, David Hayes, and Cecil Beaton. Except for Beaton, who has written principally on ballet design, the younger artists allow their work to reflect their artistic principles.[18]

* * *

From its first appearance in America, the new stagecraft received much critical acclaim from Walter Pritchard Eaton, Hiram Moderwell, and Kenneth Macgowan. Sheldon Cheney hailed the designer as a "prophet as well as practitioner" who would deliver the theatre from the "stultifying spell of Realism" to a glorious new theatrical day with abstract and symbolic settings, wherein each performance would literally be transformed into a religious rite. This notion was finally dispelled by Lee Simonson who maintained the art of the designer is only as great as the play. Stark Young not only evaluated the achievements of designers but related the aesthetics of scene design to the art of the theatre in general.

With the exception of Young's comments, which were in the context of a review of a play, discussions of scene design

[18] Several of these designers were invited to contribute expressions of their artistic beliefs to this anthology but they all begged off at the last minute, stating that they "just couldn't get their ideas down on paper."

by critics have seldom appeared. The designers themselves have made the noteworthy observations. But then, American scene designers have always been the most articulate theatre people. A few playwrights, such as Maxwell Anderson in *The Essence of Tragedy* (1938), have spoken out and spoken well, but where are the expressions of the actors, directors, or producers comparable in significance to Jones' *The Dramatic Imagination,* Simonson's *The Stage is Set,* or Gorelik's *New Theatre for Old?* Regrettably, they are not to be found.

* * *

This anthology presents the aesthetics of scene design in America beginning with the First World War. The essays are by the persons who led the development of scene design; indeed, to a degree, only men who have contributed to the movement can speak authentically about it; and we are indeed fortunate that these men have been so articulate. This is not primarily an analytic book, although principles are critically appraised, and discussions of style are incidental to the overall treatment of scene design. Several of the articles have been written especially for this anthology; namely, those by Horace Armistead, Frederick Fox, Rolf Gérard, Oliver Smith, and Syrjala. Howard Bay's article on musical comedy and Mordecai Gorelik's on Epic scene design, already published in *Theatre Arts,* were written expressly for this anthology. Articles by Mordecai Gorelik, Eugene Berman, Harry Horner, and Donald Oenslager have been amended or enlarged at the request of the editor.

The first section of the book is historical. It contains Jones' statement of 1917 and two pieces that illustrate the acclaim American critics were then heaping upon the new stagecraft. The second section presents the main currents of scene design over the past forty years. In the third section there are accounts of how aesthetic principles affect the methodology of scene design. The fourth section brings together for the

Introduction

first time a series of articles that explain the aesthetic problems of musical comedy, opera, ballet, arena theatre, motion picture, and television scene design. The fifth section contains essays outside the scope of the preceding sections, such as Alexander Bakshy's on presentational and representational theatre, Gorelik's on Epic scene design, and Eugene Berman's adieu to the theatre.

ORVILLE K. LARSON

PART ONE—BEGINNINGS

JOSEPH URBAN, FORERUNNER OF THE NEW STAGECRAFT IN AMERICA

by

Kenneth Macgowan

Kenneth Macgowan's descriptions of Joseph Urban's work with the Boston Opera Company, previous to World War I, entitled "The New Stagecraft in America," first appeared in THE CENTURY MAGAZINE, Volume 87 (January, 1914), pp. 416-21. Mr. Macgowan not only describes the influence of this pioneering Viennese artist but also indicates how the new stagecraft was being propagandized when it first appeared in America.

For a little over a year a Viennese artist, Joseph Urban, has been revolutionizing the staging of opera in America. He has brought to the Boston Opera House, and interpreted through his own fertile genius in color and line, the theories and practices in stage-settings which have transformed and reanimated the whole German theatre. His scenery, costumes, and lights have given the productions of the opera house a distinction which they could never have obtained through their singing and acting alone. His work has proved as beautiful as it is novel.

In the spring of 1912, Boston found among its conventional Italianate opera-settings a remarkable production of "Pelléas et Mélisande." It was made of strange, shadowed, and sun-flecked glimpses of wood and fountain, tower, grotto, and castle, vivid in varied color, full of the soft unworldliness of Debussy's music. The same spring came to a jolly "Hansel and Gretel," set behind a blue-checkered, toybox curtain; and a spacious "Tristan und Isolde" of beautiful solemnity.

With the next season the man who had designed these happy accidents of an otherwise dull year came from Vienna to be the permanent stage-director of the Boston Opera House. He began his work with a unique staging of "The Tales of Hoffmann." *Luther's* ruddy cellar, the blazing, golden ball-room of the opulent *Spalanzani,* a wonder-laden Venice of purples, greens, and ambers, the pale chamber of the dying *Antonia,* made the picture the most beautiful and one of the most imaginative stage-settings that America has ever seen.

3

Upon this came a production of Charpentier's "Louise" that Monet might have painted, the first truly impressionistic setting shown in America. After that "The Jewels of the Madonna" in a Naples of pulsing, yellow hill-streets and moonlit water gardens; "Djamileh," a vision of the Orient in gold and blue; and finally a "Don Giovanni" as gracefully mannered in design as Mozart's technique, as vivid in color as his melodious song, and filled with the romance and glamour of Seville.

Settings as imaginative and as distinguished, though not, perhaps, so sharply individual, you may find in a score of German and Austrian opera-houses and theatres; this work is the first expression in America of a new, but well-founded school of design.

Curiously enough, Mr. Urban did not find his schooling in those theatres but came to them full trained from a career that began in an architect's office and had made him a noted designer of exhibition rooms in art museums and in international expositions. At the St. Louis World's Fair in 1904, he designed the rooms for the Austrian Art. He had also decorated the interiors of other public buildings; he had furnished and decorated the Abdin Palace for the Khedive of Egypt; he had built castles and residences, and designed gardens, parks, monuments, and bridges, including the Czar Bridge across the Neva at St. Petersburg, for which an international prize had been offered. Out of this conglomerate work but especially from his triumphs as an interior decorator, came commissions from the Imperial Burgtheater in Vienna to design settings for a dozen plays that ran from "Faust" to "The Blue Bird." From there he went on to work at noted opera-houses and theatres in the principal German cities. To come to America he left his post as artistic adviser to the Imperial Opera-House in Vienna.

Behind his work are theories of scene design so long and thoroughly practised in Europe that they are now definitely formulated in monographs on what is called "The New Stagecraft." As definitely formulated, let us hurriedly add, as an art can be which sets its face against convention, for that is its first article of faith.

No art was so thoroughly conventionalized as the making of scenery when the new stage-craft began its reforms. There were the flimsy pretenses of reality that grace our plays even now-a-days. There were the large-sized, colored cut-outs such as ornament Christmas extravaganzas. There were land-scapes and elaborately paneled rooms after the manner of bad mid-century oil paintings in spasmodic three dimen-sions, these, of course, the favorite thing in 'grand' opera. And against all these unreal and unbeautiful conventional-isms the new stage-craft made its war.

For a positive faith the new stage-craft put imagination before everything. To take a new view, an impassioned view, and to record it fearlessly, that was its first duty. Many quali-ties hitherto little appreciated in scenic design came to its aid. There was simplicity, for instance. The stage was not to be cluttered with meaningless detail. Every 'property' was to have its use, each stretch of wall to express the one thing for which it stood. The results were productions of calm design and broad surfaces, stronger, sincerer, more direct, and so more beautiful. It crept out of simplicity. A touch or two of Eastern decoration on a flat wall surface summoned more of the orient than acres of carved filigree. A third qual-ity gave aid from the other arts, impressionism. The artist in scenic design, like the artist in oils, created an atmosphere of reality, not reality itself; the impression of things, not crude, literal representations. Flakes of color here and there brought a unity of beauty.

All these elements of the new stage-craft, in varying de-grees, have appeared in Mr. Urban's American work. Pure simplicity was the most strikingly presented in the ship scene of "Tristan und Isolde." There was no 'practicable' ship,

5

simply the couch of *Isolde* on a bare stage, shut in by a great curtain of towering yellow folds, dimly lighted, yet luminous with the sun outside. Even in the small rooms that the designer gave "Pelléas" there was a simplicity—a simplicity from which sprung a compelling suggestion of a world outside it, the massiveness of great castles, the whole rugged, fervid medieval life. The designer's impressionism, present in some degree in all his work, came out nowhere more effectively than in the realistic "Louise." The street scene of Montmartre was pure impressionism, nothing else—angular little houses in the dappled, yellow-green of many rains, set against a sky of green and blue splotches. There was no impossible pretense at a city of real mortar and a sky of true azure depths. It was simply a picture into which fitted music and personages, all in the same world of interpreted emotion.

The originality and effectiveness of Mr. Urban's new methods and individual genius showed most sharply in the varied "Tales of Hoffmann." The scenes ran from the rosy depths of *Luther's* inn cellar to the cool gray of *Antonia's* death chamber, with two remarkable settings in between. In the absence of the sketches in color, both of these deserve description.

For the first of the tales, the curtain rose upon a dim and vaporous emptiness; next came a yellow pallor; and then, with a rush of light that rose at each moment to an impossible brilliance, the golden gorgeous ball-room of *Spalanzani* burst upon you. It was a semi-circular room of rich, yellow-gold touched with a suggestion of gray. Half a dozen tall gold vases spaced the wall with splashes of purple blossoms. Through two doorways at the back glowed flat amber walls that carried the visible opulence on into a whole imagined palace.

For Venice there was an entire change of key—two wide walls of purple green at each side; formal doors and windows

6

letting in amber glows; at the back the deep night of the Mediterranean, cut at each side by a silver thread of water falling in a curve from a lion's mouth. Slowly and ceaselessly, back and forth, out of the shadows of night and into them again, passed the strangest of decorations—two turbaned negroes bearing above their heads great salvers of dark fruit. All of this was dreamy and vague with the colors of moonlight; but in the center a great glowing shaft of amber light bathed the couch of *Giulietta*. The contrast was unforgettable in its richness.

In all of this work the designer has used the new technical methods that are now a part of his own and in part the common property of all who practise the new stage-craft. Here it is, in the purely mechanical side, that they set their own conventions, not in conception, design, or creative treatment.

The 'portals' which Boston first saw in "The Tales of Hoffmann" are a characteristic new invention. They are narrow walls set at right angles to the footlights, framing in the sides of the stage and connected at the top by a strip of the same width. The portals proper, at the sides, narrow the huge stage space of our opera-houses to navigable proportions. The horizontal strip at the top rids us of the worst convention of our theatre, the 'sky borders,' or parallel strips of cloth used to represent the sky and to hide the rafters. It brings down the sight-line to the top of the cycloramic backdrop. The other purpose of the portals is more curious. They are both a new proscenium and a part of the scene. They replace the old glaring frame of gold and red draperies, and they enter into the design of the setting. For "Hoffmann" they were an unobtrusive gray with square doorways in them; for "Don Giovanni" a brighter gray-green, with the doorways curved to the Saracenic arches of Spain. Often through these doors came the people of the operas.

Mr. Urban carries us still further out of the old make-believe world of the opera-house by his novel use of plat-

7

forms. Many of the rooms in "Pelléas" were raised two or three feet above the footlights. As a consequence, the settings seemed smaller and more intimate. In the three dream-tales of "Hoffmann" on a larger scale and under skilful lighting, they give an opposite effect of distance and dreaminess.

But it is the secret of his effective, living colors that makes his walls look like something besides flapping canvas. He applies his color by the method known as "pointillage"—a method known to all artists and used more or less by the majority. Unlike the conventional scene-painter, he does not try to make a coating of glutinous paint and some shreds of canvas look like rock or air. He follows the modern artist, daubs a fleck of color here, another there, and achieves a total effect that is as suggestive of reality as is any painting by Monet, and hence the same degree of beauty. And the many flecks of mingled color carry all the prismatic glory of natural light.

Mr. Urban's method of work is curious and interesting; his studio distinctive. One finds him a largish man of early middle age, with vaguely Teutonic features touched by something of the East, the Viennese.

After reading the score and the libretto to fix impressions, he lays out the ground-plan of each scene. It is an accurate map of how much space must be used on the stage and of the general conformation of the buildings. Next he makes his sketch of the scene, a smallish, but very accurate, drawing in color of what the stage will look like from the director's chair. From the ground-plan and the sketch expert scene-painters construct and color an accurate little model of the scene. If some detail or color needs correction, he alters it on the model. From this corrected model the scene-painters produce the finished setting.

From his work he might seem a most individual artist, a man whose achievement is built on an unhampered use of exceptional talents. In reality his results spring from definite aims and are backed by a strict philosophy of his art. He is not an egotist, displaying chance moods.

In "Don Giovanni" he feels he has come nearest to his ideal. The portals became arabesques, with a curving arch between. A moonlit wall and a few cypresses as a background made them the doors of *Donna Anna's* house. They led to arbored inns, where between them glowed a hill of red and yellow above the brown wall of a street in Seville. Two columns and an evening sky made the rotunda. And so it went, to a final scene which, even in these simple confines, seemed a hall of rich proportions and beauty, the crown of an exceptional production.

How far Mr. Urban will be able to carry his theories in America is a question. Certainly prejudices will not permit him to apply his ideal method to what he feels is its goal—Wagner. Yet, in his most important production of this winter he can take a firm stand for a new and true "Meistersinger." "It is not so important that the background of the *Festeiese* for instance, should show the whole of Nuremberg, with all its Gothic details, as that it should at once give the impression of joy. When the people greet *Hans Sachs* with shouts of welcome, the sun must shine, must bathe everything in radiant splendor. This is the chief thing." Fresh conceptions, new visions, of this sort, worked out with fearless originality, will make a new stage in America—a stage of unguessed beauty and stimulus.

THE FUTURE DECORATIVE ART
OF THE THEATRE

by

Robert Edmond Jones

Writing in the NEW YORK TIMES in 1916 (December 10th, II, 1), Robert Edmond Jones declared, "The decorator, like the actor, should be translucent, like a medium. . . . He must make his work unobtrusive, in fact, invisible while discreetly and tactfully aiding, heightening in all possible ways. It should be lucid, pellucid. The finer it is, the more subservient it is. . . ." In "The Future Decorative Art of the Theatre," Jones expands this idea and defines the stage designer's position in what must be regarded as the first important manifesto on the new stagecraft by an American scene designer. This early statement of Jones' aesthetic principles originally appeared in THEATRE MAGAZINE, Volume 22 (May, 1917), p. 266.

There has recently come into the theatre what people call "the new art." European influence on various "Little Theatres" throughout the country were largely responsible for its foundation, and as a vogue this "new art" swept the theatrical world and became popular with all classes of theatregoers. Its appeal, while supposing to come from the stage as a whole, really came from the scenery, and has been the means of the establishment of a school of painters whose work is mostly known by their enjoyment of great masses of color, blended in such a manner to hold the eye and to dazzle the brain.

Ten, possibly twenty years from now this "new art" as it is known today will have disappeared, and in its place will be seen a work that is at present starting in a very humble manner; a work which is being confused in the minds of most people with ornate decoration. It is my dream that not only from a scenic standpoint will the new regime be of benefit to the theatre, but that the whole tone of stagecraft will be lifted.

Before speaking further of the "new art" I would like to present a present-day condition to aid me in explaining what I believe to be the ideal of decorative art.

Once that small idea which probably came very casually to the playwright is placed on paper, it goes to the producer, the scenic artist, the actors, the men who manage the theatre lights, even to the stagehands whose duty it is to arrange the various sets. Sometimes the idea gets to the audience as the author intended it should go—frequently it is a distorted

11

thing that does not seem akin to the thought of the play-wright.

There have been instances in the past few seasons where the idea of the play did not "get over," if I may use a slang phrase, with the scenic artist. We have all seen bits of stage pictures that were supposed to be cold and dismal spoiled by a bank of too red roses, and we have seen many conventional rooms spoiled by furniture that was too smart.

The trouble is—that is as far as I am able to analyze it—that when any play reaches the hand of the artist who is to make the backgrounds for its action it is a dead thing—something that contains words and directions for action. The artist has to visualize, to see every movement and every color, and, frequently, his conception of the scene is far different from the original idea of the playwright.

Is such a condition right? Men of the truly new art of the theatre think not. To me the ideal way of producing a play is one that seems surprising today, but one which I hope will develop with rapidity and give us an American theatre that will be second to none.

My idea of a correct production of a play is to start from the author's original idea and make it something truly alive, organic. Let producers read plots and suggestions as they now read plays. When they come on a scenario which is worthy of presentation, let the producer call a conference of the people that will make the play live on the stage so that in a body they may work up the idea. Can't you imagine the effect it would have on a play if the producer, the playwright, the painter of the scenes, and the leading actors were to talk over the idea as it was to be worked out?

While the scenery of a play is truly important, it should be so important that the audience should forget that it is painted. There should be a fusion between the play and its scenery. Scenery isn't there to be looked at, it's really there to be forgotten. The drama is the fire, the scenery is the air that lifts

12

the fire and makes it bright. If a scene is properly done it should unconsciously "get" the audience. The audience that is always conscious of the back drop is paying a doubtful compliment to the painter. It may not be that the scene is bad —the set that they are looking at may be very fine, but it may not fit that particular action of the play.

I am told that when Max Reinhardt first started to produce "Sumurun" he had his scenic artist and his composer meet the actors that were to portray the pantomime. Together they all studied it out, the artist watching each pose to see what the effect of the action of the living figure would be against the proposed background. In the same way the musicians watched, and after hearing "Sumurun's" music one can easily understand that the inspiration of its rythmetic swing with its staccato notes came as a figure danced its way across the room and came to a sudden stop.

Personally I have been very happy in my work inasmuch as I have been able to work largely along the lines I have outlined as being my ideal. When I was doing "Caliban" with Mr. Percy MacKaye for the Shakespearean celebration we worked together constantly. This, of course, was a gigantic spectacle, and offered innumerable chances for scenic effects. I think, however, that I was more satisfied with the first act set for the modern comedy for "Good Gracious Annabelle" than any piece of work I have ever done. After all, there is the same chance for scenic perfection in a vaudeville act that there is in a pageant play. It would be impossible for me to work seriously at the art of stage decoration without recognizing light comedy, farce, musical comedy, vaudeville, and even motion pictures. Just at this time I am finishing work in order that I may spend the summer with a motion picture production.

I am distinctly pro-American and I believe that in a few years we will lead the world in stagecraft. America does not have to go to Europe for plays, actors, and actresses, nor for

13

producers and artists. Also I have never seen one of the so-called "Little Theatres" that I would exchange for a chance to work on a Broadway production. I am heart and soul for Broadway, and I believe that Broadway is worthy of a far better reputation than is accorded her.

I think that the Russians' idea of the ideal stage picture comes nearer to my own picture of the ideal than any other. They believe that when they look at a stage picture they should see something that is entirely the handiwork of the artist responsible. They believe that an artist should personally—with his own hands—be responsible for every bit of color on the stage.

Even costumes should be the handiwork of the scenic artist. Yes, and if possible, he should build the very furniture.

I have only been able to do such a piece of work on one occasion. That was "The Man Who Married a Dumb Wife." For this production I made the scenery, the properties, and all the costumes. I was responsible for all the color.

This may be a strange surprise to those who look on the scenic art, and costuming, as separate departments of the drama. They are inseparable. The hands that design a room should construct the costumes of the women who live within its painted walls. Painted? Yes,—but painted so skillfully that there is no impression of the unreal; painted so well that they live and give life to the drama they surround.

So it will be in the future decorative art of the theatre. I feel that eventually the ideal I have pictured will be the ideal of the American theatre.

14

THE NEW PATH OF THE THEATRE

by

Kenneth Macgowan

The first exhibition of the new stagecraft in America devoted entirely to the work of American designers, working in art theatres as well as on Broadway, was held at the Bourgeois Galleries in New York City in April, 1919. AMERICAN STAGE DESIGNS, an elaborate catalogue was prepared which included brief statements of the participating artists outlining their attitudes toward the stage and the future of theatrical art and Kenneth Macgowan's appraisal, which reviewed and evaluated the progress of these artists since the appearance of the new stagecraft in America. Simultaneously with the exhibition, the entire series of articles including "The New Path of the Theatre," were printed in THEATRE ARTS MAGAZINE, Volume 4 (April, 1919) and reprinted in THEATRE ARTS ANTHOLOGY, New York, 1950.

Are we to emerge from the war into a new theatre? Are we to harvest in the playhouse, as we are harvesting in other fields of art, the rich seedings of Europe many years neglected? Will we find ourselves in that theatre of beauty and expressiveness towards which Russia and Germany and in less degree France and England were moving in 1914?

One thing is certain: if we go anywhere, we shall go far. If we take steps to reorganize our theatrical machine, to make it sensitive and yet strong, self-reliant and self-expressive, we can create theatrical art of a rare fulness. For we build upon a full and alive past. We build upon a past that is only yesterday and yet—by the intervention of the war—has taken on many of the rounded and summed-up qualities of tradition. More, we are building on an international past in the theatre, even as we are building towards an international future in affairs of state.

Behind the modern art of stage production loom two immense figures of theory—Gordon Craig and Adolphe Appia. Craig, an Englishman writing in English, gave us the great outlines of inspiration, filled in with the brilliant and provocative art of his pencil. Appia, an Italian-Swiss writing in French, supplied an abstract philosophy and a concrete method. Two nations—Germany and Russia—took up the task of realizing these ideas and prescriptions. Through state and city theatres, through group playhouses, where study, experiment and thoughtful accomplishment were not impossible, modern theatrical art rounded from theories into—pro-

17

ductions. From Germany rose the fame of Max Reinhardt, obscuring for us the splendid work of a dozen other producers like Schlenter, Linnebach, Hagemann. From Russia came the ballet of Bakst obscuring only less completely the theatre of Stanislawski. In Ireland, the Abbey theatre opened its eyes to vision. Barker saw in London, and minor men and playhouses in the English provinces. Rouché, of the Théâtre des Arts, showed in Paris that which made him director of the Opéra for the fated fall of 1914. And in France occurred that most remarkable birth of a literally new theatre, the Vieux Colombier of the critic-player, Jacques Copeau. At this point, the Great War wrote "finis." Russia under the Soviets has reopened the scroll. America under the Shuberts may yet write upon it.

Without the theories, progress for them or progress for us would have been impossible. Without their accomplishment, progress for us would be only a thing to dream of. For under the Shuberts—which is only an impolite and impolitic way of saying under the Broadway system of piecemeal production—America could never study, experiment and accomplish as the old world did in those German and Russian producing theatres where groups of artists worked constantly together. Fortunately that work has been done for us. Of course we need more experiment, and we need and are getting the theatres where that is possible; yet, now that we have models to work from, even our Broadway system can reproduce and to some extent develop the types of production given us by the recent and international past before the war. It had even begun to do so while Europe fought.

Indeed, America is at the point where criticism should begin to take the place of indiscriminate enthusiasm. The exhibition of sketches and models at the Bourgeois Galleries in New York and the essays by native stage artists to which this is, in a certain sense, an introduction, demonstrate how far things have already moved. We need not fear to injure

18

our cause by criticism. We are more likely now to kill it with kindness. There was a time when the faintest buds of the footlights had to be nourished with applause. We hailed much extremely bad work. Perhaps it was because we craved excitation and the bizarre, as relief from drab emotions. Perhaps it was because we knew that even from such beginnings the good art could spring—certainly better and more easily than from the old. It was thus that we applauded much of the work of the worst Washington Square Players sort. The old was so bad that we accepted an even worse version of the new. Now we must criticize.

We must appreciate the potentialities of the stage. That was what the old school didn't do. And that is what some of the new schools also are failing to do when they cling to the old theatricalism, to the old arbitrary four walls of canvas, the forced marriage of pretense and extravagance. We have fought realism. We have berated Belasco. But our fight should go back further—and further forward. Realism can emerge into the expressiveness of the new art. Behind realism lies the greater enemy, the enemy that realism and its Forty-fourth Street high priest fought for us,—yes, before us. That enemy is theatricalism. It is the dead-alive theatre of the last century, where the meagre materials of side walls, wings, and backdrops, were accepted as canvasses for the smearing of bad color and worse perspective into a "play-actory" pretense at a marvelous reality. The thing was never life. It was never poetry. It was never emotion. It was a routine rule-of-thumb fake. And in America it still lives.

Two men set themselves to demolish this thing. They were Otto Brahms and David Belasco. They produced actuality. Admirers of the Berlin producer called it naturalism. And it was this light that Reinhardt and Stanislawski first followed. These men made actual rooms and plausible exteriors. A great mass of engineering mechanism, new lights, new stages, new skies, were invented in the process of getting rid of the

19

old fake, and the easel painter was banished from the three-dimensional theatre. The footlights and the borderlights of the picture-frame stage were left to the picture gallery in all their blank staring glare.

Aesthetics, like life, does not come in water-tight compartments. There is evolution. Now it is quite possible to argue that the old theatricalism was always striving to be real, and that hard, intelligent work pushed it over into naturalism. Certainly, naturalism, as Reinhardt and Stanislawski practiced it, drifted over into the high expressiveness of the new art. There was a time when Reinhardt produced *A Midsummer Night's Dream* in a forest of real papier-mâché trees. Stanislawski made a Gorki of utter and gutter reality. But they had only to try to add beauty and meaning to their productions in order to be forced, like all the great artists of the world, into a refinement, a selection and interpretation which is best expressed through the rather awkward term abstraction. The old theatre of theatricalism had tried to reach a vivid and picturesque reality through certain rule-of-thumb abstractions which cribbed, cabined, confined and defeated the purpose. The newer theatre tries to reach beauty and meaning, to win to a vivid expressiveness of the play, through spiritual abstractions. In the old days stretched canvas, painted with pictures of leaves and branches, tried to look like a forest. In the days of realism, actual, modelled, three-dimensional forms of trees did indeed look not unlike an inferior sort of forest. In the third period, however, that same canvas of the old days, treated frankly as cloth, and either hung in loose tree-like shapes or painted with symbols of nature and draped like the curtain it actually is, becomes an abstraction of a forest, full of all the suggestive beauty of which the artist in colors, shapes and lights is capable.

In spite of the natural process of development from realism to this art of abstraction, there is such an essential break with the stiff and limited art of the past that there has come a promise of as great a break with the physical theatre itself. This is the place however, for only a hint of the reconstruction of stage and auditorium which may make a theatre as different from the present hall and niched platform as the theatre was different from the open-air cockpit of the Elizabethans and the amphitheatre of the Greeks.

The evolution which kept those utterly different theatres still The Theatre and which brings the modern art of production out of the theatricals of Garrick and Kean, also brings compromises and "sporting back." These must not confuse us. As we gain a single definite conception of the new art, we must begin to see the falsities that have crept into it. We must see and recognize, for example, the limitations of Bakst and much of the Russian method. We must note that this artist has been content with the old mechanics and methods of theatricalism. He has taken the great canvas drop and the open side wings, and he has simply sublimated them with color. He still paints perspectives on the drop, but he flings out columns and stairs and vistas with such verve and colors them with such spectacular genius that they take on a spiritual life that triumphs over the technical limitations. Bakst is a glorious compromise.

And there are many compromises that must be met and, perhaps, accepted. Banishing perspective utterly only ties us down to a setting no larger in its appearance than the actual stage. Should we then compromise by the use of set-pieces showing distant silhouettes of cities and mountains against the sky, so distant in fact as to defeat the difficulties of perspective? Or will we find a more consistent solution in symbolic representation, which turns the whole actual stage into a place without physical limitations? Similarly, shall we attempt the blue ether of the sky by that remarkable combination, electric light and plaster dome, or shall we turn the sky, too, into a symbolic and decorative thing—canvas daubed and speckled with pleasing hues?

Besides falsities that should be banned and compromises that may be accepted, there are many varieties of style and methods possible in the new art. One artist—Joseph Urban, for example—may practice an enriched and meaningful realism in *Le Prophête*, a decorative method in *Don Giovanni*, and an absolute abstraction in the "realistic" *Nju*, or he may run from realism to abstraction and symbolism in a single opera such as *St. Elizabeth*. We may have our preferences. I am personally all for the abstraction. But we must recognize the breadth of the new movement and we must see that the essential test is the effect of the particular production on the expressiveness of the play itself.

But behind all such conflicts and compromises and differences of method, there remain a few basic ideas and basic methods, without which we cannot have the beauty and expressiveness of the modern stage art. They are simplification, suggestion, and synthesis.

Simplification is the test in almost all great art. Simplification of effect always; simplification of means generally. On the stage, simplification of both effect and means are essential, because the scenery is not the only thing to be seen. Stage architecture is not architecture alone, or stage picture merely stage picture. The setting is the medium of the actor. And it is essential that he shall be properly seen. It is essential that he shall be properly set off by his background and properly fused in it. He must mean more because of the setting, not less. The case against the old setting, both the theatrical setting and the Belasco setting, is that either its garishness or its detail tends to hide the actor. On the stage we must have simplification for art's sake. But we must have it even more for the sake of the actor—therefore for the play.

The compliment to simplification is suggestion. Simplify as much as you please, you only make it more possible to suggest a wealth of spiritual and aesthetic qualities. A single Saracenic arch can do more than a half dozen to summon the passionate background of Spanish *Don Juan*. One candle-stick can carry the whole spirit of the baroque *La Tosca*. On the basis of simplification, the artist can build by suggestion a host of effects that crude and elaborate reproduction would only thrust between the audience and the actor and the play. The artist can suggest either the naturalistic or the abstract, either reality or an idea and an emotion.

Finally, the quality above all in modern stage production is synthesis. For modern stage art, in spite of all the easel artists who may care to practice the painting of scenery, is a complex and rhythmic fusion of setting, lights, actors, and play. There must be consistency that has the quality of progression in it. And there must be such consistency among them all. Half a portrait, half a landscape, cannot be in Whistler's style and the other half in Zuloaga's. The creation of a mood expressive of the play, is, after all, the final purpose in production. It can no more be a jumble of odds and ends than can be the play itself.

The achievement of this synthesized suggestion of a play's simple, essential qualities has been sought by the great theorists in very different ways. Gordon Craig would get it mainly by design, backed by color. Adolphe Appia fuses his drama in light. Jacques Copeau, whose beliefs and whose works must take a high place in the record of theatrical progress, achieves the play through restrictions of means and the re-creation of every element from the theatre building to the actor at each production.

I think a single scene of a play produced by two Americans —and a modern, realistic play, at that—can be taken as an example of the working out of the three fundamentals in a fused whole. It is the opening scene of a failure produced by Arthur Hopkins a few years ago, *The Devil's Garden*. The opening of the show showed a postal clerk hauled up for examination on charges in the room of a member of that bureaucracy, the British general post office. The setting was shallow, perhaps ten feet deep. At each end was a door set in a square wall. The wall between was without an opening and its only decoration was a buff-toned map. Three chairs and one desk. And some actors. Simplification.

But that simple room fairly breathed bureaucracy, the thing that was about to grip the clerk. Its walls were a dull gray; its door casings, map frame, narrow wainscoting and the furniture were black—the same gray and black of the morning clothes of the officials. These tones and these people made a well-composed harmonious picture, but it was a picture instinct with formality. The colors, the proportions, the map—all simple suggestions of the reality that ruled the whole great invisible building beyond.

For synthesis, there was not only the consistency of this gray and black duotone and its restrained lighting. There was the handling of the furniture and people—the stage direction. The desk and chairs were precisely and formally square with the square walls. The people entered from the end doors, moved squarely and formally up to each other, face to face, precise. It was a machine, the machine of government property. That scene, as designed by Robert Edmond Jones and directed by Arthur Hopkins, was a perfect piece of realism and a perfect piece of abstraction besides. It showed the possibilities of the new art and the drama of today as well as for the colorful and imaginative sort of plays for which so many of us are hoping and for which alone so many imagine the new stage art is fitted.

America has its artists, it even has a producer or two, that see this exacting yet catholic new art right. It is beginning to have an audience, and it must cultivate critics. We are through with imitation. Europe has taught us; we must now practice and create. We are past the Craig period when theories and rather extravagant sketches had their justification in the inspiration they gave. Now is the time for practicality, revolutionary practicality, and for accomplishment and triumph.

24

PART TWO—MATURITY

TO A YOUNG STAGE DESIGNER

by

Robert Edmond Jones

Robert Edmond Jones was often called a poet as well as an artist of the theatre and certainly no one writes on the theatre and its art in a more poetic fashion than he did. A great love for the theatre permeates all his writings and one can not help but sense the dignity and nobility with which Jones regarded his chosen profession. To him, theatre was more than a job, even more than a "calling" (as Lee Simonson recently pointed out), it was a love match, pure and simple. And nowhere does this great love shine through so much as in THE DRAMATIC IMAGINATION, a collection of "reflections" on the art of the theatre. In the essay, "To a Young Stage Designer," many of his ideas on the role of the scene designer, originally expressed in "The Future Decorative Art in the Theatre," reach maturity; set down in a more poetic yet lucid style. No essays on scenic design reveals as clearly the kind of creative thinking necessary for good stage designing as those of Jones. Reprinted by Theatre Arts Books in 1956, this essay comprises chapter four of THE DRAMATIC IMAGINATION, originally published by Duell, Sloane & Pearce, New York, 1941, pp. 69-83.

A stage designer is, in a very real sense a jack-of-all-trades. He can make blueprints and murals and patterns and light-plots. He can design fireplaces and bodices and bridges and wigs. He understands architecture, but is not an architect: can paint a portrait, but is not a painter: creates costumes, but is not a couturier. Although he is able to call upon any or all of these varied gifts at will, he is not concerned with any one of them to the exclusion of the others, nor is he interested in any one of them for its own sake. These talents are only tools of his trade. His real calling is something quite different. *He is an artist of occasions.*

Every play—or rather, every performance of a play—is an occasion, and this occasion has its own characteristic quality, its own atmosphere, so to speak. It is the task of the stage designer to enhance and intensify this characteristic quality by every means in his power. The mastery of this special art demands not only a mastery of many diverse techniques but a temperament that is peculiarly sensitive to the atmosphere of a given occasion, just as the temperament of a musician is peculiarly sensitive to the characteristic qualities of a musical composition. Stage designers, like musicians, are born and not made. One is aware of atmosphere or one isn't, just as one has a musical ear or one hasn't.

A stage setting has no independent life of its own. Its emphasis is directed toward the performance. In the absence of the actor it does not exist. Strange as it may seem, this simple and fundamental principle of stage design still seems to be widely misunderstood. How often in critics' reviews one comes upon the phrase "the settings were gorgeous." Such a statement, of course, can mean only one thing, that no one concerned with producing the drama has thought of it as an organic whole. I quote from a review recently published in one of our leading newspapers, "Of all the sets of the season, the only true surprise was. . . ." The only true surprise, indeed. Every stage designer worth his salt outgrew the idea of scenic surprises years ago. If the critics only knew how easy it is to make a scenic surprise in the theatre. Take two turntables, a good deal of—but no. Why give away the formula? It is not surprise that is wanted from the audience; it is delighted and trusting acceptance. The surprise inherent in a stage setting is only a part of the greater surprise inherent in the event itself.

And yet a stage setting holds a curious kind of suspense. Go, for instance, into an ordinary empty drawing-room as it exists normally. There is no particular suspense about this room. It is just—empty. Now imagine the same drawing-room arranged and decorated for a particular function—a Christmas party for children, let us say. It is not complete as a room, now, until the children are in it. And if we wish to visualize for ourselves how important a part of expectancy plays in such a room, let us imagine that there is a storm and that the children cannot come. A scene on the stage is filled with the same feeling of expectancy. It is like a mixture of chemical elements held in solution. The actor adds the one element that releases the hidden energy of the whole. Meanwhile, wanting the actor, the various elements remain suspended, as it were, in an indefinable tension. To create this suspense, this tension, is the essence of the problem of stage design.

The designer must strive to achieve in his settings what I can only call a high potential. The walls, the furniture, the properties, are only the facts of a setting, only the outline. The truth is in everything but these objects, in the space they enclose, in the intense vibration they create. They are fused into a kind of embodied impulse. When the curtain rises we feel a frenzy of excitement focused like a burning glass upon the actors. Everything on the stage becomes a part of the life of the instant. The play becomes a voice out of a whirlwind. The terrible and wonderful *dynamics* of the theatre pours over the footlights.

A strange, paradoxical calling, to work always behind and around, to bring into being a powerful non-being. How far removed it all is from the sense of display. One is reminded of the portraits of the Spanish noblemen painted by El Greco in the Prado in Madrid, whose faces, as Arthur Symons said, are all nerves, distinguished nerves, quieted by an effort. What a phrase for stage designers to remember. *Quieted by an effort.*

It is to the credit of our designers that they have almost made a fetish of abnegation. But let me remark parenthetically that it is sometimes difficult to go into the background where there is nothing in front of you. These pages are hardly the place in which to perpetuate the centuries-old squabble between playwrights and stage designers begun by peevish old Ben Jonson, who scolded Inigo Jones so roundly for daring to make his productions beautiful and exciting to look at. This kind of petty jealousy makes sorry reading even when recorded in verse by the great Ben himself. It is enough to say that the jealousy still persists and is as corroding in the twentieth century as it was in the seventeenth. The error lies in our conception of the theatre as something set aside for talents that are purely literary. As if the experience of the theatre had only to do with words. Our playwrights need to learn that plays are wrought, not written. There is something to be said in the theatre in terms of form and color and light than can be said in no other way.

The designer must learn to sense the atmosphere of a play with unusual clearness and exactness. He must actually live

29

in it for a time, immerse himself in it, be baptized by it. This process is in no means as easy as it seems. We are all too apt to substitute ingenuity for clairvoyance. The temptation to invent is always present. I was once asked to be one of the judges of a competition of stage designs held by the Department of Drama of one of our well-known universities. All the designers had made sketches for the same play. The setting was the interior of a peasant hut on the west coast of Ireland. It turned out that these twenty or thirty young designers had mastered the technique of using dimmers and sliding stages and projected scenery. They had also acquired a considerable amount of information concerning the latest European developments of stagecraft. Their drawings were full of expressionism from Germany, constructivism from Russia, every kind of modernism. They were compilations of everything that had been said and done in the world of scenery in the last twenty years. But not one of the designers had sensed the atmosphere of the particular play in question.

I recalled for them my memory of the setting for the same play as produced by the Abbey Theatre on its first visit to America. This setting was very simple, far simpler and far less self-conscious than any of their designs. Neutral-tinted walls, a fireplace, a door, a window, a table, a few chairs, the red homespun skirts and bare feet of the peasant girls. A fisher's net, perhaps. Nothing more. But through the little window at the back one saw a sky of enchantment. All the poetry of Ireland shone in that little square of light, moody, haunting, full of dreams, calling us to follow on, follow on. . . . By this one gesture of excelling simplicity the setting was enlarged into the region of great theatre art.

Now here is a strange thing, I said to the designers. If we can succeed in seeing the essential quality of a play others will see it too. We know the truth when we see it, Emerson said, from opinion, as we know that we are awake when we are awake. For example: you have never been in Heaven, and you have never seen an angel. But if someone produces a play about angels whose scenes are laid in Heaven you will know at a glance whether his work is right or wrong. Some curious intuition will tell you. The sense of recognition is the highest experience the theatre can give. As we work we must seek not for self-expression or for a performance for its own sake, but only to establish the dramatist's intention, knowing that when we have succeeded in doing so audiences will say to themselves, not, This is splendid, but—This is true. This is the way it is. So it is, and not otherwise. . . . There is nothing esoteric in the search for truth in the theatre. On the contrary, it is a part of the honest everyday life of the theatre.

The energy of a particular play, its emotional content, its aura, so to speak, has its own definite physical dimensions. It extends just so far in space and no farther. The walls of the setting must be placed at precisely this point. If the setting is larger than it should be, the audience gets a feeling of meagerness and hollowness; if smaller, a feeling of confusion and pressure. It is often very difficult to adjust the physical limits of a setting to its emotional limitations. But great plays exist outside the categories of dimension. Their bounty is as boundless as the air. Accordingly, we need not think of a stage setting, in a larger sense, as a matter of establishing space relations. Great plays have nothing to do with space. The setting for a great play is no more subject to the laws of space composition than music is. We may put aside once and for all the idea of a stage-setting as a glorified show-window in which actors are to be exhibited and think instead as a kind of symphonic accompaniment or obligato to the play, as evocative and intangible as music itself. Indeed, music must play a more important role than we now realize in the scenic evocations of the future.

In the last analysis the designing of stage scenery is not the problem of an architect or a painter or a sculptor or even

31

a musician, but of a poet. By a poet I do not mean, of course, an artist who is concerned only with the writing of verse. I am speaking of the poetic attitude. The recognized poet, Stedman says, is one who gives voice in expressive language to the common thought and feeling which lies deeper than ordinary speech. I will give you a very simple illustration. Here is a fragment of ordinary speech, a paraphrase of part of Hamlet's soliloquy, *To be or not to be:* I wish I were dead. I wish I could go to sleep and never wake up. But I'm afraid of what might happen afterwards, Do people dream after they are dead? . . . But Hamlet does not express himself in this way. He says, *To die, to sleep; to sleep: perchance to dream: ay, there's the rub; for in that sleep of death what dreams may come.* . . . Here are two ways of saying the same thing. The first is prose. The second is poetry. Both of them true. But Shakespeare's way—the poetic way—is somehow deeper and higher and truer and more universal. In this sense we may fairly speak of the art of stage designing as poetic, in that it seeks to give expression to the essential quality of a play rather than to its outward characteristics.

Sometime ago one of the younger stage designers was working with me on the scenes for an historical play. In the course of the production we had to design a tapestry, which was to be decorated with figures of heraldic lions. I sent him to the library to hunt up old documents, he came back presently with many sketches, copies of originals. They were all interesting enough, but somehow they were not right. They lacked something the professionals call "good theatre." They were not *theatrical.* They were accurate and—lifeless. I said as much to the designer. "Well, what shall we do about it?" he asked me. "We have got to stop copying," I said, "we must try something else. We must put our imaginations to work. Let us think now. Not about what this heraldic lion ought to look like, but what the design meant in the past, in the Middle-Ages.

"Perhaps Richard, the Lion-Hearted, carried this very device emblazoned on his banner as he marched across Europe on his way to the Holy Land. Richard, the Lion-Hearted, *Coeur de Lion.* . . . What memories of childhood this name conjures up, what images of chivalry. Knights in armour, enchanted castles, magic casements, perilous seas, oriflammes, and gonfalons. Hear the great battle-cries. See the banners floating through the smoke. *Coeur de Lion,* the Crusader, with his singing Blondel. . . . Do you remember Blondel's song, the song he sang for three long years while he sought his master in prison? *'O Richard, O mon Roi. L'Univers t'abondonne. . . .'*

"And now your imagination is free to wander, if you will allow it to do so, among the great names of romance. Richard, the Lion-Hearted, King Arthur, Sir Percival and the mystery of the Holy Grail, the Song of Roland, the magic sword, Durandal, Tristan and Isolde, the love-potion, the chant of the Cornish sailors, the ship with the black sail: the Lady Nicolette of whom Aucassin said, *Beau venir et bel aller,* lovely when you come, lovely when you go; the demoiselle Aude, who died for love; the Lady Christtable; the Ancient Mariner with the Albatross hung about his neck; the Cid, Charlemagne, Barbarossa, the Tartar, Kubla Khan, who decreed the pleasure-dome in Xanadu, in the poem Coleridge heard in a dream . . . And there are the legendary cities, too, Carcassonne, Granada, Torcello, Samarkand, the Blue City, with its facades of turquoise and palis pazuli; Carthage, Isfahan, Trebizond; and there are the places which have never existed outside the poet's imagination—Hy Brasil, Brocéliande, the Land of Luthany, the region Elenore, the Isle of Avalon, *where falls not hail, or rain, or any snow, where ever King Arthur lyeth sleeping as in peace.* . . . And there is the winged Lion of St. Mark in Venice with the device set forth fairly beneath it. *Pax Tibi, Marce, Evangelista Mesu;* and there are the mounted knights in the windows of Chartres, riding on, riding on toward Our Lady as she bends above the high altar in her glory of rose.

"These images of romance have come to our minds—all of them—out of this one little symbol of the heraldic lion. They are dear to us. They can never fade from our hearts.

"Let your fancy dwell and move among them in a kind of revery. Now, in this mood, with these images bright in your mind, draw your figure of the lion once more.

"This new drawing is different. Instead of imitating, describing what the artists of the Middle Ages thought a lion looked like, it summons up an image of medieval romance. Perhaps without knowing it I have stumbled on a definition of art in the theatre; all art in the theatre should be not descriptive but evocative. A bad actor describes a character; he explains it. He expounds it. A good actor evokes it. He summons it up. He reveals it to us. . . . This drawing is evocative. Something about it brings back memories of medieval love-songs and crusaders and high adventures. People will look at it without knowing why. In this drawing of a lion—only a detail in a magnificent, elaborate setting—there will be a quality which will attract them and disturb them and haunt them and make them dream. Your feeling is in it. Your interest is in it. You have triumphed over the mechanics of the theatre and for the time being you have become a poet."

The poetic conception of stage design bears little relation to the accepted convention of realistic scenery in the theatre. As a matter of fact it is quite the opposite. Truth in the theatre, as the masters of the theatre have always known, stands above and beyond mere accuracy to fact. In the theatre, the actual thing is never the exciting thing. Unless life is turned into art on the stage it stops being alive and goes dead.

So much for the realistic details. *The artist should omit the details, the prose of nature and give us the spirit and splendor.* When we put a star in the sky, for example, it is

34

not just a star in the sky, but a "supernal messenger, excellently bright." This is purely a question of our point of view. A star is, after all, only an electric light. The point is, how the audience will see it, what images it will call to mind. We read of Madame Pitoeff's Ophelia that in the mad scene she handled roses and the rosemary and the rue as if she were in a Paradise of flowers. We must bring into the immediate life of the theatre—"two hours traffic on our stage"—images of a larger life. The stage we inhabit is a chamber in the House of Dreams. Our work on this stage is to suggest the immanence of a visionary world all about us. In this world Hamlet dwells and Oedipus, and great Juno, known by her immortal gait, and the three witches on the blasted heath. We must learn by a deliberate effort of the will to walk in these enchanted regions. We must imagine ourselves into their vastness.

Here is the secret of the flame that burns in the work of the great artists of theatre. They seem so much more aware than we are, and so much more awake, and so much more alive that they make us feel that what we call living is not living at all, but a kind of sleep. Their knowledge, their wealth of emotion, their wonder, their elation, their swift clear seeing surrounds every occasion with a crowd of values that enriches it beyond anything which we, in our happy satisfaction, had ever imagined. In their hands it becomes not only a thing of beauty but a thing of power. And we see it all—beauty and power alike—as a part of the life of the theatre.

THREE SELECTIONS FROM
THE DRAMATIC IMAGINATION
by
Robert Edmond Jones

*The first of these selections is an excerpt from "Art in the
Theatre" (pp. 23-27, 33-34) and contains some of Jones' most
famous pronouncements on the function of scenery such as
"a feeling, an evocation, an expectancy, a foreboding, a tension," and the highly poetic "a warm wind fanning the
drama to flame." The second is a portion of "Some Thoughts
on Stage Costuming" (pp. 88-91) in which Jones differenti-
ates between imagination and ingenuity in the theatre.
Robert Edmond Jones was always praised, particularly by
his colleagues, for his ability to use light on the stage in a
most artistic and telling manner; the final selection, a con-
densation of "Light and Shadow in the Theatre" (pp. 111-
128), explains his creative approach to the art of stage lighting.*

I

There seems to be a wide divergence of opinion today as to what the theatre really is. Some people say it is a temple, some say it is a brothel, some say it is a laboratory, or a workshop, or it may be an art, or a plaything, or a corporation. But whatever it is, one thing is true about it. There is not enough fine workmanship in it. There is too much incompetence in it. The theatre demands of its craftsmen that they know their jobs. The theatre is a school. We shall never have done with studying and learning. In the theatre, as in life, we try first of all to free ourselves, as far as we can, from our own limitations. Then we can begin to practice "this noble and magical art." Then we may begin to dream.

When the curtain rises, it is the scenery that sets the key of the play. A stage setting is not a background; it is an environment. Players act in a setting, not against it. We say, in the audience, when we look at what the designer has made, before anyone on the stage has time to move or speak, "Aha, I see. It's going to be like *that*. Aha." This is true no matter whether we are looking at a realistic representation of Eliza crossing the ice or at the setting for one of Yeat's *Plays for Dancers,* carried to the limit of abstract symbolism. When I go to the theatre, I want to get an eyeful. Why not? I do not want to have to look at one of those so-called "suggestive" settings, in which a single Gothic column is made to do duty for a cathedral; it makes me feel as if I had been invited to some important ceremony and had been given a poor seat behind a post. I do not want to see any more "skeleton stages" in which a few architectural elements are combined and re-combined for the various scenes of a play, for after the first half hour I invariably discover that I have lost the thread of the drama. In spite of myself, I have become fascinated wondering whether the castle door I have seen in the first act is going to turn into a refectory table in the second act or a hope-chest in the last act. No, I don't like these clever, falsely economical contraptions. And I do not want to look at a setting that is merely smart, or novel, or *chic*, a setting that tells me that it is the latest fashion, as though its designer had taken a flying trip like a spring buyer and brought back a trunk full of the latest styles in scenery.

I want my imagination to be stimulated by what I see on the stage. But the moment I get a sense of ingenuity, a sense of effort, my imagination is not stimulated it is starved. That play is finished as far as I'm concerned. For I have come to the theatre to see a play, not to see work done on a play.

A good scene should be, not a picture, but an image. Scene-designing is not what most people imagine it is—a branch of interior decorating. There is no more reason for a room on the stage to be a reproduction of an actual room than for an actor who plays the part of Napoleon to be Napoleon or for an actor who plays Death in the old morality play to be dead. Everything that is actual must undergo a strange metamorphosis, a kind of sea-change, before it can become truth in the theatre. There is a curious mystery in this. You will remember the quotation from *Hamlet*:

> My father—methinks I see my father.
> O where, my lord?
> In my mind's eye, Horatio.

Stage-designing should be addressed to this eye of the mind. There is an outer eye that observes and there is an inner eye that sees. A setting should not be a thing to look at in itself. It can, of course, be made so powerful, so expressive, so dramatic, that the actors have nothing to do after the curtain rises but to embroider variations on the theme the scene has already given away.

The designer must always be on his guard against becoming too explicit. A good scene, I repeat, is not a picture. It is something seen, but it is something conveyed as well, a feeling, an evocation. Plato says somewhere, "It is beauty I seek, not beautiful things." This is what I mean. A setting is not just a beautiful thing, a collection of beautiful things. It is a presence, a mood, a warm wind fanning the drama to flame. It echoes, it enhances, it animates. It is an expectancy, a foreboding, a tension. It says nothing, but is gives everything.

Do not think for a moment that I am advising the designer to do away with actual objects on the stage. There is no such thing as a symbolic chair. A chair is a chair. It is in the arrangement of the chairs that the magic lies. Molière, Gordon Craig said, knew how to place the chairs on his stage so they almost seemed to speak. In the balcony scene from *Romeo and Juliet* there must be a balcony, and there must be moonlight. But it is not so important that the moon be the kind of moon that shines down on Verona as that Juliet might say of it:

> O, swear not by the moon, the inconstant moon . . .
> Lest that thy love prove likewise variable.

The point is this: it is not the knowledge of the atmospheric conditions prevailing in northern Italy which counts, but the responses to the lyric, soaring quality of Shakespeare's verse.

The designer creates an environment in which all noble emotions are possible. Then he retires. The actor enters. If the designer's work has been good, it disappears from our consciousness at that moment. We do not notice it any more.

Three Selections from "The Dramatic Imagination"

It has apparently ceased to exist. The actor has taken the stage; and the designer's only reward lies in the praise bestowed on the actor.

II

If we are to accomplish anything in any art we must first see what our problem is before we can proceed to solve it. What we do in the theatre depends upon what we see. If we are to design for the theatre we must have the clearest possible image in our minds of the nature and the purpose and the function of the theatre.

Now this theatre we are working in is a very strange place. It deals, not with logic, but with magic. It deals with witchcraft and demonic possession and forebodings and ecstasies and mystical splendors and legends and playthings and parades and suspicions and mysteries and rages and jealousies and unleashed passions and thrilling intimations and austerity and elevation and luxury and ruin and woe and exaltation and secrets "too divinely precious not to be forbidden,"— the shudder, the fission, the shaft of chill moonlight, the footfall on the stair, the knife in the heart, the face in the window, the boy's hand on the sill. . . . The air of the theatre is filled with extravagant and wheeling emotions, with what H. L. Mencken calls "the grand crash and glitter of things."

In the theatre, the supernormal is the only norm and anything less is subnormal, devitalized. If we try to bring the theatre down to our own level, it simply ceases to be. When we see *Oedipus Rex* in the theatre, when we hear *Pelléas and Mélisande,* when we examine the stage designs of Adolphe Appia, we realize that great artists like Sophocles and Debussy and Appia create as they do, not only because they are more skilled, more experienced than the rest of us, but because they think and feel differently from the way the rest of us do. Their orientation is different from our own. When we listen to what artists tell us in their work—when we

40

look at what they look at and try to see what they see—
then, and only then, do we learn from them.

There is no formula for inspiration. But to ask ourselves,
why did that artist do that thing in that particular way instead of in some other way is to take the first step toward
true creation.

Nature has endowed us all with a special faculty called
imagination, by means of which we can form mental images
of things not present to our senses. Trevisa, a seer of the late
fourteenth century, defined it as the faculty whereby "the
soul beholds the likeness of things that be absent." It is the
most precious, the most powerful, and the most unused of all
human faculties. Like the mantle of rainbow feathers in the
Japanese *Noh* drama, *Hagoromo*, it is a treasure not lightly
given to mortals. Many people confuse imagination with
ingenuity, with inventiveness. But imagination is not this
thing at all. It is the peculiar power of seeing with the eye
of the mind. And it is the very essence of the theatre.

Many of you are familiar with the region of the Ardennes,
in Belgium. Now this countryside, charming and poignant
though it is, may seem no more beautiful than many parts
of our own country, nearer and dearer to us. But Shakespeare
once went there. And in his drama *As You Like It,* the
familiar scene is no longer the Ardennes we know, but the
Forest of Arden, where on every enchanted tree hangs the
tongues that show the beauties of Orlando's Rosalind.

Atalanta's better part, sad Lucretia's modesty.

Shakespeare's imagination joins with our own to summon up
an ideal land, an image of our lost paradise. Or let us take
another example: King Lear had, I dare say, a life of his
own outside the limits of Shakespeare's play, a daily routine
very much like our own. He got up in the morning and put
on his boots and ate his breakfast and signed dull documents
and yawned and grumbled and was bored like everyone

else in the world. But the drama does not give us these moments. It gives us Lear at his highest pitch of living. It shows him in intensest action, a wild old man storming at heaven, bearing his daughter Cordelia, dead in his arms.

In these examples we may divine Shakespeare's own intention toward the theatre. His attitude—the true dramatic attitude, the mood, indeed, in which all great art is created —is one of intense awareness, of infectious excitement. If we are to create in the theatre, we must first learn to put on this creative intention, like the mantle of rainbow feathers. We must learn to feel the drive and beat of the dramatic imagination in its home. We must take the little gift we have into the hall of the gods.

III

Professor Max Reinhardt once said, "I am told, that the art of lighting a stage consists of putting light where you want it and taking it away where you don't want it." I have often had occasion to think of this remark—so often, in fact, that with the passage of time it has taken on for me something of the quality of an old proverb. Put light where you want it and take it away where you don't want it. What could be more simple?

But our real problem in the theatre is to know where to put the light and where to take it away.

* * *

Today our productions are characterized—conditioned, one might almost say—by conical shafts of colored electric light which beat down upon them from lamps placed in the flies and along the balconies of the theatre. Lighting a play today is a matter of arranging and rearranging these lamps in a variety of combinations. This is an exercise involving great technical skill and ingenuity. The craft of lighting has been developed to a high degree and it is kept to a high standard by rigorous training in schools and colleges. It has become both exacting and incredibly exact. The beam of light strikes with the precision of a *mot juste*. It bites like an etcher's needle or cuts deep like a surgeon's scalpel. Every tendency moves strongly toward creating an efficient engine behind the proscenium arch. Almost without our knowing it this wonderful invention has become a part of the general *expertise* of Broadway show-business. We handle our spotlights and gelatines and dimmers with the same delight and the same sense of mastery with which we drive a high-powered automobile or pilot an aeroplane.

But at rare moments, in the long quiet hours of light-rehearsals, a strange thing happens. We are overcome by a realization of the *livingness* of light. As we gradually bring a scene out of the shadows, sending long rays slanting across a column, touching an outline with color, animating the scene moment by moment until it seems to breathe, our work becomes an incarnation. We feel the presence of elemental energies.

There is hardly a stage designer who has not experienced at one time or another this overwhelming sense of livingness of light. I hold these moments to be among the most precious of all experiences the theatre can give us. The true life of the theatre is in them. At such moments our eyes are opened. We catch disturbing glimpses of a theatre not yet created. Our imaginations leap forward.

It is the memory of these rare moments that inspires us and guides us in our work. While we are studying to perfect ourselves in the use of the intricate mechanism of stage lighting, we are learning to transcend it. Slowly, slowly, we begin to see lighting in the theatre, not only as an exciting craft but as an art, at once visonary and exact, subtle, powerful, infinitely difficult to learn. We begin to see that a drama is not an engine, running at full speed from overture to final

43

curtain, but a living organism. And we see light as a part of that livingness.

* * *

Lighting a scene consists not only in throwing light upon objects but in throwing light upon a subject. We have our choice of lighting a drama from the outside, as a spectator, or from the inside, as a part of the drama's experience. The objects to be lighted are the forms which go to make up the physical body of the drama—the actors, the setting, the furnishings and so forth. But the subject which is to be lighted is the drama itself. We light the actors and the setting, it is true, but we illuminate the drama. We reveal the drama. We use light as we use words, to elucidate ideas and emotions. Light becomes a tool, an instrument of expression, like a paintbrush, or a sculptor's chisel, or a phrase of music. We turn inward and at once we are in the company of the great ones in the theatre. We learn from them to bathe our productions in the light that never was on sea or land.

One afternoon many years ago I was taken into the inner room of a little picture gallery and there I saw, hanging on the wall opposite me, Albert Pinkham Ryder's painting of *Macbeth and the Witches*. I knew then in a sudden flash of perception that the light that never was on sea or land was a reality and not an empty phrase. My life changed from that moment. Since then I try with all the energy of which I am capable to bring this other light into the theatre. For I know it is the light of the masters.

* * *

Lucidity, penetration, awareness, discovery, inwardness, wonder . . . these are the qualities we should try to achieve in our lighting. And there are other qualities, too. There is a quality of luster, a shine and a gleam that befits the exceptional occasion. (It would be hard perhaps to make the

44

water-front saloon setting of *Anna Christie* lustrous, but I am not sure. It is the occasion and not the setting which should be lustrous.) There is a quality which I can only describe as racy, a hidalgo quality, proud, self-contained, a bold firm stroke, an authority that puts an audience at its ease, an assurance that nothing in the performance could ever go wrong, a strength, a serenity, flowing down from some inexhaustible shining spring. Here in a little circle of clear radiance, the life of the theatre is going on, a life we can see and know, and learn to love.

But creating an ideal, exalted atmosphere, an "intenser day" in the theatre is only a part of our task, so small a part that at times it seems hardly to matter at all. However beautiful or expressive this light may be, it is still not a dramatic light. Rather it is a lyric light, more suited to feeling than to action. There is no conflict in it; there is only radiance. Great drama is given to us in terms of action, and in illuminating dramatic action we must concern ourselves not only with light, but with shadow.

How shall I convey to you the meaning of shadow in the theatre—the primitive dread, the sense of brooding, of waiting, of fatality, the shrinking, the blackness, the descent into endless night? *The valley of the Shadow . . . Ye who read are still among the living, but I who write shall have long since gone my way into the region of shadows. . . . Finish, bright lady, the long day is done, and we are for the dark. . . .* It is morning, the sun shines, the dew is on the grass, and God's in His Heaven. We have just risen from sleep. We are young, the sap runs strong in us, and we stretch ourselves and laugh. Then the sun rises higher, and it is high noon, and the light is clear, and colors are bright, and life shines out in a splendid fullness. Jack has his Jill and Benedick his Beatrice, and Millamant her Mirabell. But then the sun sinks down, the day draws to its close, the shadows gather, and the darkness comes, and voices fall lower, and we hear the whisper, and the stealthy footfall, and we see the light in the cranny of the door, and the low star reflected in the stagnant tarn. A nameless fear descends upon us. Ancient apparitions stir in the shadows. We listen spellbound to the messengers from another world, the unnatural horrors that visit us in the night.

* * *

As we dwell upon these great examples of the use of light in the theatre we cease to think of harmony and beauty and think instead of energy, contrast, violence, struggle, shock. We dream of a light that is tense and vivid and full of temperament, an impulsive, wayward, capricious light, a light "haunted with passion," a light of flame and tempest, a light which draws its inspiration from the moods of light in Nature, from the illimitable night sky, the blue dusk, the halcyon light that broods over the western prairies. We say with D'Annunzio, *I would that Nature could be round my creations as our oldest forefathers saw her: the passionate actress in an immortal drama. . . .* Here before us as we dream is the frame of the proscenium, enclosing a darkness like the darkness that quivers behind our closed eyelids. And now the dark stage begins to burn and glow under our fingers, burning like the embers of the forge of Vulcan, and shafts of light stab through the darkness, and shadows leap and shudder, and we are in the regions where splendor and terror move. We are practicing an art of light and shadow that was old before the Pyramids, an art that can shake our dispositions with thoughts beyond the reaches of our souls.

The creative approach to the problem of stage lighting—the art, in other words, of knowing where to put light on the stage and where to take it away—is not a matter of textbooks or precepts. There are no arbitrary rules. There is only a goal and a promise. We have the mechanism with which to create this ideal, exalted, dramatic light in the theatre. Whether we can do so or not is a matter of temperament as well as of technique. The secret lies in our perception of light in the theatre as something alive.

THE ROLE OF THE
SCENE DESIGNER

by

Lee Simonson

Lee Simonson wrote THE STAGE IS SET *(Harcourt, Brace & Co., New York, 1932) as a protest against those critics who throughout the twenties continued to hail the scene designer as "prophet as well as practitioner" and who would deliver the theatre from the "stultifying spell of Realism." In the chapter entitled, "The Role of the Scene Designer," (pp. 96-117) Simonson proclaimed for the first time that "the scene designer must reconcile himself to the fact that the aesthetic values of his stage settings are relative and no more important than the production for which they are designed."*

Modern scenery has been associated with "art theatres" because these have been born not of any interest in art, in its formal sense, but of an interest in ideas, and a wide-spread conviction that the theatre is, at this moment, suited to reinterpreting life and reconceiving the world. It is typical that theatrical designing rose to the rank of a separate profession, in this country, in "art theatres" like the Washington Square Players, the Provincetown Players, and the Theatre Guild—theatres that were dedicated not to providing visually beautiful spectacles, but to propagating what seemed to be important ideas in terms of dramatic stories. The importance of design in setting a stage was made plain just as often in stage pictures of drab fo'c'sles and peasant kitchens as in vistas of kings' palaces or visions of the Garden of Eden. The incentive to design has been primarily the necessity of making the world of the play as real to an audience as it was to the playwright. The scene-designer has been enlisted as part of the job of "putting the play over," of creating the backgrounds that made seeing believing. And he has been most necessary in theatres where the theme of the play, the picture of life it conveyed, was neither accepted nor obvious. Plays that arouse none of this conflict with the audience are not often mounted with beauty. Themes that are universally accepted are rarely staged with any distinction of style because they have no need to be. For an audience of editors of the Variorum Edition and the old lady to whom Shakespeare is so full of familiar quotations, any set of dull and puffy costumes and drab flats from the nearest storehouse are enough to dress any of the tragedies or the comedies.

Molière has been staged for generations with solid dullness at the Comédie Française, where he was a universally accepted classic. The backgrounds of *Don Juan* in Russia, where the world of Molière was an alien one, needed the brush of Golovin and the hand of Meyerhold and "hundreds of wax candles in three chandeliers . . . little negroes flitting on the stage here to pick up a lace handkerchief from the hands of Don Juan or there to push the chairs before the tired actors . . . handing the actors lanterns when the stage is submerged in semi-darkness." "These," writes Meyerhold, "are not tricks created for the derision of the snobs, all this is . . . the main object of the play: to show the gilded Versailles realm."

For *Peer Gynt,* backdrops no better than enlarged postcards of Norwegian fiords did well enough for years in Norway, where Peer Gynt was a national hero, his story part of a national folk-lore. The hills and valleys of his adventures first had the lure of a legend in Berlin and New York, where he was the mouthpiece of an exotic legend. If *Liliom,* as I have frequently been told, was more beautifully staged at its New York première than in Budapest, the reason was simply that to his native audience the amusement park where he flourished as a barker was as familiar as Coney Island is to us. It was, in fact, so fresh in their memory that the meanest suggestion of it in the theatre was sufficient. Here it had to be designed in order to make it live vividly as part of Liliom's life. And the impulse to invest the squalor of his world with beauty was based upon the fact that, to the Theatre Guild, the play was something more than the story of a thief, full of amusing bits of first-hand observation, twisted into a highly sentimental ending. Liliom was less recognizable as a fact than as a symbol. The play seemed worth doing not as a picture of a foreign underworld, but as an expression, through the mouth of a thief, of a romantic faith in human compassion eloquent enough to make it poignant allegory. For that reason it became necessary to give beauty even to the tumble-

50

down shack where this tough lived and the dusty corner of a city park where he fell in love with a servant girl under the light of a lamp post.

Shakespeare was first restaged in every variety of style of which the modern art theatre of its day in Germany was capable, beginning with the Duke of Saxe-Meiningen's company, long before audiences in England or America felt the necessity for anything but the backdrops of their grandfathers. It was not until the spell cast by the word-magic of *Midsummer Night's Dream* began to lose some of its potency that Granville-Barker and Wilkinson created a more magical and iridescent forest. When Hamlet's agony over his mother's incest, no longer a sin to us, began to make his tragedy seem remote, we become supremely modern, announce *Hamlet* in modern clothes, and put him in a dinner-jacket in order to make him one of us. It is only because so much of the fun of *Taming of the Shrew* begins to be heavy and meaningless that we send Petruchio and Katherine rattling from Verona to Padua in a Ford.

Stage design is part and parcel of the total effort of interpreting script, an integral factor in overcoming the resistance of an audience to dramatic ideas that transcend its stereotyped expectations. But design is necessary for staging the accepted masterpieces of the past as for plays that are assumed to be masterpieces of the present. The presentation of significant ideas where the theme of a play is based on contemporary material, because of the idea's relevance, involves a definite struggle with an audience's preconceptions and taboos. The presentation of significant ideas of the past becomes a struggle to overcome their seeming irrelevance because the audience is inclined to be not antagonistic but indifferent. Ancient kings, queens, heroes, and demi-gods can no longer be seen invested with the power or the divinity once attributed to them. Present-day labourers or harlots often obscure the dramatic value of a scene because the author gives them an

51

inherent dignity or virtue entirely at variance with popular prejudice. In accepting a current masterpiece in the theatre we must accept a new creed as we listen to the play being acted. In order to accept an ancient masterpiece we must recover a creed while its story is being played. To establish the relevance of Hedda is as difficult as to establish the relevance of Hecuba. Wedekind's Marquis of Keith in a dress-suit may be a stranger figure than Macbeth in armour.

The meaning of a classic can rarely be recovered or revived; it must nearly always be re-created. The supposedly universal ideas commonly ascribed to classics originally clarified a certain range of human experience under a particular aspect of eternity that can never again have exactly the same significance. For a Greek mother the fate of an unburied son killed in battle, doomed to a restless life in death as a perpetually wandering spirit, held the same terror that a mother today would feel for the fate of a son who had contracted leprosy and was doomed to exile of death in life at Molokai. Unless a performance of *The Supplicants* can re-create that state of terror, its lamentations will affect us less than the wails of widows at a mine-pit after an explosion. Let the same play be performed shortly after or during a great modern war, when miles of our own dead lie unburied in shell craters, and we can share the force of an ancient sorrow. The spiral of history does not create many such parallels. In most instances a stage setting must help to revive a conception of life that was part of the original background of a play existing in the mind of its original audience. It must contrive to imbue the present stage background with the emotional quality of those associations with which this lost audience invested the event enacted. The total stage picture, the choice and arrangement of its details are of aesthetic importance because they determine to a great extent the kind of emotion a performance will release. When witches were believed to exist and the sight of any old crone mumbling to herself in a twilit field was enough to send any man on a wide detour for fear of having the evil eye put upon him, three old women hunched over a black kettle, provided their noses were sufficiently beaked and their hair unkempt enough, could evoke the weird sisters of *Macbeth*. Today they must be given an added dimension of terror if we are to shudder at the sight of them and accept their power to inspire murder. The palace doors behind Clytemnestra or Jocasta must have the quality of majesty and the scale of doom that these queens can no longer convey wholly by their presence.

Shylock tends to be a victim rather than a villain for a society that subscribes to the liberation of oppressed races and is avowedly humanitarian. Hamlet seems the greatest tragic figure because inhibition is felt to be the source of so much tragic frustration in contemporary life. A bourgeois father of today may transfer to Lear his dread of old age and his fear that his property will be insufficient to retain the loyalty of his children—property still being the bulwark of his authority. In so far as the absolute authority of the father no longer seems just or desirable, Lear tends to become pathetic rather than a tragic figure. Reinhardt attempted to overcome this by making him a barbaric king, his exactions those to be expected from a tribal leader who was also a high-priest, whose whims could be received with awe by a primitive clan. To a majority of Elizabethans, Macbeth and Richard III personified upper-class privilege vested in the dominant nobility of the day, who could attain wealth and power by murdering with impunity. Envy of this effective way of rising in the world, denied to commoners, was appeased by the spectacle of aristocratic villains so corroded by ill-gotten gains that they were brought to dust before they could enjoy any of the fruits of power. Because political murder is no longer an upper-class privilege, Macbeth and Richard become more and more mechanical villains and a production of either play calls forth the greatest imaginative efforts of a designer such

53

as Robert Edmond Jones, Emil Pirchan, or Gordon Craig in order to lend it the scope of tragedy. Murder for profit has, however, recently become a low-class privilege, a certain road to millions for poor men courageous enough to run the occasional risk of being shot on sight, uneducated "wise guys" who "make good" even though they can be classed as mentally deficient in other respects. The average man's thirst for power is at present slaked in melodramas, on the stage or on the screen, that glorify successful gangsters patterned on our greatest beer-baron, Al Capone. Dime novels once glorified Jesse James' defiance of authority in the glamorous Far West and so appeased a generation unable to make millions by buying up railroad franchises or timber reserves from Western State legislatures. The interpretative power of scenery is not yet needed in order to make the gangster's relevance plain. It may be called upon by a later generation if our more plutocratic criminals are then put forward as archaic heroes, inarticulate precursors of a revolt against the entrenched hypocrisy of American legislation and the class distinctions of our present reign of Law and Order.

A director's genius depends upon his ability to understand the forces of contemporary life and to determine the emphasis of a production that in turn outlines its central idea. He relates the actor at every moment to the particular kind of reality that is being created and to the preconception of his audience. This reality is illustrated by the scene designer. He can accomplish this by the design of a drama's background because outside the theatre the pictorial quality of a background affects one's emotional reactions to whatever happens in front of it, a fact acknowledged by the amount of effort that we habitually devote to creating appropriate backgrounds for every variety of human activity that occurs in parks, gardens, public monuments, and homes. In the theatre as well as outside of it, the designer tries to give to the background of action some kind of design relevant to the experiences that it is supposed to shelter. Very largely for this reason, the practice of architecture very often proves an excellent training-school for the scene designer and conversely scenic design often provides an excellent preparation for the practice of architecture. Thus Claude Bragdon after completing the railroad terminal at Rochester can step into the theatre and almost at once become a scenic designer of authority, as Joseph Urban did when he stopped designing Viennese villas. And Urban, like Norman Bel Geddes, after an apprenticeship of ten years or more in the theatre, finds himself equipped to solve architectural problems imposed by modern ways of living. However, although stage settings, as structures housing human activity, perform many of the functions of architecture, they are also pictorial in immediate effect. And as pictures modern stage settings are able to provide the kind of aesthetic satisfaction that painting no longer affords.

The applause that often greets a stage setting at the rise of the curtain measures the appetite of a public for pictorial interpretations of human experience which modern easel-pictures do not provide. Since the middle of the last century, after Géricault dramatized the survivors of the wrecked frigate Medusa perishing on a raft and Delacroix completed *The Massacre at Scio,* drama has been eschewed by painters of the first rank. The doctrine was established that painting was to interpret nothing but itself, and the literary subject was exorcised as a temptation of the devil. In consequence galleries of modern art are filled with episodic masterpieces: jockeys pirouetting at the starting-post of Longchamps and not horsemen winning a battle, canoeists lunching at an inn on the Marne instead of guests feasting at Cana, elderly women climbing out of tin tubs rather than Susanna in her bath or Venus rising from the sea. Peasant wenches, wading or washing in a stream, replace nymphs and nereids. Milliners trimming hats are substituted for Flora and the Graces ushering in spring. Instead of portraits of saints and saviour we contemplate the portraits of barmaids, nurse-girls, and village letter-carriers. Modern painting has been acclaimed as great and imperishable without ever touching the same popular imagination that has been stirred by contemporary poets, novelists, and scientists, for the reason that so many masterpieces of graphic delineation intensify no experiences more important than those of a man about town or the distractions of a week-end in the country. The villages of modern landscape-painting are, as a rule, deserted villages. An occasional picnicker piles his punt in a bend of the Seine but no one embarks for Cythera.

Dramatists of genius, however, continue to exploit themes that painters of genius have abandoned. They set themselves to interpret the meaning of fate and the rewards and punishments of human behavior by reviving ancient myths to point new morals, retelling the doom of princes, the doctrines of prophets, and the deeds of saviours. Painters of easel-pictures were once willing to illustrate such themes; their imagery fixed the types of gods and heroes, their pictorial compositions dramatized the crucial vicissitudes of the human race. Today it is in the theatre that we can most easily enter the Garden of Eden, interrogate the Sphinx, sit at the feet of Gamaliel, or with Marco Polo set sail for Cathay. We witness a Day of Judgment as machine made men destroy the fabric of machine production and with it the human race; we listen to an invisible Pan piping the goat-song of revolution and tremble at an apocalypse as his shadow leaps across the sky and swallows the stars. When the stage designer helps to stage the mob movements of *Danton's Death, Goat Song,* or *The Weavers* he faces problems of pictorial composition once solved by Tintoretto and Goya. The necessity of costuming the trolls of *Peer Gynt* brings him face to face with the necessity of devising appropriate masks of evil analogous to those evolved by Van der Weyden and hundreds of his contempo-

56

raries when they painted altar pieces such as the triptych at Beaume, where graves open and Hell sucks in the damned. In setting important modern plays the scene designer is forced to interpret significant themes and recovers the painter's historic role of image-maker. His imagery, like that of the fine arts of the past, achieves beauty not by appealing to a supposedly separate aesthetic sense but as part of the process of illustrating the meaning of life.

The conventions of modern painting often achieve a relevance in the theatre that is not apparent in the field of their origin. A human body made of metal tubes or pipe-joints, a face articulated like a machine, have no obvious importance in establishing a likeness of Mr. X. But they acquire an immediate and obvious value as the costume of an actor playing the part of a mechanized factory-hand in a play projecting our fear that machine production may destroy the soul of man. The angular clash of opposing planes may not make the fact of a guitar reposing on a table more important, but they can intensify the tragic conflict of Macbeth or Electra at war with their environment as well as with themselves. The picture of a street in Paris, Dusseldorf, or Canton, Ohio, so distorted that windows are awry and houses lean from the perpendicular, may in a picture-frame, be an irrelevant nightmare. But the same distortion acquires new meaning as the background of a play where the frenzy of a modern city drives the hero to the point of madness and a megalopolis of sky-scrapers is felt to be on the brink of destruction. The fresh values that so many novelties of modern art acquire on the stage is due to the fact that they can effectively illustrate or symbolize ideas that revaluate or reinterpret the forces felt to underlie existence today.

* * *

My conviction that the designing of stage settings is integrally a part of and so subordinate to the values of a play as interpreted and acted, has not been arrived at entirely by a process of dispassionate analysis. Most of my designing, having been done for the Theatre Guild, has necessarily been a part of an effort to project ideas not already obvious to New York theatre-goers. Some of these ideas have proved less significant than they seemed at first. But at the time no other management competed for scripts that seemed morbid, precious, oversubtle, or obscure—as a whole undramatic and unactable. Shaw himself, when he learned of our determination to produce *Back to Methuselah,* considered a contract unnecessary, remarking, "It isn't likely that any other lunatics will want to produce it." Both *John Ferguson* and *Jane Clegg* by St. John Ervine, were rescued by Lawrence Langner from the comparative obscurity of a shelf of miscellaneous drama at Brentano's. *Liliom,* one of Molnar's first plays, was regarded as a fledgling failure and had been all but forgotten despite the success of other plays such as *The Wolf* and *The Devil. The Guardsman* had been attempted by another management and abandoned as preposterous. Not even the endowed Burgtheater considered *Goat Song* an acting play, although Werfel's reputation as a poet was already established in Vienna. I do not, of course, pretend that we were always Daniels come to judgment. We selected many scripts that when acted turned out to be superficial and unimportant. But in the main the scripts we chose were free from stereotypes that could be expected to win easy recognition from New York audiences.

Our first ten years were animated by the nightly adventure of convincing an audience by the time the curtain fell of the importance of some theme that seemed remote or irrelevant when the curtain rose. Ibsen had proved to enlightened theatre-goers that any wife had the right to run away from a fatuous husband. Would they grant the same right to Jane Clegg, a forty year old domestic drudge, whose home had never been a doll's house and who could not dance her way into the heart of the next man by performing the Tarantella?

Or would they dismiss her as an elderly fool who had better make the best of it? It is notoriously difficult for American democracy to grant the same freedom to working-men and their wives that it accords to a bourgeoise and to millionaires. "Find God and be cleansed of your sins," is a doctrine entirely acceptable to American church-goers provided the sinner does not object to going to jail as part of the process. But how would they react to a play where the act of finding God was enough? After struggling with the powers of darkness, a peasant is cleansed of sin at the moment that the child he murdered is supposedly in the cellar under his feet. A wife-beater is an object of contempt to all right-minded Americans who subscribe to the Anglo-Saxon code of conduct befitting an officer and a gentleman. Could they accept the truth of a parable in which a wife-beater is absolved after he returns from Heaven to beat his posthumous child? During our first seasons at the Garrick Theatre such reflections were not literary exercises in experimenting with progress from the particular to the universal. We had at times less than a thousand dollars in the bank. To outrage our audiences without convincing them meant the closing of our theatre and the end of our experiment.

The same excitement of challenging audiences continues today. Could we make them accept Nina Leeds, who deliberately connives at the abortion of her legitimate child, breeds a bastard, and takes a lover not as indulgence to sin, but as her inherent right? What purgation could prosperous New Yorkers bobbing like happy picnickers on the tides of post-war prosperity, feel when faced with the *tragos* of revolution in *Goat Song* or the dreams and dirges of a battling proletariat in *Man and the Masses*?

Having designed settings as a part of such experiments that at times succeeded and at times failed, I conclude that a scene designer must reconcile himself to the fact that a stage setting is no more important than the production of which it is a

59

part. It fails or succeeds to the degree that a total cohesion of lights, forms, gestures, and voices succeeds in illuminating the script as performed. We continually forget that no play, even when written by a master dramatist, will play itself. The words themselves, the most minute stage-directions, furnish no more than a clue as to how it is to be acted. To have a script read by a dozen voices rather than by one does not make a performance. To turn dramatic dialogue into drama that can be accepted even by the most uncritical audience as an imitation of life or an interpretation of it requires an immense effort of co-ordinating the intonations of speech, the pantomime of facial expression, subtle variations of gesture and movement, and by incessant repetition, fixing their emphasis, rhythm and interplay. In the language of Broadway, a play must "get across the footlights." And even where footlights are obsolete, there is always an invisible line, marking the frontier of any stage, that separates the pretensions of the players from the expectations of their audience. Every performance is a battle with spectators which must be won again every night. Stage settings, realistic or symbolic, abstract or imitative, are nothing more than the ramparts of a battlefield where a victory over an audience has been won or lost.

No one method of setting a stage can be repeated everywhere as an aesthetic formula. The most radically different ways of staging may, in different environments, be equally good theatre art. Pitoev mounted *Liliom* in Paris in a deliberately fantastic manner, the park, the shack, and the street fair, as well as Heaven. *He Who Gets Slapped* was staged almost diagrammatically with a single poster and the outline of a tent indicated by a red ribbon. If one wanted to compare these settings with the more realistic ones made for the Theatre Guild, one would have to ask not whether formalism as a picture is superior to realism, but against which background Liliom became more significant. *He* more articulate? I have seen Richard III storm up and down the blood-red stairway provided for him by Jessner and Pirchan at the Berlin State Theatre, but his malignity was as successfully dramatized by Arthur Hopkins and Robert Edmond Jones in New York where a reproduction of the gate at the Bloody Tower backed every scene like a fanged jowl that alternately menaced and devoured. The single background of the prison that was the background of every character's fears and ambitions became as effective a symbol as a single stairway. To compare settings as pictures is to forget that their pictorial qualities exist only as a part of interpreting a play to the public. There are as many ways of setting a play as there are effective ways of acting.

Any setting that I have designed might have been done equally well, if not better, in an entirely different manner. Had I been faced successively with the necessity of expressing Copeau's, Reinhardt's, and Jessner's ideas of how the meaning of the plays mounted by the Theatre Guild could be projected, the backgrounds I designed for them would have been different from those I evolved in expressing the convictions of Emmanuel Reicher, Feodor Komisarshevsky, Herbert Biberman, Jacob Ben-Ami, and Philip Moeller. The realism of *Liliom* is not inevitable, nor the formalism of *The Tidings Brought to Mary,* nor the isolated vignettes of *The Failures,* the roofless house and church of *Goat Song,* the unit frame that held *Faust, Marco Millions,* and *Volpone.* The justification of these settings was the total impact, the value and the meaning of each play as performed.

*   *   *

Directors are often criticized for depending too much on the scenic background of a play in order to illustrate its meaning. No doubt this happens occasionally, although playwrights often do not realize the full implications of what they have written. But the increasing emphasis placed upon stage scenery is due not only to the director's reliance upon it, but to the fact that playwrights themselves use it more and more as a prop to playwrighting and depend on the details of stage setting to do the work they formerly had to do entirely with words. The careful specifications of the details of Roebuck Ramsden's or the Reverend James Morell's studies, such as the portraits of Cobden, Spencer, and Huxley, or a conspicuous "autotype of the chief figure in Titian's Virgin of the Assumption," let an audience know at a glance, in conjunction with all other details of furnishing, the education, approximate income, habits, and social class of the leading character and prepare his entrance much less clumsily than by marking time while the audience listens to the maid and a butler discussing the master and telling each other what they already know: "What a lot of books the Master has—" (business of dusting) "a learned man for sure," and "How he worships the blessed saints" or "honours the grand old men of England." Molière's leading characters usually establish their position by their costumes, their manners, elaborate verbal explanations of themselves or equally elaborate verbal descriptions of the other characters in the play. But in these days when costumes are standardized and there is so little that can distinguish a duke in a one-button cut-away from an undertaker in a one-button cut-away or a successful sculptor in a blue double-breasted suit from a successful travelling salesman in a blue double-breasted suit, every object on the stage serves not only the purpose of being used by the actors, handled or sat upon, but also the ultimate purpose of characterizing a social milieu that underlines everything that the actors do.

As an example read the stage directions of an unpublished manuscript:

A living room in W——'s house within easy commuting distance of New York (This cannot be specifically expressed, but the author plainly invites the designer to make the room unmistakably suburban.) *The room is comfortable, much lived in. All the evidence of a cultured family, a grand piano open with music on it, books everywhere, flowers, etc.*

W——— is a patient idealist of the Carl Schurz period and the room if given the proper atmosphere underscores the restlessness and incipient revolt of his two children, long before he makes his appearance toward the end of the act.

In *Meteor,* where S. N. Behrman tells the story of the rise of a penniless young college student to the dazzling position of "a captain of industry" and multimillionaire, Act I takes place in the study of the professor who encourages his confidences. But when Act II begins he is already the Napoleon of Finance that he bragged of becoming. The fact is announced by the stage setting at the rise of the curtain:

ACT II: Three years have elapsed. The scene is in a living room of a house off Fifth Avenue in New York, a nobly proportioned room with great dull yellow curtained windows in the rear. A carved ceiling, a chastely square marble fireplace. Old Florentine pieces—a richly mellow rather sombre room that could only have been achieved by a person of opulence and exquisite taste.

There is no more awkward problem for a playwright than to make convincing any such sudden metamorphosis, particularly one that takes place offstage between the acts. And there is no doubt that the setting called for saves a good many pages of equally awkward exposition, and by presenting tangible evidence of a meteoric change says as convincingly as the words of any character or chorus, "Lo—look what has happened—what a change is here."

Settings have become more than backgrounds for plays. They are often so much a part of a play that the meaning of dialogue depends on them. In *Hotel Universe* Philip Barry attempts to create a mood of mystic insight into life and death, and to express transcendent intuitions of their nature.

But he does not attempt to do so by words alone. The particular shape of the terrace is almost as important as the words spoken on it; in fact it prompts them, and recurs as a symbolic *leit-motif*. The stage directions carefully specify its shape:

> *Over and beyond the wall nothing is visible: sea meets sky without a line to mark the meeting. There the angle of the terrace is like a wedge into space.*

A director or designer who, for pictorial reasons, preferred a terrace with a curved wall, a railing parallel to the footlights, or an illusion of a deep-blue expanse of the Mediterranean Sea, as I did when first planning the setting, (by way of disguising the line that sea and sky make in meeting on a stage floor, at least to the balcony seats), would find, as I did, that nothing but the particular shape and the horizonless sea called for could be used, because the dialogue continues to refer to them.

Hope: *I tell you, you're all in a state.*
Pat: *I don't doubt that the people who used to come here were too. Lord knows it's on the edge of the world.*

A few minutes later:

Ann: *... What are you doing there, Pat?*
Pat: *Me? Oh, just looking—*
Ann: *But I thought you didn't like views.*
Pat: *This isn't a view. For a view you've got to have a horizon. There's not a sign of one out here. The sea meets the sky without a line to make the meeting. The dome begins under your feet. The arc's perfect.*

Shortly after this the complete picture of the terrace is made a symbol.

Lilly: *It's fantastic, this terrace. It just hangs here. Someday it'll float off into space ... like an island in time.*

After the announcement by

Stephen: . . . *Space is an endless sea, and time the waves that swell within it . . . Now and again the waves are still and one may venture any way one wishes . . . They seem to be still now . . .*

the terrace does become this island in space; past and present are jumbled as one character after the other re-enact a crucial scene of his or her youth. The effective movement of the actors depended, we found, and as Barry had intended, upon the triangular shape of the terrace railing, so that one or another of them could, at a given moment, stand there as on the prow of a ship, voyaging silently on an ocean of time between two worlds. The terrace plays its role to the end. A few moments before the curtain, Lilly repeats her refrain:

It's fantastic, this terrace. It just hangs here. Some day it will float off into space and anchor there, like an island in time.

By rights the terrace should not have appeared in the stage-directions but at the head of the program:
   Characters (In Order of Their Appearance)
   A Terrace, of triangular shape, that seems to hang in space.
   Pat Farley
   Tom Ames, etc.
Even such minor details as a fan-backed cane chair and a fig-tree are indispensably tied up with the action. Artificial foliage is always ugly. A high-backed garden chair takes up a great deal of the playing space, already cut down by the triangular boundaries of the set. Why not eliminate both, and instead of cluttering the setting, simplify it so that its symbolic outline is austere and apparent? Again the dialogue intervenes:

Alice: . . . *Last night I woke up and couldn't get back to sleep . . . so I came out on the balcony. It was a funny light.*

The Role of the Scene-Designer

Everything was—I don't know—awfully pale. For instance,
the fig-tree didn't seem to have any colour.

If not a fig-tree, some other variety of tree must be used, for
more important than a single line—which might be cut—is
the fact that twelve pages before the final curtain, Stephen
Field, presumably exhausted by his efforts to play Prospero
to a set of sentimental and intellectually shallow souls, dies of
apoplexy on stage. The effect of the final scenes depends very
largely upon the contrast of the presence of death unsuspected
by the departing guests and the daughter, who, hand in hand
with her lover Pat, says, "Thank you Father," as a cock
crows. Pat says, "It must be dawn somewhere," and she re-
plies, "But of course, dear, always," unaware of the corpse
within a few feet of her on an open terrace. Unless this seems
plausible to an audience, any suspense to which the scene can
build snaps. The shadow of the tree and the high fan-back
of the chair helps to establish this plausibility. If the playwright had not thought of them the director would have had
to invent their equivalent.

My point is not that such dependence on scenic details is
to be deplored or that the play would necessarily have been
better if it had ignored them. I see no reason why Barry or
any other playwright should not have his characters affected
by the sight of a terrace rather than by such dusty stage
properties as the first evening star, a rose, or a daisy. If metaphors are part of dramatic love-making, they can be made
effectively poetic and possibly more so, by apostrophizing a
terrace that seems to hang in space as by alluding to a star
that also seems to hang there. My point is, on the contrary,
that the designer cannot be expected to put less emphasis
upon a play's scenic background than the author has already
placed on it.

Hotel Universe is a typical, not an exceptional instance. A
director, instead of playing the first two acts of *The Lonely*

Way successively in Professor Wegrath's suburban garden and his living room, may simplify his setting by having them played in a room that overlooks a garden. But unless he wishes to change the script he cannot eliminate a pear tree *en espalier,* which Schnitzler thought important enough to mention specifically in the lines of the opening scene. In Romain Rolland's *The Game of Love and Death,* the eighteenth-century salon cannot be reduced to an abstract design, symbolic of the aristocratic intellectuals who find refuge in it. A painting must be hung, so that when the mob of sans-culottes breaks in, it can prompt the line, "Spare that fragile work of art." The fireplace must be built so that the same mob can stuff it with straw and attempt to smoke out a Jacobin supposed to be hidden there. But the play is a romantic homily, full of rhetoric that aspires to poetic significance, and not a "transcript from life." *Berkeley Square* is a dream play about a room quite as much as about its hero—a Georgian room in an old London mansion that hypnotizes its American tenant into re-living the love affair of one of his ancestors. A portrait, presumably by Reynolds, but painted so as to be startling in its resemblance to the leading actor, must be conspicuously hung, for it supplies the first clue. And the details of the room itself, from its period furniture to its panel moulding, as well as its general atmosphere of a bygone century, are dramatically indispensable in building the situations that lead to a flight into the past. *Street Scene* is meaningless without the complete reproduction of the facade of a typical tenement-house. The role of scenery is occasionally pushed to such absurd lengths as in *Recapture,* given a few seasons ago, where an old-fashioned open *ascenseur* in a small French hotel cued most of the action by sticking between floors and brought about the denouement by snapping a cable, falling and killing its dummy occupant.

One cannot point to dependence on scenic detail as the mark of realistic playwrighting. *Berkeley Square* and *Hotel*

Universe are dream plays, the former praised for having achieved metaphysical subtlety in romantic terms, the latter commended for having attempted it. Nor can one point to the usual moral and say that only plays dramatically feeble are dependent on scenery and invariably fail for that reason. If *The Game of Love and Death* and *Recapture* were financial failures, *Berkeley Square* and *Street Scene* were hailed by the press as little short of masterpieces and ran through two seasons. Such a traditionally decorative and picturesque background as the Sphinx can be made a purely decorative silhouette in *Peer Gynt* but not in *Caesar and Cleopatra*. Its paws must be modelled to hold Cleopatra, be large enough to half hide her during Caesar's soliloquy and not distract the audience's attention. But once he has finished, Cleopatra must be obvious enough in a shaft of moonlight to attract Caesar's eye instantly. A shaft of light is often as tangible an aid to playwrighting as the less ambient elements of a scene. To take only one instance out of a possible hundred: In *Fata Morgana* a *mondaine* friend of a country family arrives unexpected and finds the house empty except for the son studying under the dining-room lamp. The act ends by her deliberate seduction of the boy. "Turn out the lamp," she says. He obeys. As it goes out she is covered by a shaft of moonlight that strikes her from a near-by window. And that romantic transfiguration is conceived to be the final touch of romantic excitement which entices the youngster. Deliver the setting of *Le Misanthrope* for a performance of *Le Malade Imaginaire* and the play could still go on. But deliver the wrong set of scenery for a production of a modern playwright and the curtain could not go up. Let an electrician miss his cue, so that a lamp or a candle does not go out on the instant, and the curtain may as well come down.

Occasionally a designer, too timid to look modern playwrighting in the eye and face the consequences, affects an attitude of humility, asserts that scenery is purely a background, to be forgotten five minutes after the curtain is up. But playwrights today, bored with such self-effacement, are continually asking the setting to speak up and lend a helping hand. *Marco Millions* is of course a scene-designer's holiday and nowhere more so than in its opening scenes before a mosque, a Buddhist temple, and the Great Wall of China. In each of these O'Neill calls for the figures of a ruler, a priest, a soldier, in a semi-circle consisting of a mother nursing a baby, two children playing, a young couple in loving embrace, a middle-aged couple, an old couple, and a coffin. Three times these figures are repeated in different costumes. In order to make the production financially feasible, the Guild, with O'Neill's consent, omitted them, with the exception of one or two in each lot who had lines to speak. But as a result each scene was made dramatically feeble. For this recurring circle of figures placed Marco not in a particular temple of the Far East or at one gate in China, but in the presence of the patient pattern of Eastern civilization. His trivial conversation was given point by being addressed to a circle of human beings most of whom were too wise, too indifferent, and too contemptuous of his inanities to open their mouths. By the time this had been repeated three times, the ironic climax that O'Neill had in mind was achieved. These mute figures were no more than scenery, conceived as statues and supposed to have some of the monumental quality of Oriental sculpture. But with O'Neill's complete picture the sequence of scenes had dramatic force. Without it they seemed pointless and the play did not begin as drama until the second act.

The situation is not, as is often maintained, the result of a world conspiracy of modern scene-designers to enslave the dramatists, but the consequences of the methods that modern dramatists adopt in order to dramatize their experiences.

THREE SELECTIONS FROM
THE STAGE IS SET
by
Lee Simonson

The first two selections, "Motion and Meaning" and "Plan of Action," are excerpts from Simonson's exposition of Georg II, Duke of Saxe-Meiningen's contributions to the modern theory of play production (pp. 272-277, 284-290). In the first Simonson explains "the dynamic relationship between the mobile actor and the immobile setting in continuous interaction." Realizing this relationship, he evolves in the second selection his most famous definition of a setting, namely, "a setting can be best defined as a plan of action." The third excerpt, "Translation," from Simonson's scathing attack on Edward Gordon Craig's contributions to modern theatrical art (pp. 309-311), reveals one designer's attitude toward the scenic sketches designers create to illustrate their scenic concept. At best, according to Simonson, the scenic sketch is merely a notation of an idea.

The Duke of Saxe-Meiningen's claim to the title of theatrical innovator rests upon two accomplishments; he established the dramatic value of the stage picture as an indispensable factor in interpreting a script and he demonstrated that scenic effects must be fundamentally related to the actor. The human figure in movement was made the pictorial unit. Instead of first making a picture and then letting his actors wander about in it as best they could, taking care not to lean on canvas tree-trunks and to keep it free of the painted gables under their elbows, he planned his setting to fit their movements both as individuals and as groups, movements carefully planned before the work of stage setting was begun. His career inaugurated a new epoch in theatrical production and made the subsequent development of modern stagecraft possible because he eventually convinced every important director in Europe, including Antoine and Stanislavsky, that the fundamental problem to be answered by the scene-designer is not, What will my setting look like and how will the actors look in it? but, What will my setting make the actor do? More than this, he made plain that the dramatic action of a performance was an organic whole, a continuous pattern of movement, complex but unified like the symphonic rhythms of orchestral music. At the end of his career the dynamic relation of a mobile actor and an immobile setting in continuous interaction was an accepted axiom, and it is upon this assumption that experiments in production have proceeded since his day.

71

Three Selections from The Stage Is Set

Georg II was for his time an accomplished painter and draftsman. He designed every detail of his productions, including the costumes complete to the minutiae of hats and head-dresses and such accessories as swords, canes, pikes, and helmets. The settings used were enlarged from his own pencil-drawings. Their graphic method would be classed today as tight and academic, but they were revolutionary drawings nevertheless, for they are not pictures of settings but always of settings filled with human beings, grouped as they were to be at climactic moments. The Duke of Saxe-Meiningen's pictures demonstrate that stage pictures can have no independent existence, that a stage setting is not complete until the actor has taken his place in it. The lines of one cannot be set until the movements of the other are determined.

How fundamental and far-reaching this insight was it is difficult for the layman, even the habitual theatre-goer, to realize unless, by sitting in at rehearsals, he has learned how directly the motions of actors, not only particular gestures, but also their movements back and forth across the stage, affect the meaning of what they say. We think of plays of action as distinguished by the violent movements of murder, combat, flight, despair, love-making—raising of swords, parrying of blows, embraces on a bench or a balcony. But even in plays of violent action such extended gestures occur only occasionally. The action of a play is continuous. The cumulative effect of human movement on a stage is equally decisive when they are casual and consist of nothing more than rising from one chair, sitting down on another, moving to a door, looking out of a window, moving from right to left and back again. For the actor must not only speak and gesticulate; he must move from one spot to another. And it is precisely this succession of movements that make a performance out of the process of speaking the words of a script. Directing a play involves not only directing vocal inflexions and the individual gestures that center in the actor's body; it involves also direct-

72

ing motion, moving bodies from one position to the next. Leave actors rooted in a single spot and the most dramatic scene ever penned becomes not drama but recitation.

Imagine that you are about to rehearse a comedy, the first act of *Arms and the Man*. Forget Shaw's stage-directions for the moment and take the act after Bluntschli has broken into Raina's bedroom and she has decided not to rouse the house. Do not consider the scene beyond the moment that she leaves to call her Mother. Here are two people quietly talking to each other. Now select your ideal players: Bernhardt in her youth and Coquelin cadet, Katharine Cornell and Roland Young, Alfred Lunt and Lynn Fontaine. Keep them seated. They may recite the lines flawlessly, achieve every comic innuendo, laugh and weep to perfection. But keep them seated. The effect will be not of an incident lived but of a reading, a perfect piece of elocution with gestures attached. Keep them standing but never allow them to move from the same spot, and the effect will be the same.

You meet what seems to be a simple problem by telling your two players to move about as they have a mind to. Immediately you discover how subtle the problem is. For they cannot move about aimlessly unless you wish to convey a general impression of restlessness and nothing more. But if they move, where are they to move to? You find yourself obliged to set the essential parts of your scene: a window leading from a balcony (through which the artillery officer can break in), the young lady's bed, a door leading to the rest of the house, a table or tables to hold two essential properties, a candle and the photograph of the young lady's fiancé. Now begin to move your actors, and it will not be long before you discover that the positions of these two openings and the few pieces of furniture determine not only how your actors move, but also the implications of everything they say, and after a while, the entire mood of the scene.

Analyze the problem more closely, and consider at the out-

73

set only the relative positions of the balcony window, the door, and the bed. And assume you get no more help from Shaw than Shakespeare or Molière gives a director. Raina blows out the candle and goes to bed. Where will the candle be? Next to the bed seems the logical place. But that cannot be set until the director has made up his mind what Raina does when she discovers a man silhouetted against her window and lights the candle again. If the candle is within easy reach the lady will be discovered in bed by the soldier. If the rest of the act were purely melodramatic this might be an excellent arrangement, for the soldier could then threaten the lady at pistol's point. It might do equally well if the act were entirely of the blood-and-thunder variety, and Bluntschli a long-lost lover, banned by the family and determined either to force himself into Raina's bed or to drag her off with him down the balcony. But the act is nothing of the sort. Its words are a comedy of *rapprochement* between a terrified young lady and a terrified young soldier, who find that they both have been needlessly afraid of each other and finally take each other for granted. Even an amateur director would discover that this cannot be conveyed if the two continue to talk eye to eye on the bed or immediately plump themselves down on a near-by settee. Hence it becomes important to separate the lady and the soldier as soon as possible. The position of the table with the candle on it is therefore decisive. If it is not next to the bed but half-way across the room, Raina can leap out of bed to light it and she and Bluntschli can face each other, he on the opposite side of the stage as he locks the door to the room. But until the director is certain of these positions of his actors he cannot set the position of a bed or a night-table.

Until he is equally certain of their positions in what follows he cannot fix the relative distance of his window and the one door, or set the remaining pieces of furniture. The lady and the soldier come to an understanding when she realizes that

74

he is not a military brute but a gentleman and he perceives that she is romantic enough to be chivalrous, after which it is plausible that they sit down and talk the situation over. But that can be accomplished in several ways, each of which will determine or be determined by the position of two chairs or a settee. A settee may be near enough to Raina for her to reach it first while Bluntschli is still at the door uncertain of what he is in for. In that case Raina will take command of the situation and the comedy of their uncertainty will be played with the soldier tottering on his feet with fatigue but all the while proving that he has the instincts of a gentleman by not sitting down until he is asked to, eyeing the empty bed longingly, but not going near it. Or the settee may be near to Bluntschli for him to drop into it with a sigh of relief the moment he sees he has only a frightened girl to deal with. This leaves the man in command of the situation. He must then convince her that he is a gentleman although he does not behave like one, and the lady capitulates when she finds him a harmless chocolate cream soldier. If it strikes the director that sitting down beside a grimy stranger on a settee really makes it plain that Raina has been won over, there will be no other furniture in the room. If this seems unimportant, there may be several other chairs and they may talk to each other across the room, both gradually edging nearer each other as their mutual panic subsides. On the other hand, it is not inconceivable that the director might have Bluntschli throw himself on the bed—his fatigue makes this plausible enough—and play the entire scene with deliberate disingenuousness, knowing that the lady, feeling herself more compromised every minute, must come to terms with him if she is not willing to have him shot. The bed will then have to be brought more or less prominently down stage, whereas before it could be left up stage, as it is needed only for a moment at the beginning and end of the act. In each case the humour of the scene has a different overtone and different implications.

Three Selections from The Stage Is Set

I have by no means exhausted the possibilities of the simplest kind of setting or the dramatic consequences of placing a door, a window, a bed, a table, and a settee. But until the director visualizes them and places them so that he is sure of their effect on the movements of his actors, no amount of characteristic detail of Bulgarian architecture is of any importance whatsoever.

This visualizing of motion and planning of setting that will induce it may be done for the director by the author, it may be inadequately done, it may have to be added to, or it may have to be invented from start to finish. But in no case can the job be avoided. The kind of imagination involved in anticipating the connection between the physical properties of a stage setting and the kind of action that is to take place within it, and the kind of inventiveness necessary to relate the two, are an essential part of every director's equipment. For the implications of certain lines, the ability of others to provoke a laugh, the very meaning of certain lines, will depend on what the actors do at the moment of speaking them. Their meaning will depend on the way two people stalk each other about a room, converse side by side, the precise moment when they stop doing one thing and beginning the other, and also whether the transition is abrupt or direct. For the effect of a single line may be changed by the kind of physical motion that accompanies it.

Take the moment when Raina shows Bluntschli the portrait of the Bulgarian major whom he has been ridiculing: "That is the photograph of the gentleman—the patriot and the hero—to whom I am betrothed." Shall the lady rise, get the photograph from across the room, and present it with a great flounce and flourish. The effect of this is to underline her romantic heroics and the next instant to spoil her attitude completely when Bluntschli stifles a laugh. This is what Shaw calls for and it undoubtedly heightens the effect of Bluntschli's amusement more than if Raina, without getting up, did nothing more than reach for the picture on a near-by

76

tabouret. But if at this point in the scene Bluntschli were still standing and Raina seated, her gesture of confidently playing her trump-card as she showed the photograph of her fiancé might be the very thing to make Bluntschli capitulate on the lines:

I'm really very sorry. Was it fair to lead me on?

However, the way he crosses to her as he says these words can colour their implications. The printed speech with its stage-directions reads: (Looking at it) I'm really very sorry. (Looking at her) Was it fair to lead me on?

But even these directions do not fix the way this single moment is to be acted. Its effect has still to be determined by the precise timing of the cross. It makes a decided difference whether Bluntschli says, "I'm really very sorry," and then crosses to Raina, or whether he goes over to her before saying anything. Shaw doesn't direct him to speak "with sincere remorse" until a few seconds later. But if he does so now, if immediately upon seeing the photograph of the major he is genuinely apologetic and crosses to Raina on that impulse, what registers is the fact that he sympathizes with her predicament. What becomes important is his look at the photograph, not his look at her. That can be quick and casual. But if his apology is the usual polite and colourless formula and he goes to her only after having seen the look in her eyes, what registers is the fact that it is the genuineness of her feelings that moves him, not the mere fact that she is engaged. His look at the photograph is therefore casual, not the look into her eyes. And if that is prolonged only a second more than seems necessary, it conveys to the audience that Bluntschli, without knowing it, is beginning to fall in love. His laughter a few minutes later is, in spite of himself, kindly because an undercurrent of sympathy has been established. If this is not established his amusement may sound malicious and leave him a cynical professional soldier laughing at a romantic young girl, condescending to her to the end of the act. On the other hand a director may find at a much earlier moment in the act an opportunity for the two to be naturally drawn together. They may already be seated side by side by the time the photograph is shown and the scene can then be played against the tableau of a tete-a-tete. Precisely because their most violent differences of opinion do not separate them, their unconscious attraction for each other will be emphasized. It then becomes important to avoid a cross on the words "I'm really very sorry," whereas with another way of playing the scene it was important to plan it to the second.

Such niceties involved in co-ordinating motion and meaning in the theatre is called stage business. The nuances I have been describing are not confined to realistic comedy or realistic playwrighting in general. They are as necessary for a production of *Hamlet,* as decisive on a larger and more complicated scale, in building the mood and qualifying the emotions expressed by any particular scene. The total effect of a production depends largely on the cumulative force of the business that a director is able to invent. A play's action often consists less of its overt acts than of the movements (not specifically called for by the text) that accompany speeches in a way that enlarges or underlines their import. The subtleties of stage business are what prevent a play's being ready for performance the moment that the actors know their lines. Most of the time consumed in rehearsals goes to relating a continuous pattern of movement that must accompany words if they are to be acted and not simply spoken. Moments of violent action rarely offer any problems. The business of hiding Bluntschli behind the window-curtain, when a Bulgarian officer enters to search the house for fugitives, can be easily set in ten minutes, like the business of Hamlet stabbing Polonius behind the arras. But the movements that will be significant when Hamlet shows a miniature of his father to the queen have to be searched for, precisely like

78

those needed when Raina shows Bluntschli a photograph. When Hamlet sees Ophelia gone mad there is nothing in the text to indicate which lines are spoken "with genuine remorse" and between what lines he looks at her. The climax of the players' scene depends on where Hamlet crouches spying for the first sign of terror in the king's face, how he leaps forth in accusation, where and how he moves until that moment, and every movement of the queen, the court, the players, throughout the scene until they break up in confusion.

II PLAN OF ACTION

The theatrical value of stage business not mentioned in a script, the dramatic importance of the total stage picture as established by the Duke of Saxe-Meiningen, was built up not only by actors but by a stage setting directly related to them. His work as director-designer is an irrefutable demonstration of the fact that scenic design is fundamentally related to architecture, not because it reproduces architectural forms, but because it is based on architectural plan and like the plan of a building, directs whatever human activity it shelters. As sightseers we may identify architecture with façades but as householders we hold the architect to account if he has planned a layout of rooms that do not help us through our daily routine. Any housewife knows that the placing of a sink, a kitchen cabinet, a stove, a pantry, and a broom closet, if correctly spaced, directly affect the ease with which she can cook for the family; if incorrectly placed, they can make it difficult to keep a servant. A real estate agent would have difficulty renting an apartment where the bedrooms open directly into the dining room, which had to be crossed in order to get to the bath. The most perfect Georgian detail in window frames and panelling would not reconcile a single tenant to the fact that two sets of activities had not been segregated, those of sleeping and getting dressed, those of eating and entertaining. The first and the most important question that an architect, like a scene-designer, puts to himself, is, "What will the people who inhabit my building do?" He often spends far more time developing the plan of his building, invisible underfoot, but nevertheless directing every future step to be taken in it, than he does in elaborating the ornament of his façade, obvious to every passer-by. In larger structures, such as banks, hotels, office buildings, and railway terminals, the arrangement of the main units of a ground plan is of crucial importance. It organizes the circulation of crowds, prevents them from doubling on their tracks, leads them without detours to the objects that bring them into the building, sets up a current of activity and controls it almost as directly as a traffic-light does a stream of automobiles. A single mistake in the relation of entrances and exits to a main lobby or a bank of elevators can create a traffic-jam as quickly as too narrow a street placed between main thoroughfares. It is the plan of a building, not its façade, that helps people to achieve their purpose or impedes them.

The value of a building depends upon the architect's ability to plan intelligently, and this ability to plan depends in turn upon his capacity to anticipate the typical movements made in carrying out the purpose that brings the average person to an art museum, an office building, or a railway terminal. The museum visitor must be guided without a guide. The commuter, without bucking streams of people going in opposite directions, must be led on the shortest axis to the train platform, picking up his evening paper, an extra ticket, or a new timetable on the way. The mediocrity of its neoclassic ornament does not prevent the Grand Central Terminal in New York from being so excellently planned that the commonest rendevouz is the information desk, where any two people can find each other easily even at the peak of a rush hour.

80

The vertical planes of architecture that carry its ornament are rooted in its horizontal ground-plans. The historic styles of such monuments as cathedrals, temples, and mosques grow out of a typical arrangement of space made to direct the path of a votary towards a priest or god, hidden or revealed, a characteristic pattern of worship made up of a certain sequence of steps, genuflections, ablutions. The design of the ground-plan organizes this sequence about a point of central interest. The design of the enclosing walls attempts to symbolize or enhance the emotion that is supposed to accompany the typical progressions of each form of devotion. The design of a stage setting is built up by a strictly analogous process. Its plan, unseen by the audience, controls the pattern of movement made by a group of players; its façade, which immediately strikes the audience's eye by its choice of shapes and colours, expresses the prevailing emotions of the players as they move through this pattern. This is what is meant by the current dictum, "A setting should express the mood of the play," a thoroughly superficial statement unless one realizes that the basis of stage setting is architectonic. Whatever mood is evoked by its pictorial effect is created by a fundamental relation of façade and plan. A stage setting can be best defined as a plan of action.

The great contribution of the Duke of Saxe-Meiningen to the development of stagecraft was his insistence on the continuous and direct relation between the design of a setting and the actor's movements within it. His power of imagination lay in his ability to control this interaction to its last detail and develop both elements of it simultaneously. If his conceptions seem realistic to us today, it is only because we have foolishly restricted the field of imagination in the theatre to the creation of stage pictures that have the tenuous and slightly ambiguous quality of dreams. The effect of this school of stagecraft, at present so fashionable, is often to

81

make the event enacted on the stage more remote. The effect of the Duke of Saxe-Meiningen's methods was to achieve an intensified reality and give remote events the quality of actuality of being lived for the first time.

* * *

The details of the Duke of Saxe-Meiningen's settings were significant, even when literal, because they were so directly related to the dramatic action. Five studies were made for the opening scene of *The Maid of Orleans,* involving the relative positions of a chapel and an ancient tree. In the same play an abandoned wagon, piled high with military paraphernalia, was dragged on stage, not only for its value as an accent in a pictorial composition, but also to hide the approach of the French troops whose surprise attack is the climax of the scene. In the scene in *Macbeth* in which Macduff's children are butchered, the room where they were seen playing with their mother was entered by a long stairway from a balcony. The assassins were discerned there in half-shadows by the audience and the horror of the moment was immeasureably heightened by their slow, silent descent, waiting for the moment to strike. This stairway is the prototype of many that have been used since, including the staircase in Copeau's masterful production of *The Brothers Karamazov,* where Smerdiakov darted up and down like a malignant spider. Much of *The Merchant of Venice* was played on a bridge over one of the Ghetto's canals. On it the masqueraders danced in a frenzy of excitement as Jessica eloped, hidden in a gondola below it. This same scenic scheme formed the basis for Reinhardt's revival of the play some thirty years later. The doge's courtroom was enclosed by a loggia balcony, not only for the decorative effect on its characteristic architecture, but also to hold a crowd of onlookers who watched the trial and added to its excitement by reacting to Gratiano's jibes and Portia's casuistry. Silence was

82

dramatized as well as sound: the scene of conspiracy in Brutus's garden was played almost entirely in whispers. Light and colour were used to achieve dramatic climaxes: Brutus's tent was deep vermilion, lighted only by a candle, filled with deep shadows. The actor playing Caesar's ghost, clad in vermilion toga, was lost in them until one of the then new electric spotlights, shot through the tent's flap, struck him in the face. His vermilion robes still merging with the colour of the tent gave him the appearance of hanging in the air, and the ghost disappeared as uncannily into the murky shadows when the spotlight was turned off. The Duke seized every opportunity to play with varied intensities of light: in one scene he lighted a loggia with the gas light still in general use, then had a tapestry drawn and showed a garden brilliantly lighted with electric lamps, thus achieving the effect of sunlight. For the scene in *Mary Stuart* where Elizabeth signs Mary's death warrant, the table was lighted by four candles and the rest of the stage lost in shadow. But directly back of the table, dimly caught by reflected candlelight, was a copy of Holbein's portrait of Henry VIII, who seemed to preside smiling over the occasion. Antoine cites one lighting effect that he saw in Brussels as an example of "epic naivete": a shaft of sunlight, coming through a high window, strikes an old man at the very moment that he dies. But such a deliberate timing of stage lighting to accent the pathos of a scene, like all of the Duke's lighting effects that I have described, are now commonplaces of staging. The interpretative value of varying intensities of light and the contrast of light and shadow are assumed by every director and designer. But they were almost apocalyptic revelations of the possibilities of stagecraft at a time when every other stage was filled with a bland radiance and actors singed their trousers at the footlights in order to be seen.

Another interesting aspect of the Meiningen productions was the Duke's consistent effort to add to the plastic possibilities of stage setting by breaking the monotonous surface of the stage floor into different levels. In the *Hermannsschlacht* where a delegation of Roman generals come to parley with a German chieftain in his native forest, the primeval world which they are invading was emphasized by the unevenness of the stage itself, the hummocks and fallen logs that had to be clambered over in order to reach the chieftain's hut. In *Fiesko* the movement of a court fete was carried up and down a double stairway in a palace courtyard. Antoine complained that the Alpine paths in *William Tell* resounded like wood and thought that the use of platforms was overdone. We should probably find that they were not used enough. For an entire range of movement, valuable dramatically, is lost when actors are kept shuttling back and forth on an unbroken stage floor. The vertical relationships of higher and lower have the capacity to symbolize purely emotional relationships of one person to another and even of a person to an idea. The yearning of lovers is heightened by the use of the traditional balcony. A king or lawgiver pronounces his judgements more appropriately from on high and his figurative fall is symbolized when he falls from an actual throne or a rostrum. The pull of gravity suggested by the act of climbing a height emphasizes the pull of tradition, the burden of matter opposed to the élan of spirit. These physical ups and downs are important aids to the interpretations in the theatre because outside of it we respond to them with mimetic responses often so subtle that we are only half aware of them, as when we look up to a President on a balcony or a preacher in a pulpit, whom we are supposed to look up to as a political or moral superior. The sight of an aeroplane rising from a field gives us a sense of elation, of release from our bondage to earth. We soar with a bird in flight. We rise with the sky-rocket, involuntarily say, Ah, as it bursts, and then sigh as though we were fluttering down with its tinsel stars. Dramatic performances have always exploited similar devices. The Greek gods appeared above the palace roof. In the mystery at Mons, Pilate does not go to the upper of his two thrones until the climactic moment when he condemns Christ. But the Duke of Saxe-Meiningen's originality lay in his ability to show how movement up and down could be used to dramatize scenes where the possibility of utilizing it had not been suspected, how much more often it could be effectively used than on the few occasions where a playwright called for it. On this intuition alone the dogmas of various modern schools of production have been founded so that an entire play is now often performed up and down stairways, terraces, plinths, and trestles.

III TRANSLATION

What designer has not, at one time or another, on seeing one of his scenes set up, felt like Quince when he beheld his friend in ass's ears and exclaimed, "Bless thee, Bottom, bless thee, thou art transformed." When scenic projects are carried out they are in the literal sense of the word translated, carried over from one medium to another. In this process lies all the unavoidable technical problems of stage craft which have preoccupied the designers of every epoch in the theatre's history. The technical problem in its fundamentals is always the same: How are the form, colour, texture, atmosphere, and light of a design to be preserved when enlarged and erected in a theatre? A scenic drawing is no more than an intention; it is no better than the methods eventually used to embody it. Paper, as the Germans say, is patient. A swirl of the brush can create atmospheric distance in a watercolour, the sense of physical liberation that a landscape gives when one walks in it. But the space evoked by a watercolour wash or perspective drawing is the very quality most easily lost when the design is translated to a broad floor that meets a canvas backdrop or a plaster wall. Space was never

85

more convincingly evoked than by the perspective scenic drawings of the nineteenth century, which caricatured their intentions when executed. Any number of designs that as drawing seem to express the spirit of a play, once in the theatre, are transformed into something as grotesque as a donkey trying to make love to a fairy queen.

The dramatic poet evokes the full sweep and the scale of nature at every turn, lifts his heart to the hills, testifies to the glory of the firmament, opens his window on the foam of perilous or silver seas. A playwright can say, with Edna St. Vincent Millay:

> All I could see from where I stood
> Was three long mountains and a wood.
> I turned and looked the other way
> And saw three islands in a bay.

A designer can project the scene and recapture the mood in which such a scene is viewed, in a drawing that may be worth preserving in an art museum. But if an audience in a theatre must share this vista with Iseult at Tintagel or Ariadne on Naxos, all that it sees from where it sits will, in all probability, be something very like the enlargement of a lithographed calendar advertising the advantages of spending the summer in Maine. The overwhelming chances are that the audience will not see massiveness and mobility of natural forms, the downward thrust of cliffs and headlands interlocked with the upward thrust of mountains, holding the sea in their arms. Iseult or Ariadne will command the vista, so dramatically appropriate for love in exile, on a wrinkled hummock of padded canvas that has lost all semblance to the elastic tension of a hillside and the easy undulations of the earth. It is of course a simple matter to solve the problem by evading it and say that an audience need see nothing more than a woman on a flight of steps looking into a void. But as I have pointed out, both playwrights and audiences

86

for more than twenty centuries have been insistent in their demands that the stage be a world and that the backgrounds of action be visualized. If a designer decides that the problem is insoluble, he finds himself in the position of Bernard Shaw at a lecture when a solitary hearer booed him while the rest of the house applauded furiously, "I agree with you," said Shaw, "but what can we do against so many?"

The designer who declares that the technical problems presented to him every day in the year by every dramatist, whether poet or realist, genius or hack, have nothing to do with art, decrees his own exile. If he cannot invent a technical method more certain to create beauty in the theatre than the prevailing one and put it into practice, he does nothing more than surrender the field to those who manufacture ugliness. The technical problems of stagecraft may never be satisfactorily solved until the playwrights and the audiences become what they have never been. But in a living theatre the technical problem of finding ways and means to embody a microcosm of the natural world has to be solved daily.

Every stroke of the designer's pencil or of his brush must be enlarged at least twenty-four times on the stage. And the scene-designer's art consists not in being able to record his intentions as skillfully as the painter of easel pictures, but in being able to make a picture that, once it is enlarged, retains its original values of texture, colour, and form. Mathematical enlargement by itself is of no use because in every square inch of a drawing colour, form, and texture are inextricably combined. They can be translated to the stage only by being disintegrated and then recombined. How can this be done so that they retain their original effect? In a sketch a plaster wall scintillates in sunlight. The plaster surface must be translated into canvas, wood, veneer, or some composite building-board solid enough to be carpentered, light enough to handle. The modulations of white have to be organized in entirely different scale if the wall is not to be as monotonously flat as the side wall of a newly painted barn. The light that was part of a brush-stroke becomes actual light that hits a surface so painted that it will vibrate as the original sketch did. In a scenic sketch "little aspens dusk and shiver," we find ourselves in a gloomy wood astray or in Philomel's bower. How are we to recapture the resilient massiveness of clumps of trees so that on the stage they can seem an appropriate refuge for a poet or two lovers? Cut down a grove, transport it; it becomes a collection of dead limbs and faggots. Reproduce each tree with canvas stretched over wire frames and hung with imitation leaves, and each becomes a bedraggled mummy of a living tree. Suggest a forest with columns of canvas hung in folds and you lose the grace and lightness of the kind of grove that a given scene calls for. Project the grove with a stereopticon: you keep a semblance of its palpitant life but lose the essential forms that gave the original drawing its design.

In a scenic sketch a hero meditates on a hill-top crowned by a soaring cumulus cloud. How impressive as a picture. It might be as effective on the stage if one could find a way of translating the cloud. Paint it on the back-drop and it loses its effulgence. Cut it out of cardboard and hang it on a wire: it has a wire-line edge and soars no more freely than an angel on a Christmas tree. Project it with a lantern-slide. How then, precisely because it has some of the ambience and transparency of a cloud in nature, are you to avoid making it seem conspicuous because its forms are paralyzed and do not dissolve and then rebuild themselves? At the same time you discover that if the cloud projection is to be seen, the rest of the stage will have to be dark; enough light on your actors will wipe it out of the heavens. Resolve these difficulties with a moving-picture machine and project a cloud in motion; your stage seems a photograph that has no relation to the other parts of your stage setting.

Renounce your attempt to translate the landscape forms to the stage and limit your effort to translating the forms of architecture. You have restricted the number of your problems but you have not made solution of any one of them easier. The actual forms of architecture can be approximated by stage carpentry. But their actual scale cannot be absolute even on the largest stage ever planned; and once scale has been made relative, the very proportions that make an architectural drawing dramatic are often lost. The actor cannot be led up a flight of a hundred steps, down the immense depth of a cathedral nave; the eye cannot be led into the soaring heights of its groined arches, or through an entire temple colonnade. These distances can of course be suggested, but in the process much of the effect of a total architectural pattern is sacrificed. The base of a column or of one archway can be given its full scale but the rest of the architectural picture, so easily indicated in a scenic drawing, must be stunted or truncated. Throw the carpenter out of your theatre, call back the painter. Let him paint in perspective or in flat formal patterns; both will seem transparent artifice as soon as the first actually three-dimensional actor, an organic piece of nature, appears.

Drawings for the theatre are desires. They should all be signed with a question mark, for they are, even the best of them, pretences until they are fulfilled. A designer for the stage is a pretentious counterfeit of the Creator in miniature. Not being a god, he must attempt to create a world by one system of mechanics or another—each inadequate, each more or less clumsy—which tries to hide its inherent defects by striking a new balance between fact and illusion, truth and deception. And every attempt, whether its aim be reproduction or illusion, must be translated into materials that may in themselves easily destroy the aesthetic quality of the original design. The life of a scenic idea is inextricably bound up with the search for the purely mechanical means by which it can be projected on the stage without being destroyed in the process. The drawing of a stage setting is largely a dream. Its realization is often nothing less than a nightmare.

DESIGN IN THE THEATRE TODAY

by

Donald Oenslager

Donald Oenslager has successfully combined academic and professional careers, working simultaneously on Broadway and teaching scene design at Yale University ever since 1925. Although he has written extensively on the art of the theatre, the best summation of the aesthetic principles he practices and teaches are contained in this essay which Mr. Oenslager wrote for the catalogue of the retrospective exhibition of his work in the theatre, DONALD OEN-SLAGER, STAGE DESIGNER AND TEACHER, sponsored by the Detroit Institute of Art, September 25th through November 4th, 1956 which the American Federation of Arts circulated throughout America in 1957. Oenslager describes the American scene designer as "an eclectic and a mannerist" working within the limitations of stage, script and production. Retitled "Stage Design: New Directions or Dead End?" this essay was reprinted in THEATRE ARTS, Volume 40 (October, 1956) pp. 24-28.

THE DESIGNER'S INTENTION

In our theatre the stage designer is essentially an artist-craftsman. He uses his head and hands. He has many facets of knowledge—architecture and sculpture, painting and engineering, decorating and the graphic arts. He is at once a woodworker, a weaver, a florist, a dressmaker, a plumber, an upholsterer. He is accustomed to design settings for all medium of theatrical expression—drama, opera, musical, ballet, motion pictures and television. He assumes many styles working on one production as a realist or surrealist, on another as an expressionist or an impressionist.

Creating his sketches is the happiest and briefest part of the designer's work. Working as a craftsman and projecting his sketches onto the stage is the full-time burden of his responsibility. The easel painter and the designer in the theatre are different breeds of men. The former, working alone, expresses himself on his own canvas with his personal style, his own thoughts and views of the world. When his painting is finished, his work is accomplished. The latter is a collaborator working with playwright, producer, director, and actor. The painter needs an audience of one. The designer, an audience of hundreds. With fortune the painter's work may survive for centuries. The designer's work is ephemeral and with the best of luck lasts only as long as an audience will applaud the production. While Picasso, Tchelitchew, Chagall, and other painters have designed original and distinguished settings for the theatre, I suspect they think of

93

these works only as occasional forays into the theatre's Elysian Fields. Similarly, the designer removed from his scenic beatitudes finds relaxation before his easel.

The designer is an eclectic and a mannerist. He is always subject to the criticism of the unfinished sketch, for he can never make a final statement of a play. This year he will design *Macbeth* from one point of view. Ten years from now, with other collaborators, he will design *Macbeth* from some totally different inner compulsion. The stage designer works with the limitations of the stage, not with the freedom of the easel. Yet within his limitations he enjoys limitless freedom.

WHAT TO DESIGN

After setting up and lighting a production and the labours of dress rehearsal, there is stimulating contrast the next morning in catching the early Thursday train, as I have had the privilege of doing for many years, to lecture on the art of the theatre and criticize and discuss the work of growing designers at the Yale School of Drama. Teaching design in the theatre is midway between the practical and the ideal world, and therefore affords another area of interest for me. Those students who bring talent with lofty intentions should not be subjected to studying technique alone. In the University School of Drama not *how* to design or *to be able* to design should be emphasized, but *what* to design—above all, content. Young designers must learn to discriminate; they must learn "how to know the waking vision from the idle dream"—that rarest of gifts, Aeschylus tells us, Prometheus gave to man. Good scene designing is good thinking, with freedom of imagination supplemented by reasonable performance in execution. A proper climate is essential where practical experience is balanced by an imaginative approach to the theatre of both the past and the present. This implies facilities where technical guidance is provided and where students work together. Often the best criticism may be the comparison of one's own work with that of other students. They are side by side at the post together, ready for the race. But it is not all running. Young designers must also enjoy the opportunity and the advantage of discovering within the university community much for themselves besides theatre—stimulus to the eye and to the mind. In working with student designers I have always tried to set my course to conform with the changing barometer of the times, and however bromidic it may sound, I have found that teaching can be almost as exciting and stimulating as designing.

I frequently urge a young designer to make projects to test his trial-and-error insistence on new forms of expression. Some of the busiest designers' works do not always reach the stage of the theatre. These are his projects—the things he dreams of for tomorrow's theatre. The malcontent designer finds pleasure in a project which he designs for himself as producer and also audience. No contacts are required. These projects are ideas for productions—experiments in form and research in the styles of scenery of the past and of new directions in lighting which are not demanded by the average production the designer is likely to devise for Broadway. These projects are self-imposed exercises. They cost no more than the pleasure of planning and sketching them. Such dreams may communicate an idea to a director, a young playwright, or a producer for the newer freedoms of tomorrow's theatre. That is what the stage designer of today should care about and search for, believing with Gordon Craig that the "big Dream recurs again and again till it becomes in years the reality."

THE DESIGNER'S ROLE

Occasionally, the practical question is asked, "How do you go about designing a scene for a play?" Indeed, the designer sometimes wonders himself. He can answer in terms of feet and inches, dollars and cents, minutes and hours. That is easy. But first let the designer pause and ask himself just how *should* the scene look, first to himself and then to the audience. A stage setting is rather like a "still life" on the stage—*Nature Morte,* the French call it. The scene does not come to life until it is peopled with actors. Therefore, the designer's primary intention is to allow the playwright to help design his scenes. These scenes are more than backgrounds. They are the silent characters of the designer—the realization of all that is in the mind's eye of the dramatist. Thus his imagination peoples the place. He makes soundings in the hearts of the characters, observing them in conflict. What kind of theatrical dress will these characters wear? What external atmosphere best suits the necessities of this inner drama?

The designer's own feeling for the play will determine the direction away from imitating reality which the production will follow. He will be guided by his own compass of intuition toward a determined feeling or mood for the production. By evoking in himself a feeling he has once experienced, he proceeds to dramatize that feeling for others who have experienced a similar feeling. The designer translates this feeling onto the stage in theatrical terms of color, form, line and light so that an audience will realize clearly as the curtain rises that this scene before it is no ordinary eyewitness scene, but something deeply felt, seen for the first time on any stage. This scene *is* the heath of Lear's imagination, or the haunting rookery of the *Madwoman of Chaillot,* or the ominous dwelling of *The Crucible*'s rockbound Puritans. The designer has wrought these scenes from the hearts of the characters who are to inhabit them. Yet while he has made these scenes inseparable with the actors, he has also identified them clearly with the audience's imagination. This is the contribution of the designer's role in our theatre today.

METAPHORICALLY SPEAKING

by

Mordecai Gorelik

Mordecai Gorelik is another designer who is concerned with the quality of imagination necessary in scenic design. This concern with the kind of creative thinking that must engage a designer has led Mr. Gorelik to formulate the principle of the dramatic metaphor. The dramatic metaphor may be defined as the central scenic image of each setting which summarizes all the creative thought the designer has on that setting. This theory does not propose a particular style of design but is intended instead as an aid in the creative process of evolving the design. This essay originally appeared in THEATRE ARTS, Volume 38 (November, 1954), pp. 78-80.

Some stage designers begin with a sketch, others with a ground plan or a preliminary model. It may be notorious by now that I start with a metaphor. I began that way with the Robert Whitehead production of Bernard Shaw's *Saint Joan* for which I designed both settings and costumes in 1954.

The metaphor idea is simple enough, once understood. But it is not too easy to explain. A metaphor, according to the dictionary is "a word used in an unusual way to suggest a likeness between ideas." At Biarritz American University —surely one of the most unusual and impressive of all teaching ventures—I was in charge of a capacity class in scene design. The students were G.I.'s fresh from the beachheads and foxholes of Europe and Africa, an attentive, serious minded group. They were all ready to learn about the stipple technique in scene painting and how to mask the horizon strips of a cyclorama. But this metaphor notion stumped them for a while. I insisted that a girl's bedroom could also be the scene of a raging fever (Chekhov's *The Three Sisters*); that a tenement parlor could be a prize fight ring (Odet's *Golden Boy*); that a lighthouse was a candle in the darkness (Audrey's *Thunder Rock*). Most of them got the point eventually. At the end of the term one of the toughest-minded students conceded that "there is something to this here metaphor drill."

A good actor can give infinite variation to a single line of speech. A good setting is equally subtle. Just as an actress may remark, "Good morning dear," while intending mayhem

99

and murder, so a designer may portray a bloodsoaked battle-field while evoking a lovely spring morning. Furthermore, a setting is a dynamic creation, one that has a development of its own. Thus, in Arthur Miller's *All My Sons*, my setting changed from a David Belasco type of folksiness in Act I to an Edward Hopper starkness in Act III.

It seems to be popularly believed that the setting is a background. Most designers don't care for that term, which is not only inadequate but misleading. As *documentation*, the setting records the geography and history of the locale. As environment, the setting represents a place that has been made by human beings, or that has an effect on human lives or both. As *machine for theatre*, the setting answers to the sightlines of the auditorium and the physical limitations, the machinery of the stage; it serves the actors who in turn act upon it. But it is as the *scenic metaphor* that the stage design is most nearly related to the script. It seems to me that a setting can have no greater usefulness or distinction than to be poetically right for a given play. However, the design should not be "poetically right" in a merely general way; the relationship must be precise, the meaning pin-pointed. The designer must have in mind a definite scenic image, a creative, poetic thought which transfigures the his-toric and geographic documentation of the setting. This im-agery must affect the audience subtly; it must never be obvi-ous. (Crude, obvious imagery has long since had its day in the professional theatre in the era of expressionism. Unfor-tunately it lingers on in the educational and community theatres, perhaps because it seems to offer an easy road to "imagination" and "experiment.")

If it is true that every playscript is—or should be—unique, then perhaps one should be allowed to say that a Shaw play is still more unique. Certainly it presents the designer with more than his usual number of problems. If I remember correctly, *Saint Joan* is the only tragedy Shaw wrote; yet it

100

reads like high comedy. It documents the Middle Ages while remaining modern, even in this Atomic Age. Its story is not only a biography of a warrior-saint, but follows G.B.S. in all his wide-ranging survey of manners, ethics, religion, politics and art. In the theatre the play contains eight scenes— a notable extravagance these days for any show other than a musical. And this Robert Whitehead production was scheduled from the first as a touring company—meaning it must attain a maximum of scenic effectiveness with a minimum of bulk and weight.

Faced with a job as formidable as this, the designer gives the script as thorough a scrutiny as any monk or Talmudist ever gave the Bible. At the same time he steeps himself in the history of Saint Joan and her period, trying through pictures, written accounts and museum exhibits to recover the otherness of those days, which were so like and yet so completely unlike our own. But the severest test of the designer —this side of opening night—is not his ability to do research. It is his choice of metaphors for each scene and for the play in general. Whether the artist knows he is using them or not, they are there; and they must be simple, accurate and somehow exciting. They must be vivid to him but never obvious to the audience. Unless as I am doing this moment—he chooses to reveal them.

Some of my own metaphors for *Saint Joan* I developed consciously, after much brooding over the author's lines. Others came by sheer instinct. (The latter sort are hereby recommended as relatively painless. Unfortunately, I do not know of any normal way to induce them into one's mind; one must trust to fate.)

Here then, is a brief index to my own thinking:

Act I, Scene 1. A room in a castle of Vancouleurs. We are high up. Weathervanes, a gargoyle, a wooden balcony overlooking the barnyard. If this were a movie I would specify swallows darting overhead, droves in the rafters. A spring

101

sky, feathery trees, the color bright, lighthearted, youthful. Joan is only seventeen or eighteen, a little peasant girl with heaven-high ideals. The humor is broad, even farcical—Shaw himself is poking fun at the minor miracle of the hens laying eggs like mad. Metaphor: the bright sky overhead.

Act I, Scene 2. Antechamber of the throne room, Chinon. "Behind the scenes," and in direct contrast to Scene 1; the seamy side of the Dauphin's court. A rather tawdry set of curtains before which Trémouille, especially, can posture like a phony theatrical manager. "A monstrous, arrogant wineskin of a man," says the author. That means a purple complexion, of course; fingers covered with massive rings; and Mme. de la Trémouille is probably a luscious blonde, formerly in the chorus of whatever corresponded to a leading nitery in those days.

Act I, Scene 3. The throne room itself. Metaphor: a meager elegance. The Dauphin is pinched for money. The Bishop of Rheims remarks, "He never has a suit of clothes that I would throw to a curate." A large baronial hall, indicated mainly by ample space and shafts of light. Very thin columns. Expensive-looking costumes in contrast to Joan's hard-riding, soldier-girl appearance. This crude provincial, Joan of Domrémy, is a match for the elegantly upholstered court.

Act II, Scene 1. A new note. The River Loire, outside of Orléans. Palisade fortifications. Engines of war. Across the river the beleaguered castle. The Bastard, Dunois, in armour; Joan armed top to toe. But the whole scene has the metaphor of peace. Twilight along the river. Shimmering water mirroring the castle, slender trees, a lance with a fluttering pennant. Dunois' page aims his slingshot at an invisible kingfisher.

Act II, Scene 2. Warwick's tent. A scene different in quality from any other in the play—more abstract and intellectual, a typical Shavian discussion. Metaphor: church and state. The tent, as stylized as a coat of arms. In the background a view of army tents, almost abstractly painted, like a plaque.

Act II, Scene 3. Rheims Cathedral after the coronation. Metaphor: stained glass. The stage ought to be like a cube of crystal, viewed by the thin piers and arches and stained through with the deep, rich colors of the spectrum—Roualt, Picasso's black-line period, Matisse's cathedral designs. The color splinters against the backdrop, spatters over the actors. In contrast Joan kneels by herself in the somber blue light as though outside the church, in the ambulatory.

Act III, Scene 1. The trial, Rouen. Metaphor: fire. The assessors' boxes: skeleton construction with blackened graining, as of charred wood. The costumes: red, black, gray, white, yellow. We do not see the burning, but the stage itself seems to burn: Fire rises as though from the floor and sweeps across the black wall: sparks hover in the air. De Stogumber, the chaplain, stumbles in, weeping, as though his tears could put out the fire.

Act III, Scene 2. The room is hung in red and yellow tapestries, "somewhat flamelike," notes Shaw, "when the folds breathe in the wind." The breeze that stirs them is a breath of the lower regions, whence comes the rough English soldier who gave Joan her rough wooden cross. The Dauphin, now Charles VII, lolls in bed reading Fouquet's *Boccaccio,* but he is plagued with thoughts that rise to disquiet him; his bed is a bed of embers. Now the theme of red and yellow tapestries becomes clear. Metaphor: the hell of war. A Lurcat tapestry, the *Guernica* of Picasso—depicting a world of combat and carnage, the world of the armoured past which is still the continuing world of the present. Joan asks, "O God that madest this beautiful earth, when will it be ready to receive thy saints? How long, O Lord, how long?"

Thus the separate scenes. What of the scenic quality of the whole play? Tragedy and comedy so fused together that they cannot be separated, the comedy occupying the foreground. One almost feels the gaiety and color of a musical. Why do so many designers handle Gothic as though it consisted of the gray walls of a dungeon? Gothic is fundamentally graceful, with the upward thrust of a tree; its color is brave with red, blue, green, silver and gold, the color of illuminated books; it has the fanciful humor of scrolls and gargoyles. Let's have the Gothic of Bernard Shaw here. And let the cubic area of the stage seem crystalline, segmented by the slender columns. Make the proscenium opening very high—a vertical stage picture, every scenic element thin and vertical.

For the allover metaphor is a straight descent: the journey of Joan of Lorraine from the time of her naive, heavenly visions to the hell of her martyrdom; the amused, devilish dismay lest she ever return to trouble the well-intentioned, plodding citizens of this earth.

SCENERY OR STAGE SETTING

by

Leo Kerz

In this short article, which appeared originally in the NEW YORK TIMES (August 2, 1954, II, 1), Leo Kerz succinctly illustrates there is more than a semantical differential between the terms "scenery" and "stage setting." Scenery, according to Mr. Kerz, no matter how beautifully designed, remains a decorative background, often leading a more or less attractive life of its own. The stage setting, on the other hand, does not live by itself but is a constant compromise between the artist's impulses and the playwright's story, resulting in a simple and sparse design based upon an understanding of the play's content, form and spirit.

Scenery or stage setting? To most people, even to the professionals of the theatre, this is one and the same thing. Yet, there is a difference.

When the proscenium arch came into being with its curtain and the "transparent wall" through which the audience was allowed to have a glimpse of a strange world, scenery was the means by which this world was created: First in the form of backdrops and painted wings, such as are still used in the classical ballet. Then, over a period of two hundred years, in order to make this world more believeable, more and more three-dimensional scenery was added until, today, we are not too surprised if the curtain opens on a swimming pool with real water in it, a station complete with train and signals, or a city in all its architectural detail made of aluminum, lumber, velour and paint.

This literal approach is a direct result of a style of acting which pretends that there is no audience present, even though the house may be sold out to capacity. Here, scenery has the purpose of masking off the bare walls and the steampipes of the backstage area so that the audience can forget that they are in a theatre, watching a performance by actors. Why we would want to do that when, today, we have to work so hard to get an audience into the theatre remains one of the foremost contradictions of our theatrical history. Of course, scenery also indicates the locale, and the mood of a scene, an act or the entire play, but apart from this superficial link with the play, it leads a more or less attractive life of its own.

The stage setting, on the other hand, does not live by

itself. It is a carefully designed instrument for the purpose of lifting the play from paper to life. As such, it will prove its effectiveness only to the degree in which the stage director and the actor use it. Good stage design strives to integrate with the action; it must fuse the inner life of a play with the work of the actor. During this process it may become quite unnoticeable as a setting because it has become an organic part of the play itself.

Scenery, no matter how attractive it is designed, remains a decorative background and often, unless this is the desired effect (in a musical production number, for instance) it is a disturbing factor in establishing an intimate relationship between the audience and the play.

The stage designer uses scenery too, but to him the scenic elements are only means to an end. He does not depend entirely upon scenery, however, and will use any material, textures, color or objects in order to create the setting. His ground plan and his elevations are not only specifications for the carpenters and the paint shop, they also pick up the unwritten words of the playwright and make them a coherent part of the production. The working drawings are helpful tools with which the director can plan his strategy.

It is quite surprising how few producers are aware of this basic difference between scenery and stage setting. Directors, too, for that matter, and authors. They call in a designer; they give him the play to read. Often they only give him the page to read which describes the place of action, exits and entrances, and the general mood. They ask him how much money he thinks the scenery will cost and what color he would paint it in. If the price is right and the designer can guess the producer's favorite color he will, in all probability, get the contract.

I remember a scene in a well-known producer's office where after I had read the play and studied it for about a week, I outlined my ideas of combining all the different locales of the play into a single setting: A single setting which was to produce all the phases and scenes of the play by means of lighting and some slight maneuvering of certain props and elements in full view of the audience. I was convinced that in the final analysis such a setting would project a far greater reality into the minds of the viewer than six truckloads of scenery. When I had finished my presentation, the producer gazed into the drawer of his desk and said, "I want this to look very beautiful, you know. I see this setting painted in the colors of *Oklahoma!*."

Of course, there is nothing wrong with the colors of *Oklahoma!*—for *Oklahoma!*. This play happened to be, however, a psychological drama. Needless to say, the producer found himself a designer who saw this play as another *Oklahoma!*.

I am telling this story here only because it was this incident which made me realize the difference between scenic design and set design.

While the scenic designer is satisfied to be called in a week or two before the show goes into rehearsal, the designer of stage settings likes to be consulted right at the start of production activities—earlier than that, if possible, when the play is conceived, or when the author sketches the first draft of a novel's adaptation for the stage; when the playright feels frustrated because he cannot fit the play into the same old living room; when, on the other hand, he also fears the prohibitive cost of too much scenery and too many scene changes.

That is where the set designer can do his job most effectively. Since he does not, as most authors do, think in terms of individual settings, but always in terms of an over-all design, format and style, and since he regards the stage setting as an implement rather than a visual enrichment, he will usually come up with an idea for a single setting which can encompass all the phases and which can produce all the locales with a minimum of scenery.

109

Scenery or Stage Setting

Where the scenic designer illustrates in literal or abstract terms what the author has already written, there the set designer will try to arouse the playgoer's imagination. By calling for this active participation on the part of the playgoer, he is making him alert and interested, where the scenic designer would bow to the mistaken idea that the audience is an essentially lazy group of people.

Stage setting in the modern theatre is a constant compromise between the designer's artistic impulse to tell his version of the author's story in visual terms and his conscience, which will always remind him that the visual is only part of the theatre and that the other part is for the ear. The result, therefore, is a simple and sparse design based upon an understanding of the play's content, form and spirit. Fused with the director's approach, it will emerge as a real contribution toward the play's success and stature. As such, it may, in retrospect, assume a character and a face, within the framework of the production, more beautiful and more memorable than any amount of scenery.

PART THREE—METHODOLOGY

THE DESIGNER SETS THE STAGE
by
Norris Houghton

These interviews with prominent American scene designers were conducted by Norris Houghton for THEATRE ARTS MONTHLY in 1936. Although written more than twenty years ago, taken as a group, these accounts of the aesthetic attitudes and working methods of Norman Bel Geddes (pp. 766-83), Lee Simonson (pp. 879-85), Donald Oenslager (pp. 885-91), Robert Edmond Jones (pp. 966-70) and Mordecai Gorelik (pp. 970-75) reveal still the predominant attitudes and methods of American scene designers. Donald Oenslager and Mordecai Gorelik, who are still active on Broadway have written new conclusions to bring their interviews up to date.

1. NORMAN BEL GEDDES

To Norman Bel Geddes the art of design and the art of direction are inextricably part of one scenic pattern. When he talks of design, it is in terms of the movement of actors in three-dimensional space, the ideas contained in their speech, and light; when he speaks of direction it is in terms of these same things. An examination of his methods of work shows how natural it is for him to be both designer and director, how necessary for him to have one foot on each bank.

Like every worker in the theatre, Geddes begins his work on production with the script of the play. But unlike many workers, it is only a part of the script that he studies. Before he starts an assistant eliminates every stage direction of the author, every description of locale or movement. All Bel Geddes has before him are the speeches of the characters and the indicated facts of entrance or exit. Any play worth doing at all, he feels, contains within itself sufficient evidence of these physical elements to give the designer all his necessary clues. Then he is free to allow his imagination to create whatever mise-en-scene it will, unfettered by the author's superimposed vision. For once he has read the description of the setting which the playwright has visualized, it is hard for him to erase it from his mind and create something which will be in its stead his own. In *Dead End,* for instance, because he never read Sidney Kingsley's original stage direction, Geddes did not know that the author had called for a setting which

113

would look *down* the dead-end street toward the river instead of *up* the street away from the waterfront. If he had studied these directions, then as he read the play he would unconsciously have tried to fit it to this structure. But since he did not, he was free to build up a picture based on the action and dialogue of the play itself, a picture wherein the activity of the pier's end became the focal point and rightly so, a setting just the reverse of the one the author had described in his manuscript, but not out of keeping with what the author had visualized.

Geddes had arrived at this solution by studying the action of the play, and that is his invariable approach. The actor on the stage is the important fact to him and the actor's movements are his basic consideration. For about three-fourths of the productions he has designed—"at least for the great majority in the last fifteen years"—he has worked out the action for the director. Even in an English drawing room comedy like *The Truth About Blayds,* which he himself did not direct, he provided a set with "avenues of entrance and areas of action" which proved themselves inevitable to Winthrop Ames who did direct. Incidentally, in this play likewise his setting bore no relation to the directions of the author. Milne's manuscript had indicated a room having five entrances. Geddes, reading the play with descriptions deleted, visualized a setting with but a single entrance— again to "point up" the action more effectively—and such a room it became.

In his more abstract productions, *Lysistrata, Hamlet* (*"Hamlet* was the best thing I've ever done"), this relationship of the actor to the setting becomes so intimate that a study of Geddes' processes of creation goes directly to his rehearsal script rather than to the drafting board. With *Hamlet,* which serves perhaps as the best illustration, he again began with the text, this time trying to "visualize the scenes so that a way might be found to have no pauses between them

114

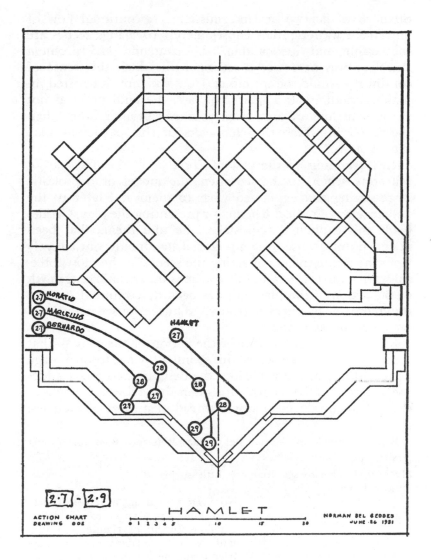

HAMLET

ACTION CHART
DRAWING 002

2·7 - 2·9

NORMAN BEL GEDDES
JUNE 26 1931

115

other than the two act intermissions. A continual flow of movement was essential. Pauses merely to change scenes are intolerable and inexcusable," he contends. His problem therefore was to devise a setting with which this sense of continuity would be possible. He "was not interested in making pictures; as a matter of fact, the audience was not to be conscious of any scenery or background other than the mood in which the characters of this particular play should move."

In his address to the cast of *Hamlet* on the first day of rehearsal, when he showed them the model of the plastic stage setting and explained what to them and later to the audience was a radical scheme for presenting the play, Geddes made this explicit. "This stage," he told them, "has been designed in no sense from a pictorial standpoint, but entirely from the requirements of acting the scenes in the most forceful way. . . . Every detail of this stage is the organic outgrowth of the action of the play and has been determined from the standpoint of practical necessity." Thus, "the set is imposed on the actor, as it were."

"The organic outgrowth of the action of the play"—that seems to be the essence of his point of view toward stage design; it suggests how Geddes the designer becomes Geddes the director. That is why he offers his rehearsal book to explain his processes of work instead of a sheaf of sketches.

A Page of script from Norman Bel Geddes' **Rehearsal Book for Hamlet**
HORATIO

My lord, I came to see your father's funeral.	A little surprised.
	Note: Horatio is not a native of Denmark and is a stranger to this court; a fellow student of Hamlet's at Wittenberg; his confidant and intimate friend; and he is more a listener than a talker.

HAMLET
I pray thee, do not mock me, fellow-student; I think it was to see my mother's wedding.

Bitterly but witty.

Bernardo and Marcellus glance at each other.

HORATIO
Indeed, my lord, it follow'd hard upon.

Sad, as it is, Horatio sees humor in the point.

HAMLET
Thrift, thrift, Horatio. the funeral baked-meats did coldly furnish forth the marriage tables. Would I had met my dearest foe in heaven or ever I had seen that day, Horatio. My father—methinks I see my father.

Seriously, but even so, a flash of humor.

Pause.

Thoughtfully—his hands float ethereally as his imagination carries him away.

HORATIO
O where, my lord?

Having just returned from seeing the Ghost, and thinking that Hamlet is seeing it now—Horatio half rises in terror.

HAMLET
In my mind's eye, Horatio.

Lightly, casually letting his hands drop.

HORATIO
I saw him *once*: he was a goodly king.

LIGHT: Out—Circuits 11, 31, 34.

HAMLET
He was a man, take him for all in all.
I shall not look upon his like again.

With poignant sadness.
He loved and admired his father; his language about him is always the language of genuine affection and respect.

This prompt script is complete in every detail. There is nothing to compare with it in scope save the monumental *regiebucher* of the great European regisseurs. All of it— every movement, every voice variation, every light cue, every sound effect—is worked out to the minutest degree before a

117

single rehearsal takes place. Then it is followed verbatim as far as the mechanics of it are concerned—"just as an orchestra conductor follows the notes of his score;" and the artists, like the musicians who have no need to worry about what the next note will be, are free to devote themselves entirely to the interpretation of the score before them. The action is worked out in advance on a small cork model, cork so that pins with the names of the different characters may be stuck around on it. Then as the action is developed it is transferred to ground-plan diagrams of the setting which are spaced at three or four page intervals throughout the script.

From these diagrams one can see at any given point in the play the position of every character on the stage, whence he came and whither he goes. One can see, too, how Geddes works at making compositions with his actors, how, in fact, they become in themselves his scenery. One can see from the diagrams how one scene changes into another, not by the addition of a new wall or backdrop, but by the withdrawal of actors from one area of the stage, by the appearance of other actors in another area, by a change in the direction of a beam of light (the lights, too, are carefully plotted in this script and on these diagrams). Geddes, the director-designer, becomes a great general marshaling his troops into strategic formations over the terrain which is his setting. The character of the place determines the maneuvering of his forces; at the same time he chooses for these movements the most telling position he can find.

Since his settings are predicated on the action (though in the case of *Hamlet* he "would not wish one to think that action is dominant over the spiritual and intellectual side of the play, rather is it subservient to it," and since his sets are in no sense pictorial backgrounds, Geddes does not make sketches or drawings. He is "least interested in the visual aspect." His work is in three dimensions, in elements of plasticity. The stage model assumes with him a position of

118

far greater importance than it does with any other outstanding American designer, for it is the most satisfactory way of rendering a plastic, architectonic or sculpturesque stage. From it come the working drawings for the carpenter, the painter can follow its coloring, the actor can trace the pattern of his movements throughout any scene, the director can plot his entire production. With the model as his guide, the director (Geddes) can plan that a platform may in turn become a throne dias, a grave, a player's stage; an aperture between two towering blocks may become now a dark corridor, now an empty abyss separating Hamlet from the supernatural world. None of these physical elements of the set is changed, yet each is charged with a new meaning every time the action of the play changes its function. Before the characters come alive in rehearsal or performance, these meanings can exist only in the imagination of the creator. "Picture" drawings of the setting would therefore, if made, have in themselves no active value at all. So Geddes would rather use pins stuck in cork.

Scenery for Norman Bel Geddes consists of three things: "this three-dimensional plastic space, lighting, and clothing." The last two are more important than any conventional decorative scenic background. Therefore, he believes that the designer must unquestionably devise both lighting and costumes himself. Geddes uses strong and positive color. In naturalistic productions like *Dead End* his actors wear no make-up. He works out all the sources of light, their intensity, their quality, their color, before a single piece of scenery is constructed, before a rehearsal takes place. The firm which supplies his lighting equipment says he is the only designer who never has to change the location of a lamp, angle of throw, or color of medium, in rehearsals.

In costume he is equally interested. Because of the strong color which he uses in light, his costumes must be planned together with that light, so that their colors will be heightened and not made negative. Even in a modern play he designs the clothes. Although it is contrary to custom, he bought and paid for all the men's as well as women's clothes in *Dead End* himself so that he might have exactly what he wanted. "It is part of the designer's task," he believes, "not only to provide an actor with his clothes but to show him the way to wear them. The effectiveness of a costume depends in a large measure upon the way it is worn." Again Geddes the designer becomes the director.

When asked what he considers the greatest limitations which the designer faced in the theatre, he countered by remarking, "The greater the limitations, the better the results." . . . After only a few hour's talk with Bel Geddes it becomes understandable why he makes such a statement, why he is impatient; for him the possibilities of the theatre are limitless.

II. LEE SIMONSON

Although Lee Simonson was a painter first, a theatrical designer afterwards, his talk of stage design nowadays is in terms of architecture. His method of procedure, as he conceives and executes the settings for plays reminds one repeatedly of the architect at work and seldom of the painter at his easel. Like one building a house, he works from the ground up; like one planning the living environment for people, he seeks to surround actors with a mise-en-scene that may be comfortable, flexible, adequate to their physical needs, as well as reflecting their aesthetic sensibilities. His definition of scenery is almost the same as that of Norman Bel Geddes —"a setting is a plan of action"—but, as he proceeds to his work, he translates this definition more literally than Bel Geddes does, and he places the emphasis differently. From the very beginning there are plans, plans in the architectural sense.

"My first step in designing almost any production," Simon-

120

son says, "is to find a solution to its technical problems."
Harking back to his work for an illustration, he points out
how in *Call It a Day* his first consideration in designing was
to invent a series of settings which could be rapidly shifted.
In every act there were a number of different scenes, each
requiring a more or less elaborate realistic set. A scheme to
handle the changes from one to another had to be devised
before anything else about the setting could be ascertained.
This was essentially a scheme related to the floor area and its
treatment; so here, as in almost every Simonson production,
the floor plans were the first stage in the evolution of the
production.

Finding the technical aspects of *End of Summer* negligible
and quickly determined, Simonson the architect became
almost from the beginning Simonson the decorator. To create
a charming room for Ina Claire was his problem. Now the
color of the walls became his first consideration, the details
of the fireplace of primary importance (he did over the latter
four times). The rest of the creation consisted of what Simonson calls "piling up bibelot," and then lighting the whole.

His work on the background for *Idiot's Delight* illustrates
his emphatic statement that "the design of a setting depends
upon the acting that fills it." Such a contention demands a
close relationship between the work of the designer and the
director, and the production of *Idiot's Delight* is the story
of such a collaboration. Together directors and designer
began with the technical problems which had to be solved
through ground plans: where and how to handle the entrances and exits (would one large entrance be enough, as
Alfred Lunt insisted?), where to place the window with its
view of Alpine peaks, where to put the piano around which
Alfred Lunt played much of the time and at which the last
scene of the play took place, how to handle the staircase so
that scenes could be played on and from it with maximum
effectiveness, how to do all these things and still have room

for a chorus to dance. These were not problems of the designer alone, they were also of vital concern to the directors.

Lunt and Bretaigne Windust envisioned many of the solutions, Simonson says. When Simonson felt that a setting with some feeling of closeness and intimacy was required, Lunt insisted on great height and vastness, so sure was he of the ability of Lynn Fontaine and himself to project their comedy in space. With other actors playing, this same setting might have engulfed the action completely and ruined the performance, Simonson pointed out. That is part of what he means when he says—why he lays emphasis on the importance of the designer's cooperation with imaginative direction.

When these technical difficulties were surmounted, Simonson moved on to a consideration of detail and color. He sought the curves of modern streamlining, the sure, hard accuracy of steel and chromium, he coupled them with color equally hard and dynamic. He "invented" the stairs, the built-in seats, the turbine-like motifs of decoration, the piano-case. "Invented" is a word which Simonson frequently uses when referring to his creation of scenic devices. It was he who "invented" the runway in *He Who Gets Slapped* years ago. It seems to be a word of particular appropriateness.

When Simonson talks of his earlier productions it is to illustrate further these two points: his use of the technical problems of production as his point of departure in designing, and the collaboration of designer and director. The foundations of his settings for *Marco Millions, Volpone, Faust* were laid in a unit set—a technical solution used in multiple variations. Again, his famous setting of the railroad bridge scene in *Liliom* was designed, Simonson says, not by beginning with a decorative approach toward a pictorial effect, but as a solution of the complicated problem of how to make a railroad crossing convincing on the stage. From considerations of such matter-of-fact things as sight-lines and entrances and exits for actors, there emerged a setting highly imaginative and theatrical.

Just returned from Europe before *He Who Gets Slapped* went into production, he was filled with enthusiasm for the use of levels, then much in vogue abroad, and he persuaded the director that a setting with levels and a runway was necessary for *He*. So, working both pictorially and dramatically, he helped the director to mould the form of the production. In *The Power of Darkness* this situation was reversed. Then it was the director who, sensing the need of something beautiful at the very end and by demanding it of Simonson, contributed to the scenic structure of the play. In *Liliom* Joseph Schildkraut was a source of inspiration to the designer. Thus, by illustration after illustration, Simonson points out how he begins his work—first through careful conversation and interchange of ideas with the director, and then, to quote him directly, in summary, "I begin with the technical problems; that leads me to the acting problems; then to the mood and the style. I ask myself, 'Can the play be stylized?' If so, I go to the director and see how such a stylization will affect the actors concerned."

* * *

It is in connection with these two aspects of his work, so strongly emphasized already—solution of technical problems and cooperative creation with the director—that Simonson finds his greatest limitations. His first quarrel is with the physical conditions, the architecture of New York's theatres, particularly the lack of depth of most of their stages. He longs for a little more room to do what he would like to do. His second limitation he feels to be "directors" lack of power to visualize, their inability sufficiently to realize dynamic patterns, and their difficulty in being able to talk in terms of ground plans.

The fact that he almost never makes sketches or pictorial

123

drawings of his settings testifies to how completely Lee Simonson has turned from painter to architect of the stage. He may start with a rough sketch or two, for his own eyes alone, (he shows them to no one), but it is with the ground plans that his setting actually gets under way. "The architect makes his plans first, his renderings last," Simonson remarks, but in practice he rarely gets to the rendering. As he works from the ground plan he thinks of the elevation that goes with it; when the former is finished he raises the structure upon it in elevation and stops with that. "You may have noticed," he says, "that exhibitions contain only photographs of my finished settings, never my own original drawings or sketches; the reason is that I never make any. I could if I tried, I suppose, but it would be a terrible chore for me."

Not only does Simonson seldom make sketches and devise projects but he never or at least rarely makes models of his settings. When he does, it is only to check against his sense of proportion and he seldom feels called upon to do that. He admits, however, that his work in executing his designs, which takes place only with sets of geometrical plans to guide to the finished effect, has been made easier by the fact that most of his execution is handled through the permanent staff of the Theatre Guild for which he has done his principle designing. Schooled in his methods of work over many seasons, the technical director and his department heads have understood Simonson's intentions and have been better able to help him to realize the visions of his mind's eye than would strange and constantly changing technical assistants. For, like many another American designer, Lee Simonson is very dependent upon seeing things in his "mind's eye." In his case, it is an eye that sees with sureness and exactness the past and the present, that knows near places and far, an imaginative eye that can translate reality or fancy into the idiom of the theatre.

124

III. DONALD OENSLAGER

The architectural, technical approach to stage designing, which the study of Lee Simonson's methods have revealed his to be, is not his alone. A more inclusive study of designer's methods would undoubtedly show that a good number of our artists create, like Simonson, "from the ground up." Therefore, it may be coincidental, or it may be indicative of the similarity of mind and talent that academicians might call a "school," that, as Donald Oenslager describes his process of work, he tells, step by step the same story that Simonson has told. It is not that the one artist has followed in the footsteps of the other, it is rather that both men have faced the same problems and undertaken the same solution.

When I asked how he begins his designing, Oenslager answers, like Simonson, "I begin by working out a ground plan. As an architect lays out the plans for a room, determines the way in which it connects with other rooms, its sources of illumination, the position of fireplace or stairs or closet, so I plot out the space upon the stage." From plan Oenslager proceeds to elevation: having determined the position of window and door, arch, bay, or column on the floor, so to speak, he now considers them vertically, giving them form and proportion. He finds that he works in certain definite proportions which have become characteristic of his style.

In preparing these plans and elevations Oenslager makes use of squared graph paper. There are no sketches now or at any time in the course of mounting the production. Perhaps after everything else has been completed he will make a rendering of the finished effect, but this will be as a record of the thing accomplished and not as a guide to its accomplishment. What is more, he almost never makes any models of his projected settings unless he is faced with a particular intricate technical problem which a three-dimensional visualization can help to clear. Instead of "pictures" or models he concentrates on carefully drawn and painted elevations for the scene painter to copy exactly.

Digressing from discussion of methods to more general considerations of intention, theory, and approach to the art of designing—a digression all designers are more than willing to make (all these scenic fellows find it very trivial and uninteresting to recount their actual processes of work)—Oenslager remarks that he seeks constantly an approach to stage design which may be without individualism; his desire is to sublimate himself so that his setting may appear to be the creation of, or at least an expression of, the characters in the play. The fact that he works in definite proportions, as he has mentioned, he again insists is not a conscious striving for style, but an unconscious expression for taste of which he was unaware until it was pointed out.

Color, should not however, come out of the characters, Oenslager believes. That, he says, is a theatrical part of the setting. Furthermore, he does not agree with the accepted tradition that comedy requires a light decor and that tragedy should be played in the dark. Comedy can as well be done against a dark background (he proved the point to himself by using a deep blue-violet wall in *Forsaking All Others*), and he would willingly set a tragedy against white.

From the very beginning of a production, Oenslager feels, the designer should be one step ahead of the director. He should be prepared to show the director the plans of the settings, should be able to indicate the most workable schemes, for mounting the production, the logical color plots, lighting effects, before the director, out of his preconceived ideas, is able to dictate to the designer how these things should be ordered. Incidentally, designers must be skillful psychologists, Oenslager points out. They must be able to convince actresses that colors which they imagine are unflattering are quite the contrary, urge some producers that they should spend more money for certain effects, persuade other and more lavish producers that a cheaper material might be more effective than a rich one. They must be able to keep on good terms with painters, prop men, carpenters, electricians, as well as the directors. The designer does not work alone; in fact he is at the mercy of all of these others.

"I suppose," said Oenslager, after describing his manner of creation, "that essentially my approach is that of a craftsman." The comment, . . . motivates a new consideration. Stage design is a curious blend of craft and art. It might be well to enumerate some of the details of the craft—methods common to all scenic artists. . . . Oenslager can be used as an example.

Roughly speaking, the stage designer's work has two aspects: the creation of designs and their execution into scenery on the stage. The former has to do with art, the latter with craft. The assembling of his ideas—out of the script, out of himself, out of conversations with the director, out of the visualizations of their "mind's eye" as Simonson, Oenslager, Jones and others claim—this assembling of ideas from one source or another seems to be the first step in creation. Their notation in some visual form, either in water-color sketches, or sepia renderings, in scaled models or mechanical ground plans and elevations, is the second and final stage. Now the realization of the setting commences.

Oenslager first calls scenic construction shops and painting shops to estimate the cost of execution of his plans. The bids he thus receives he places before the producer who awards the contracts for this work. During the weeks that follow he makes almost daily trips to these shops supervising the building, choosing special mouldings, door knobs, cornices, checking the color and the texture of the paint job, the staining and the finishing of the wood, approving minor readjustments or revising dimensions.

When this work is under way, he makes the rounds of furniture stores, auction or antique shops, property studios, assembling the furnishings for his setting. (Oenslager believes that furniture for the stage must be slightly exaggerated to make its full effect there.) He goes to artificial-flower houses to select from their stock or to order such specially-made plants or trees or flowers as he may need. He visits electrical shops to find chandeliers or wall brackets or lamps that suit him. He goes to the upholsterers' to choose materials for the re-covering of those pieces of furniture which may require it. He makes trips to the drapers' to select drapery material, to give them plans for the way curtains are to hang, valances or swags to be cut.

With the department heads he holds conferences: he plans with the electrician the amount of equipment that will be required, the number of lamps and their location, the sources of light and their quality and intensity; he discusses with the carpenter the method of handling and shifting the scenery, he describes to the property man the kind of ink-well, the shape of a bolster, or the size of a tea-tray that must be provided.

Fashions in settings for the theatre change in a fluid process of healthy evolution. After two decades, the emphasis on designing drawing rooms and average interiors remains the same, requiring only taste and craftsmanship for their routine execution. The longer one designs, the more apparent it appears that only the imaginative play (all too rare today) becomes the pivotal point of departure for ways and means of achieving a new visual expression in our theatre. Today, more than ever, the designer must believe in and make tangible the imaginative contribution of the playwright and actors, matching his belief with his dream of how the production will appear on tomorrow's stage. Lewis Carroll's Queen, who, on hearing Alice say, "One *can't* believe in impossible things," retorted, "I daresay you haven't had much practice. When I was your age, I did it for half an hour a day. Why, sometimes, I've believed as many as six

128

impossible things before breakfast." Surely the Queen must have at one time been on the stage, where make-believe is essential to the audience's belief in the impossible.

IV. ROBERT EDMOND JONES

It is difficult to write an account of an interview with Robert Edmond Jones; it is difficult in the first place to conduct the interview at all. For Jones is an artist, a poet, a visionary, and, as you sit watching him pace the room as he conjures forth visions, you are magnetized by a kind of electrical discharge which he emanates; yet when you attempt in later tranquility to put those ideas into common prose, to set down the glowing image that he has somehow seemed to snatch from the air about him, the result is stale, flat and unprofitable. And when you try, through conning your notes, to decide what his answers to specific questions were you find he has made no answers.

It is quite understandable for Mr. Jones was in little sympathy with my purpose of the moment. "All us designers work the same way," he said, when I explained what I wished him to tell me, "Nobody is interested in these processes: the important things are the deeper ones, things that have to do with our ideas about the theatre, the ideas and the dreams that motivate our work. It is in them that we differ. You must try to extract the essence of each of us. That sort of thing is significant, but it has little to do with our methods." In that argument itself there is already revealed some of the essence of Robert Edmond Jones.

* * *

Robert Edmond Jones' first, his constant, desire as he designs is "to carry the audience into that other region where the ideal play takes place." Hence, to "find the simplest, broadest, boldest, grandest way to take the audience there and to keep them there" is at the same time his principal preoccupation and his point of departure. Jones, never satisfied however, and always seeking and questioning, asks at once, "Is this simplest, broadest, grandest way to carry the audience out of reality always and necessarily to be found in the scenic decorations? Need it, indeed, ever be the designer's way? May it not quite as probably be acting, even in an empty space, which uplifts the spectators?"

In Elizabethan times words had the power to transport audiences, Jones points out. "The spoken word of literary description could evoke in the imagination of the Elizabethan's scenery far more satisfying than any created with paint and cloth. So settings were *indicated,* but not *represented* or even *suggested.* Yet the theatre was very broad, bold and grand. Words have in some measure lost their meanings for us these days." Jones wonders, however, whether the radio may not revive in our times the value of words spoken and thus do the theatre great service. Indeed, he envisions one kind of theatre in which the loudspeaker of the radio could be used to replace scenery: "There might be only an empty dome, beautiful lights, and the amplifier of music and other sounds and words might provide the rest of the atmosphere. So once again the background for drama might become evocative and indicative instead of suggestive.

"One must continue to bear in mind, however, that we are nowadays particularly eye-conscious." Jones went on, "People's visual responses are much more acutely sensitized than their aural responses: so a theatre in which words and sounds might replace scenery as we know it is perhaps only a dream. If realized in our day, one would want, I suppose, to combine with it color in light and costumes." (One is reminded of Norman Bel Geddes' comment that scenery for him consisted of "three-dimensional plastic space, lighting and clothes.")

Color is important to Jones and when he says that "color is emotion" one concludes that its usefulness to him is far

130

greater than in its realistic application—blue for sky, green for grass, red for bricks. He remarks that he has long wished to design a production for a play of Bernard Shaw entirely in black and white—"Color, being emotional, has no place in the Shavian theatre of intellect." At last Jones reveals where he actually begins his designing. His conception comes from the feeling, the quality, the mood and intention of the play and the playwright. The ground plan, the director, the technical problems involved, all are of little importance compared to the establishment of a kind of *rapport* between Robert Edmond Jones and the play. Several years ago he prepared a production of *Much Ado About Nothing* which, although carried out even to a dress rehearsal, was never presented. In it he dressed the actors in a kind of actor's uniform—all the men alike and all the women alike—and the entire company appeared before the play as *actors*. They put on hats, cloaks, swords, and so forth, in full view of the audience and at the end laid their trappings aside and appeared again as actors. As Jones read Shakespeare's text, it seemed to him that "such a scheme came closer than any other to carrying out the intention of the poet in this play."

This relationship of Jones to the play is so close that Jones admits to doing bad settings for a play he does not like—not intentionally of course, he simply cannot help but express his reaction in that way. Therefore in past years he has tried, whenever possible, to design only for plays with which he was in love. When this has been the case, then his setting has occurred to him suddenly as he sat reading the script. "All at once the people, their groupings, their clothes, the light, the background, appear to me complete in detail." Thus, reading, he envisions the play as though it were being acted out before him. It then but remains to make drawings of these pictures of his imagination which he will take to the producer.

How different is Robert Edmond Jones' process of creation

from those designers already interviewed in this series. While the men who work from ground plans or with architectural or plastic units in space may arrange their designs a dozen times until they find the most satisfying position for a door or a window, a platform or an action area, Jones has before his mind's eye a complete picture which requires but slight adjustment to be executed and allows little rearrangement. The accuracy of his imagination may be judged by a comparison of his finished products with his sketches. The latter in their proportions, perspective and atmosphere almost perfectly presage their realization on the stage, and this seems possible only because he conceives them pictorially rather than structurally or architecturally. Thus he reverses the procedure of those designers who raise their settings from the ground into the air, by creating his scenery in the air and then mooring it to the floor. Jones moves from picture to plan instead of from plan to picture.

As he develops his setting, Jones seeks to "avoid in scenery the idea behind type casting"—that is, representation (in acting, an old man cast as an old man) as opposed to presentation (which is the essence of real acting, Jones claims). So he contrives decors which may be presentations rather than representations—suggestive rather than literal. "A setting should say nothing but give everything. Scenery as a rule seems to me to be too definite. It should possess powerful atmosphere but with little detail. It must be important but unobtrusive." Such dictums may help to explain his palette and his use of light—much black and gray and chiaroscuro which seem to sink his backgrounds into remote detachment from the world of his scarlet-or-golden-clad actors. "Above all else," says Jones, "I seek to avoid doing a 'Jones setting'."

If certain of these remarks lead one to imagine Robert Edmond Jones as an abstract visionary conceiving in some cloudland of art, that thought should be dispelled immediately. Although perhaps he may dream more dreams than some of our designers, he is adept in the craft as well as the art of stage decoration. His costume sketches are usually complete only when there are pinned to it samples, chosen by Jones himself, of all the fabrics that compose it; his ground plans and his painter's sketches are prepared with the greatest of care and display an accurate knowledge of stagecraft and construction. His fingers have fashioned headdresses and fitted sandals for as many years as his "mind's eye" has been busy seeing visions of the stage.

v. MORDECAI GORELIK

Another visionary in the theatre, although his dreams are of another world than Robert Edmond Jones, is Mordecai Gorelik, and as "visionary" was used of the former with no intended opprobrium, so it is again used as an observation and not as a criticism of this outstanding artist on the social front. Both men are visionaries in that they long to make the theatre what it is not, and each bends every energy to the fulfillment of his dreams. But whereas Jones seeks to make the theatre more splendid in unreality—through that ideal to touch the real—Gorelik strives to bring the theatre into strongest possible grips with the realities of the day, to make it a force in the solution of the social problems which so manifoldly beset us.

Gorelik starts his work on a production with a threefold inquiry. Primarily he "considers the audience—who they are: what their purpose is in coming to the theatre, how they can best be appealed to." Second, he tries "to penetrate to the social meaning of the play and of the playwright." Third and last, he attempts, whenever possible, "to discover the purpose of the producer in presenting the play."

In connection with the second aspect of this initial inquiry, Gorelik observes that "Broadway has too much respect for manuscripts of plays and too little realization of what the correlative arts of the theatre may contribute to the script."

He considers that this over-regard for the script at the present time has developed from the mad bargaining and buying and selling of plays as pieces of property by managers, who look at the works of dramatists as though they were race-horses, who "consider the theatre as a commodity." As for his relations with the producer, his third initial consideration, Gorelik remarks that a theatre production is within itself a kind of little class war. When the play goes into rehearsal, everyone involved has his own interpretation of the ideas of the play (if it has ideas). In a truly collective theatre, the conclusion deduced from these varying interpretations would be arrived at democratically. Under the existing system of our professional theatre, however, each production becomes a dictatorship; the ruling opinion and idea of the producer, Gorelik claims, is the one which receives voice.

Time, this designer feels, is the great limitation of our theatre. From the shortness of time allowed for the preparation of productions, Gorelik feels that shallow talents too often result. He himself tries to find time for ample experimentation with a production. He makes both sketches and models. For a production in many scenes, he makes "quantities of sketches that are more or less cinematic"; for a play of few scenes he will "picture a number of the different episodes that take place in the same setting." He attacks each scene by asking first, "What are we trying to say in this one?" It is important to him that his scenery should say something, that it should be in itself a commentary on the drama.

"A production is, in a sense, a machine for the theatre," says Gorelik. "Scenery is the chassis and the actors are the engine. The scenery must be thought of as moving toward the audience. Flat scenery and box settings are essentially static," Gorelik contends. "Therefore they are the proper medium for plays of introspection, plays concerned with the activities of those essentially sedentary individuals whose lives are led in the office or the parlor and whose thoughts are

134

concentrated therein. But plays that are more active should be performed in settings that have a more active form. The oblique line is active," says Gorelik, who therefore bases much of his design on the oblique or zigzag line.

As Gorelik designs the various "chassis" for production, he employs many different styles. "The designer must suit his medium to his audience, just as a speaker adjusts his delivery to the temper of his auditors." He is now back at his first consideration, the audience. Some crowds must be addressed calmly, reasoned with, if the speaker wishes to make his point, Gorelik says. Other crowds need to be swayed by fiery oratory. Gorelik uses different styles of scenery for the same reason that a skilled speaker changes his mode of delivery. But always, be it noted, the style is used "to make a point," and to make it most effectively. In the play *Little Ol' Boy,* Gorelik considered it necessary for the scenery to help arouse the audience's indignation. His projected settings for *They Shall Not Die* were designed to expand the meaning of the play-wright into a document of racial warfare, the photographic medium serving to strengthen the implications of the Theatre Guild performance as presented to an audience that expected such introspective treatment. "To expand the playwright's meaning" becomes a significant comment in Gorelik's dis-cussion of the use of scenery.

Of the various styles which this designer has adopted, most frequent use has been made of constructivism. In fact, he has "always used a kind of constructivism" since he first attempted it in John Howard Lawson's *Loud Speaker.* What Gorelik means by constructivism is "a form that proposes to fill the whole space of the stage." He was also one of the earliest designers to work with industrial materials, using them first in 1922 in a production of *King Hunger.*

"The important thing for the designer to remember as he works," reiterates Gorelik, "is not merely that a produc-tion is the amplification of the script or the transference of the script to the stage, but that it must consist of the script *plus* all the other elements of the theatre."

I still believe that the purpose of worthwhile theatre is to clarify life; that stage production must exist for the welfare of its audiences, not merely to show how well someone can write, act, direct or design. Therefore the designer must know what the play will mean to its public, and how he can contribute to that meaning. I define the setting as a documentation of environment (historically and geographically) and as machine-for-theatre (acting, along with the actors, throughout a performance). In the largest sense the relation of the setting to the play is an imaginative, poetic one (the *metaphor* of the setting).

This leaves open the question of what purpose the play shall have. On Broadway this purpose has become, increasingly, one of nostalgia or mere titillation. In spite of its smash hits the American commercial theatre as a whole appears to be shrinking and weakening. At the same time the university, community and off-Broadway theatres are expanding. Thematically and artistically these playhouses are still largely dependent on Broadway; still I remain hopeful that they will give rise, some day, to a renewed, vigorous leadership of the American theatre.

DESIGNER IN ACTION

by

Harry Horner

Harry Horner's account of how the settings for Lady In The Dark *were created substantiates Lee Simonson's contention that "the first step in designing almost any production is to find a solution to its technical problems." That* Lady In The Dark *is still remembered as a triumph of "show biz" and ingenuity reflects how competently Mr. Horner was able to solve his technical problems. This exposé appeared in* THEATRE ARTS MONTHLY, *Volume 25, (April, 1941), pp. 265-273.*

A new play goes through a full cycle of exciting phases before it comes to life. The opening night of a production is for everyone connected with it like the thrill of watching the blossoming of the Victoria Royal which blooms only once in a hundred years. In these two hours is unfolded the accumulated craftsmanship of weeks and months. The opening night belongs to the cast, the crew, the artists, far more than to the audience.

It is an indescribable feeling—that of being connected with a show and waiting backstage for it to unroll. Among the many waiting anxiously that first night is the designer of the set. Tensely he watches for the technical cues to come, for the lights to dim, the machinery to work. And as he waits and watches, he remembers all the drawings, the many blueprints that have suddenly come to life. He feels like the Sorcerer's Apprentice, and hopes that his own invention will not betray him.

The opportunity to create a set comes to the designer in different ways. Sometimes he seeks the job, sometimes the job seeks him. Often a designer is type-cast, just like an actor. If he has once designed a biblical play, he will probably be asked to design five more; if he attempts to obtain a commission for a musical, he may well be told, "I will give you a chance when I do a biblical play." Yet a designer is good only if he is versatile; his style must be adaptable enough to fit any type of play, realistic or fantastic, light or heavy.

The designer first talks to the producer and director. Usually it is the director who chooses the designer, for the two

139

must work together cooperatively. Their ideas must compliment each other, and their work will be most effective if the designer is able to give the director additional inspiration and visual ideas.

Once the job is his, the designer is handed a script. This valuable property, brainchild of the author, created during months or years of work, is often presented with the words, "We have only two scripts in the office, read it right away and bring it back tonight at six. Tell us what you think about it and give us your ideas." It is difficult for the designer to explain how absurd it is to be given such a short time for the visual creation of a mood that took the author so many months to establish. A knowledge of the script is an absolute necessity in planning the physical production. When the designer has read it he waits anxiously for an inspiration. He succeeds only when the situation in the play and the layout of the set melt into one unit which fills the audience with the complete illusion required by the author.

Take for example, the script of *Lady in the Dark* and follow the designer, step by step, from start to finish. He has read the script once. He has analyzed the general problem of the play—the contrast between stark reality and a world of fantasy and dreams born in the mind of the leading character. How can this problem be translated into technical terms? The stage directions read: "Glamour theme as apartment fades out and we fade in on 'Boudoir' "; "The stage blossoms into a night club"; "The magazine cover comes to life."

The technique of writing used so many filmic elements that one of the designer's first decisions was to use such effects in the setting. First he tried to create the ideal production mentally. Then he eliminated as technical problems narrowed him down. To obtain the effect of changing dream sequences, it seemed to him that the scenes should change like a kaleidoscope, moving from one sequence into the next.

Thus he decided on the use of turntables. With sketching paper as his memorandum sheet, he jotted down several ideas, none of them ideal, but all approaching a definite goal. One of the principal limitations lay in the small size of the theatre for which the show had to be designed.

Before the final scheme crystallized, page after page was covered with possibilities. The plan was to use two turntables and to put the two realistic settings on them, so that half of each room was on each turntable. This was tried on a small ground-plan sketch. It showed that with some juggling there was still half a turntable on each side for the dream sequence. It soon became evident that the two empty parts were not sufficient for the thirty necessary scenes, if the realistic scenes were not to be shifted. It was necessary, therefore, to put one small turntable on top of the empty half of each large one. Screen-shaped walls were introduced to divide the turntables in half and placing these screens in a zig-zag pattern proved to give the best effect while at the same time serving to hide the turning points of the turntables. It was further essential, for the effect of the show and for the necessary surprise element, to obtain a method by which scenes could split without leaving a gap on the floor between platforms, by which scene changes could be made quickly without bringing down the curtain, and by which these changes could form surprising and different combinations.

Once the realistic settings were established it was sufficient to create a few but effective and representative pieces to indicate the locale of the different dream scenes. While the designer's hand still worked on the perfection of the technical scheme, his mind was already one step ahead—inventing typical forms, sufficiently fantastic, to represent a dream apartment house entrance, a dream boudoir, a dream night club, and so forth.

A big moment came. The scheme was accepted. Only after all this work did the designer draw the pictorial effects, al-

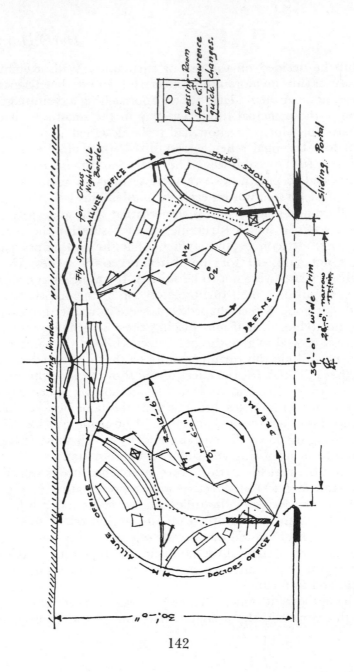

142

though he had been working on them mentally while he was busy with the technical design.

The work on the visual approach started. Even considering the restrictions of the scheme, there was still a large field of possibilities for the scenery. The script was taken off the shelf. The designer, this time, was not asked to return it after one day. It called for the office of a psychoanalyst and the office of an editor of a fashion magazine. Both required knowledge of the surroundings and atmosphere of such places. The best way to understand a locale is to seek it out. There are always typical details which a photograph or description might fail to reveal, a lamp in a certain position always used by a psychoanalyst, certain books, minor details which give a touch of life. It is the interesting experience of almost every designer that in his first rough sketch, made before any research has been done, he will have focused on something which he will find later to his amazement, is a part of the real place. His imagination often proves a confirmation of reality.

Along with such research went a careful study of the script of *Lady in the Dark*. How would the characters in these rooms move? Would it be more effective to have them enter through a centre door or by a side door? An entrance in the centre might give a person entering more weight and importance, an entrance from the side might be faster and more surprising.

It seems important to point out that the designer is not merely concerned with creating an atmospheric background. In modern productions he becomes the visual director. He goes through the movements of the actors and weighs the effect these actions have on the audience. His task is similar to that of the cameraman in motion pictures. He must focus attention on certain scenes by grouping the furniture not merely to please the eye, but also to fit the idea of the scene. (How fortunate it is if director and designer merge into one

143

cooperative unit. How unfortunate if the designer's duty is reduced to the background painter of the eighteenth century.)

After the research had been completed, the designer created color sketches to free his mind of the pictures he had so long withheld. These looked like the impressions the audience would receive. They served to show the producer what the finished setting would look like, although later the designer made more carefully executed color details to serve the painters as a guide line.

At this stage of any production changes are very painful to a designer. The work has become an integral part of his final conception. He has discussed his plans many times with the director. Many of his suggestions have been incorporated. When a script is suddenly revised there are many new problems. In a complicated set in which everything is worked out like a jig-saw puzzle, it gives the designer a shock to hear that another door is needed or that a window must be larger, changes which can be easily expressed in words, but which take weeks to execute properly. Often an entire set is cut out of the play and out of the bleeding heart of the designer, even though he realizes that such changes do excellent service to the play as a whole.

Happily few such changes were made in *Lady in the Dark*. The sketches were finished and the designer constructed a model of the proposed set which was shown before an audience of critical experts: the producer, director, author, composer, lyricist, dance director, costume designer and leading actors. The designer performed with trembling hands. He shifted the little model from scene to scene through the play. It worked. Everyone was satisfied.

To accentuate the contrast between reality and the dream world, the use of new materials and new forms for the dream sequences was important. There was a hunt all over the city for something that looked like glass to give the strange transparency associated with dreams. Finally a new plastic was found, but weeks passed before it was approved. It had to be fireproofed and it had to react favorably to light. It was tried out under spotlights for reflections. One sample after another was discarded. New materials were tried, new consistencies mixed, until finally a plastic was found that was fireproof, heat resisting, flexible, unbreakable and usable in different variations.

The design of each piece in the dream sequences took pages and pages of the designer's sketch book. Finally a general note was found for the entire dream. In order to tie the dreams to the heroine's sphere of thought, elements of her real life were used. Ribbons, out of the world of fashion, go through her dreams: the chairs, the automobile, the couches, all were designed to look like fantastically arranged lace ribbons, shaped into the desired form. Every shape was worked out in a technical drawing. Blueprints were made of these pieces as well as of the rooms and the screens and the turntables. All the details were specified in special plans— sixty-eight of them for this show.

The upholstery materials were then chosen. The designer had to select a fabric to cover certain large construction pieces, like the gold leather for the fairy-tale castle and the silver foil for the circus scene, as well as those materials that covered the chairs in the offices and the couches in the dream night club.

When the construction started, everything had to be organized into a careful schedule and handed out to everybody concerned. A detailed property list was made out, containing everything in the production from the large pieces of furniture (many of them specially designed for size, style, mood, etc.) down to the signed picture of Freud which hung in the doctor's outer office. Even the pictures must be in keeping with the spirit of the characters in the play. Special properties were designed and made: glass flowers, glass lyres, glass palettes.

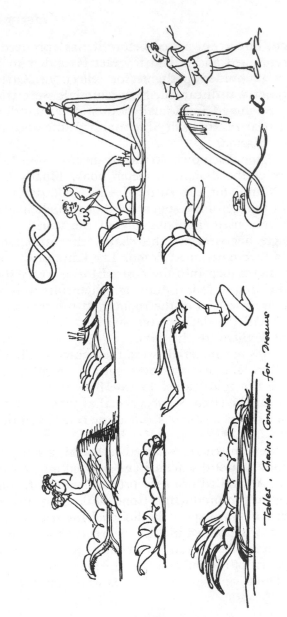

Tables, Chairs, Consoles for Dreams

Finally, the machinery of assembling the work rolled along. The designer and his assistants ran in and out of painting shops, construction studios, plastic shops, property shops, book shops and furniture factories, supplying everyone with plans and keeping the wheels greased.

The sign that the production was nearing completion came when the time of departure was discussed. Even then one could still have observed the designer and the property man chasing through department stores selecting desk sets, ashtrays, books, and so forth.

Finally the scenery, crew and designer left for Boston. When the designer entered the theatre to watch the stage-hands set up the scenery, he had a strange sensation. Suddenly he felt diminished to thumb-nail size, and imagined that he was standing in his own model. The pieces that once looked small and fragile in his hands were towering walls. The wild mass of low-hanging light pipes on which electricians fastened spots, of free standing windows and of velour hangings without apparent purpose finally took shape. The platforms and turntables were laid with linoleum. The lights were hung. The sets were up; the property men placed the furniture, hung the pictures, put the vases in their places. The wooden walls came to life. The director arrived, and the complicated mechanism was synchronized. The stagehands were the heroes of the hour. On one single cue the following moves had to be made: two big portals slid to each side, a border raised, two large turntables turned in one direction, two small turntables turned in another, the bookcase of the doctor's office split in the center and slid apart, and a curtain border moved to a higher trim. They managed it all.

The opening night arrived. Everybody backstage was tense, waiting for the cues to come, the machinery to work. The designer had his fingers crossed. A cycle of this new little life was closing.

For the moment he felt the let-down that comes in the

147

theatre at the end of a piece of work. He hated to think how little permanent value lay in all the energies and effort he had used. Then, suddenly, he heard the actors on the stage. He heard the audience applaud. He saw the stagehands turn the tables to another scene. He realized what happiness lay in the hearts of all these people, and knew that this was the purpose for which he had worked.

SCRIPT TO STAGE: CASE HISTORY OF A SET

by

Aline Louchheim

*Paul Osborn's dramatization of the J. P. Marquand novel,
POINT OF NO RETURN, produced by Leland Hayward
and starring Henry Fonda in the role of Charles Gray,
opened at the Alvin theatre in New York City, December
13, 1951. This case history of how Jo Mielziner created the
settings for this production not only devulges the intricacies
of the scene designer's art but also reveals Mr. Mielziner as
a man of the theatre in the true Craigian sense, concerned
not only with the settings but every facet of production.
Aline Louchheim discloses also how his aesthetic approach
to the problems in POINT OF NO RETURN vividly
illustrates Jo Mielziner's own statement that "an imaginative
theatrical designer often strategically influences a whole
production." Miss Louchheim's account appeared in the
NEW YORK TIMES MAGAZINE, December 9, 1951, pp.
24ff.*

To design a stage set is to create a world. It is a special world, one brought into being for the sake of a few individuals and one intended only to reflect their moods, their emotions and their experience. It is a world which must be created within stringent limits: its maximum depth is about twenty-eight feet; its maximum width forty, its maximum height fifty. Everything in it must be functional, flexible and telling. It is a world of illusion, yet its construction involves the most tangible of realities; it is a world of magic built on the most precise blueprints, a world of fantasy put together out of multitudinous practical details. The man who brings it into being must have visual imagination and artistic skill. But he must also have the structural knowledge of the architect, and the technical knowledge of the electrician. He must have the generous patience of a true collaborator.

Above all, he must be able to understand the script from the point of view of director and actor. For, although he is what Jo Mielziner calls the director's "extra eye," an imaginative theatrical designer often strategically influences a whole production. Mielziner's techniques of two revolving stages and center set piece in *Dodsworth* and the projections and flexible use of the full stage in *Death of a Salesman* not only made the telling of these retrospective stories possible in the theatre but also played an influential part in their scripts and direction.

A case history of the designer's infinite tasks and his effective role provided by Jo Mielziner's 195th Broadway produc-

151

tion—the six settings for the Osborn dramatization of the Marquand novel *Point of No Return.*

Jo Mielziner's first connection with this play took place in the fall of 1950 in Newtown, Conn. His neighbor, Paul Osborn wanted to dramatize J. P. Marquand's story of Charles Gray, a man for whom the difference between climbing and crawling to a goal (the vice-presidency of his bank) becomes clear only as he relives the past he has never understood. In January and February they discussed the book in terms of the theatre, and, by early April, Osborn showed him the first script.

Mielziner was intrigued at how interesting Osborn had made the characters, but he worried about the physical staging. Acts I and III were essentially conventional as to scenic demands, but in Act II the audience would have to be carried back and forth in a difficult sequence of scenes from reality to reverie. He knew that whatever *technique* he chose, the *style* would be "selective realism," the reduction of everything to the simplest possible terms.

The designer liked the challenge of a multi-scene, episodic story which would move from events in the present to incidents twenty years in the past. An ordinary multi-scene production going from one scene to another would require many men and much time. "Twenty-five years ago," Mielziner says, "audiences would sit patiently for two or three minutes before a lowered curtain, accepting over-long scene changes. But radio, TV and movies have quickened the pace of storytelling. That long pause that refreshes—only it doesn't refresh."

He believes that whereas the American theatre has become progressive, imaginative and original in musicals, it has been "creaking with the conventional three-act form" in legitimate shows. Musicals have inspired experimental, expressive means where actors, music, lyrics, book and dancing all move together.

152

When he conferred with producer Leland Hayward, director H. C. Potter and Osborn in June about presentation techniques, he asked, "Why not use musical play techniques to tell this story?" One such technique is keeping important action in full stage, but allowing the story to progress by putting the transitional action "down in one"—the front six feet of the stage—thus providing time for scenic changes without story interruption. In *South Pacific,* for instance, The Company Street was "down in one." It seemed logical here to make the "one" device a place that represented Johnson street, the street symbolic of the right side of the railroad tracks to which Charles Gray aspired as a youth. Other possibilities included reducing several scenes to telephone conversations "in one" and using slide projections in another. By using drops (painted curtains hanging from above the stage and reaching to the floor) and flats (framed pieces covered with canvas or other material) with a minimum number of highly expressive props, scenic changes could be reduced to as little as thirty to forty seconds. Osborn reworked his script completely to conform to such production schemes.

Fearful of creating static pictures and aware always of the "fourth dimension"—the actor's living and moving within a set—Mielziner first reads a script as director and audience. On second reading, he makes a breakdown. "In military school," he says, "I learned you had to guess the intention of an unseen enemy before you dealt with what is in full sight. Reading a script, the author is the unseen enemy. What is he driving at? What does he want to say? When I reach the basic intent of a scene, I reduce it to a few simple objects, and a light effect."

Thus, on odd sheets of paper, are: "Act I, Scene I, Charles Gray's living room—4 people—fireplace?—symbols of family shipping. Omit stairs?" or "Railroad scene—2 seats." Accompanying these notes are quick sketches in black and blue

153

pencil, rough, but in scale, each with a lighting notation, each with a ground plan.

There would be six sets, framed by a misty gray color on the portal (or inner proscenium) to suggest reverie, Charles Gray's living room would be a chintzy, upholstered, suburban room. As the symbol of family shipping, Mielziner felt a carved figurehead eagle would be more evocative and visually arresting than the script-specified clipper-ship painting.

The bank where Charles worked would suggest gentility, refinement and solidity. Spacious scale, arched windows, a few Corinthian columns, the fragment of a railing—simulated marble, red velvet and gilt—would convey the atmosphere. The railroad he took back to his home town would be reduced to a pair of old-fashioned, well-worn seats—a fragment to dramatize the whole. This set would be constructed, for "anything an actor works with or touches becomes furniture and must be three-dimensional."

In Act II Charles Gray would see a glamorized stylized version of symbolic Johnson street and its evocative character would set the mood of reverie. Johnson street would be a "traveler"—a curtain which can pull offstage to right or left—made of rectangular-meshed net (scrim curtain), opaque when light was thrown on it from the front and transparent when lighted from behind. As Charles looked at Johnson street lights would come on in the scene behind the traveler and the audience would "X-ray" into this room. Johnson street would float away, and as Charles walked into the room he would be the Charles of twenty years ago.

The first of these rooms of the past was the so-called "Wallpaper room" of Jessica Lovell, Charles' old love—the quintessence of "upper-upper-class" Johnson street homes, immediately proclaiming luxury, distinction, beauty and unobtrusively expensive good taste. The Chinese painted wallpaper would be a refulgent blue-green. There would be a Chippendale settee, a wing chair and a table—elegant, cold and formal.

Charles' father's study, in contrast, would indicate a man for whom the "refinements of life" meant books, pictures and the warmth of well-worn things. The color would be golden brown, the furniture a pleasing, haphazard combination of Victorian and Early American. A desk lamp would cast shadows on picture-covered walls.[1]

Working in his orderly, tasteful, book-lined studio, Mielziner began quarter-inch scale drawings which became a springboard for extensive research. His assistant, John Harvey, helped him scan books, magazines and photographs for Johnson street's New England architecture and inevitable elms. Museum files were consulted for Chinese wallpapers. A visit to the Fifth Avenue Bank had nothing to do with accounts.

By July 1st, Mielziner had a ground plan showing at exactly which stage depth each drop and flat would go and where lights would be hung. Harvey, who was trained as an architect, made structural blueprints and details of such elements as Johnson street's houses and church.

Mielziner converted the penciled blurs of his roughs to exquisite water-color sketches which the scenic painters would ultimately translate into actual scenery. Because he believes lighting is a basic, integral element in good stage design Miel-

---

[1] This, Mielziner cited as an example of what he called "freezing." To explain what he meant, Mielziner went on to explain that the scenic designer must work far ahead and can have no second chance. Thus he must frequently force the director into advance decisions on props, their placement and even stage movement, often in turn, influencing their decisions. In *Point of No Return*, for example, before the director had the John Gray scene "on its feet," the eerie, mood-setting shadows in this room— presumably cast by the desk lamp—were already being painted into the set. This meant "freezing" the director into deciding the lamp's exact, unalterable position.

155

ziner took paint samples, fabrics (dyed or plain) into a little room where, under the rainbow gelatins of his own lighting unit, they were subjected to the effects they would receive on stage.

At a mid-August conference the director requested that the Charles Gray living room be changed to a symmetrical, fireplaceless, window-centered scheme with the ship painting. The conforming new version was to prove later the least successful and only troublesome set.

By September 24th a major part of the activity shifted downtown to National Scenery Service's long, narrow building. On the ground floor whizzing jigsaws cut out the intricate luggage-rack brackets. Up two flights of a tortuous spiral staircase three men, crouched as if in a crap game, were enlarging one-inch scale blueprints to full-size cartoons to be transferred to drops and flats. Four men, busy with sponges, enormous brushes and airbrushes, were painting the bank-scene drop, stippling on a dozen colors so that under the lights the apparently even tan tone would have vitality rather than drab flatness.

The tempo quickened. The designer made almost daily trips to the National Scenery Service, supervising painting and construction, constantly reminding the painters, "Please remember I am aiming frankly at stylization." With Harvey and the electrician he plotted the lighting in its final form. He examined every object which the property man had tracked down, for the fewer the props the more important the rightness of each in telling a story of a way of life.

During the next two weeks action accelerated: painters at the National Scenery Service were recreating the spirit and suggestiveness of Mielziner's sketches; a department store truck carted off floor samples for Charles Gray's room; furniture was being upholstered and boards put under seats of chairs and sofas, for if actors sink too deeply into upholstered furniture they cannot rise and sit with ease; bank desks were

156

having their innards removed so they could be handled easily; the designer went to rehearsals of the cast which included Henry Fonda, Leora Dana, John Cromwell, Frank Conroy, Colin Keith-Johnston and Robert Ross, noting where important action took place in order to verify positions of pin-spots, snap-on lights and so on. When he discovered John Gray would lie down on his sofa in the death scene, a hurry-up call went out to have the two-seater Victorian sofa cut in half and extended to accommodate actor John Cromwell who is 6 feet 2 inches tall.

On Sunday, October 21st, Mielziner and his assistant Harvey, checked into rooms at the Hotel Taft in New Haven where the show was to open its try out run at the Shubert theatre. They were to spend at least sixteen out of each twenty-four hours in the Shubert theatre next door. Backstage, against the pipe-covered white-brick wall, props were meticulously arranged on the "prop table." Furniture, draped in dustcloths, suggested a house whose occupants were away on vacation. Johnson street was a filmy curtain hanging limply at stage right. Lamps and their gelatins hung, barnacle-like, from nine overhead parallel pipes, from hatrack-like standards between the "tormentors" or wings, and from the outer face of the first balcony railing. In the tenth row of the darkened theatre, at an improvised desk, Jo Mielziner talked through the intercom system to the electrical crews.

As an artist lays out his pigments on a palette, so Mielziner checked each lamp for angle, intensity and area on each set. One man went aloft a devil-daring ladder. "Blues are pretty even, but the amber is hot on the third pipe." "Tell me when you're tight," "Let it tickle the bases." The painstaking, tedious process continued until midnight: the palette was ready.

At 8 o'clock the next morning Mielziner started the creative steps—"painting with lights." Some lamps were used for bringing actors in; others were employed to create atmosphere. The effect of lighting in establishing and explaining mood is one of the most subtle but potent elements in any production. Each moment received its special treatment. Intensity, timing—each was cued. "Come up with your blues to 5 to the count of 6, then add the center amber on the rail to the count of 4. O.K. Call that cue 14."

All the while the painted scenery came more and more magically alive. Scriptless, actorless, this became a play of moods, strangely communicative and dramatic in itself, step by step, hour by hour—while, simultaneously prop men marked furniture positions on the stage floor. Mielziner watched vigilantly, lest a small detail ruin a carefully planned illusion. "Please make the railroad car seats sag in the middle, as if people had used them for years, and dirty them where their hands and heads would have been." Artists worked immediately with a chlorine compound and alcohol to get this effect.

After an hour's break for supper at 6, Mielziner returns. Directors and cast straggle in. The calm, mutually respectful talk between designer and electrical crew drones on. The actors move on stage, reading cues, going through rehearsed motions so lighting can be adjusted to them. They falter in surroundings that seem strange after the folding chairs and tables of rehearsal weeks. An upholstered chair seems a mountainous barrier to Leora Dana. Without makeup Colin Keith-Johnston looks skeletal. The light cues go on. The playwright wanders restlessly.

In a mumbled conference in row M, Mielziner confides to the producer his disappointment with Charles Gray's living room. "We can have a new flat," Leland Hayward says quietly, "I trust you, Jo. The rest is beautiful." From 8 A.M. to after lunch rehearsal calls the next days, Mielziner and Harvey do "clean-up jobs" with the crews. From 1 P.M. to midnight the technical rehearsals continue. Patiently, the actors repeat entrance and exit cues, tirelessly re-doing bits of business.

Each directorial change requires changes in lighting. A designer can make suggestions, but like everyone else in the theatre, he is, as Mielziner puts it, "a spoke in the wheel of which the director is the hub. If his visual sense and yours don't agree, your job is still to give him all you can."

By Wednesday noon in Mielziner's hotel room there are a mass of crumpled paper, a toothbrush glass of muddily colored water and the new Charles Gray sketch (using all existing framework) to be rushed to National Scenery Service so that it will be ready for Monday's opening. It is less drab, but as the designer admits "the least thoughtful." That night there is a complete run-through. For the third night the designer joins the producer, playwright and director for a conference until 3 A.M.

After the New Haven opening Mielziner returned to New York (starting sketches for a new show—*A Month of Sundays*) and kept in telephonic communication with the show. Two days before the Boston opening he conducted technical rehearsals.

During the second week of the Boston run and again before the Nov. 27th opening in Philadelphia, Mielziner was on hand. The management had decided that the transitions from the present to the past were not satisfactory. Important changes in the direction and vast alterations in the script were constantly in work, so that actors, story, scenery and lighting could move together in a continuous flow.

Instead of walking "through" Johnson street for his first entrance into his past, Charles was now to make a conversational transition from present to past as his train blacked out into a tunnel and was to walk directly into the "Wallpaper room." Only the flexibility of the sets and the possibility of changing them with incredible speed allowed this and other drastic script changes in the last few weeks of out-of-town try-outs. And it was in turn, the very flexibility and ingenuity of the scenery which suggested such changes, all made in the interests of ·creating a continuous and fast-paced story flow.

On Tuesday (December 11, 1951) Mielziner will begin another technical rehearsal at the Alvin theatre. At the opening, on Thursday night, he will sit in the audience, quiet and composed, objective. If he feels he has been successful, the scenery will appear to him, not as a beautiful spectacle, but as an integral part of the production. It will be a magic world, "aiding and abetting the actor," subtly giving hints, suggestions, information about the people who inhabit this world and the emotional experiences they will undergo. The wearisome hours, the arduous detail will be forgotten: only the imaginative illusion will remain.

PART FOUR—FACETS

DEATH OF A PAINTER

by

Jo Mielziner

In addition to explaining how he became interested in the theatre, in this autobiographical essay Jo Mielziner reviews the principles and working methods he used to solve the scenic problems of Death of a Salesman. *In so doing, Mr. Mielziner reveals how completely he fulfills his own definition of the theatre artist: one part painter and draftsman, one part architect, one part sculptor, one part couturier, one part electrical engineer and finally and most important, one part dramatist. Mr. Mielziner's explanations appeared in* AMERICAN ARTIST, *Volume 13 (November, 1949), pp. 33ff.*

From early childhood I was determined to be an artist. I was born in my father's studio in the Latin Quarter of Paris, and handling clay and paint and creating imaginative toys was my normal routine. From boyhood it was an accepted fact by both my parents and myself that I too would be a painter. When I was old enough to be conscious of economic necessities, I realized that many artists had difficulty earning a decent living and a good artist like my father often went through periods of real financial hardship. How the future painter could support himself was the subject of many family discussions. Like most art students of forty years ago I had a vague and yet fanatical abhorrence of having to turn to what I called "commercial art." Earning one's living at anything would be better for a young artist than to "prostitute his art" in such a Philistine field as advertising or illustration. The possibility of my entering these fields even for temporary economic support was never considered.

At this time my mother was an active journalist and the main breadwinner of the family. One of her assignments was a monthly letter for *Vogue* covering the artistic life of Paris— theatres, music, painting, in fact, all the liberal arts. Two of Mother's ancestors, Charlotte Cushman and Dan McGinnis, had achieved considerable fame in the American nineteenth-century theatre, and Mother was an avid theatregoer. My brother and I were exposed to the dramatic arts at an age when most of our contemporaries were only seeing an occasional Christmas pantomime or children's entertainment. Practical Mother very naturally suggested that during Jo's

163

Death of a Painter

future apprenticeship as an artist he might get a part-time job as a "scene painter" in the theatre. This idea seemed attractive and in no way interfered with my ultimate ambition and, in a vague sense, seemed a pleasant means or making ends meet.

The family moved to America and I continued painting and drawing in Father's studio. By the time I started high school I was taking serious academic work after hours at the Art Students League. I was offered a full-time scholarship by the Pennsylvania Academy of Fine Arts. To accept this meant giving up all further formal academic education but so certain was I of the inevitability of my career that, against the advice of family friends, I accepted this scholarship. Four years followed of concentrated academic study of painting and the winning of two scholarships for painting and study in Europe. However, the time finally arrived when scholarship funds were no longer available and a bread-and-butter job became a necessity.

In the intervening years my older brother, Kenneth Mac-Kenna, had been on the professional stage making a success as a young leading juvenile. On his advice I took a job as an apprentice in the Bonstelle Stock Company in Detroit. I learned the technique of stagecraft the hard way, but also the best way, by playing bit parts, acting as assistant stage manager, working with stage carpenters and stage electricians. From the Bonstelle Stock Company I went on to apprenticeship at the Theatre Guild in New York working as bit actor and technical assistant, and finally as an apprentice to Robert Edmond Jones. All this time I kept repeating to myself, "Once I get a little money ahead I'll give up the theatre and do nothing but paint." By the time I had actually started to design my own settings, I realized that the art of scenic design was a field rich in expression and emotionally satisfying. The technical complexities were as demanding as the combined skill required by an expert etcher and engraver, or the physical and technical dexterity required by a painter of frescos. Suddenly, I no longer looked upon the theatre as merely an economic expedient.

Upon analyzing my feelings about my childhood ambition, I saw that the canvas on which I wanted to express myself was not necessarily limited to 30x40 inches but, as I believed at that time, could very easily be expanded to a stage opening of 30x40 feet. However, the transposition from the easel painter to the scenic designer is not a direct one. Neither is the relationship between an architect and a theatre craftsman too closely allied. The ideal background for a theatre artist is a composite of many arts and crafts. But these component parts must be as skillfully blended as the smoothest cocktail —a good recipe might be: one part painter and draftsman, one part architect, one part sculptor, one part couturier, one part electrical engineer, and the final and most important part, the dramatist. This concoction has no potency unless shaken so violently that no single part, with the possible exception of the dramatist, dominates the brew.

The prime difference between the art of an easel painter and that of a theatre designer (and for that matter architect and sculptor, too) is that the theatre designer is practicing an interpretive art which deals in four dimensions at the same time. The first three dimensions are those normal to both the painter and the sculptor, but the theatre artist employs the fourth dimension of time-space. No matter how pictorially compelling a stage set is when the curtain is raised, it only has life when it continues to develop in relationship to the continuing movement and theme of the play. This may be accomplished by a change of lighting as the mood of the drama fluctuates. It may also change in pure composition by the relationship and movement of actors on the stage. In some cases the scenery itself changes shape before the spectator's eye. In other words, there is nothing static in a really dramatic stage setting. To be a perfect foil for living actors in a vibrant drama all the arts of the theatre must be combined to accomplish the ultimate aim. The three-dimensional elements of a stage design as the artist draws them cannot be realized except as viewed from one seat in the theatre. There are hundreds of other picture planes and angles of vision. Each of these compositions must be to some degree satisfying. Naturally, the view of the top-most gallery patron must by necessity be a compromise as compared to the observer in the sixth row center. The theatre designer's handling of color, unlike the painter's, must be in terms not only of local color on the canvas but in terms of the constant and varying effects of controlled light and projected color. Surface textures of fabrics and costume materials sometimes are more important than the actual pigment in which they are dyed or painted. A cast shadow on one part of the scene can be more telling than the rest of the set put together. During the progress of a play, by the simple expedient of lighting control, a three-dimensional plastic setting can be, as if by magic, changed to a flat two-dimensional design.

In designing Arthur Miller's dynamic play, *Death of a Salesman,* I first had to work on a careful analysis of the manuscript to determine the author's basic intent of each scene of the play. By listing what I felt was Miller's dramatic motivation in each scene, I could analyze the requirements in terms of scenic space relationship to the actor in movement, in other words, the third- and fourth-dimensional requirements of a setting in which this drama could live freely and expressively. Miller stated that he wanted the "simplest possible scenic solution" to the play, but in his first draft of the script he implied the need for some nine or ten separate settings or locations. In several cases, two or three of these areas were to be used simultaneously. The author and Elia Kazan, the director, agreed with me that even the most rapid mechanical method of scene changing might impair the flow of the action and the unity of the play.

The basic problem was to create a symbolic frame of a Salesman's house built in suburban outskirts and now over-shadowed by apartment houses. Important scenes had to be played in the kitchen, the master bedroom, the boy's attic bedroom, and the backyard. Another vital acting area, as finally devised, was a forestage where by the use of a few simple properties, such as a round table and a couple of chairs, scenes from the past life of this family could be enacted.

In actuality, my major contribution as a designer to this production was made before I went near my drafting board or my paint table. In getting the approval of author and director of my plan I naturally made quick, rough pencil-and-pen sketches in order to help them visualize my ideas, not to mention the fact that I think better in that medium. After their approval, my next job was to put my ideas down on quarter-inch-to-the-foot plans and elevations. Even these early sketch plans included specific notations of lighting equipment: the type of instrument to be used; from what source and location difficult areas could be lit: even notations of color filter. I mention this because it is another indication that the painter in the theatre must really look like the eight-armed Hindu god, blending from the beginning all the technical elements with which he can best realize his eventual production. Before builder's drawings were too far advanced, my assistant was making a model of wire, cardboard, wood and clay. This sculptoral study of the setting was not a cute little "exhibition model" to intrigue the author or producer, but a three-dimensional work model to clarify in my own mind the strange blending which this final setting achieved of structural form, painted form, and that illusionary quality achieved by the use of painted gauzes—all transposed under constantly moving and controlled lighting. In the actual realization of the setting some of the skeletonized frames suggesting the structure of the Salesman's house were covered in gauze to intensify the sense of intimacy when they were lit from within and at the same time to isolate them when lit from without.

In my early analysis of the play I was somewhat doubtful that the audience would always be certain when, during the action of the play, the Salesman went off into daydreams so compelling both to him and to the audience that his house appeared to him as it had looked twenty-five years before. Miller referred in the script to the fact that the house once had been surrounded by living trees but at the time of the opening scene of the play the trees had been cut down and in their place were ugly apartment houses crowding in and around the house. This was a clue to a scenic device to assist the audience in making the transition with the Salesman. The effect was achieved by covering the stage with green leaves projected from numerous magic lanterns. As the projection was slowly brought up on the dimmer and the leaves became visible, the painted apartment houses on the backdrop slowly faded from sight, in a sense visually liberating the Salesman's house from their oppression and giving the stage a feeling of outdoor freedom.

In this particular play a highly complicated engineering problem presented itself. The manuscript indicated that the two boys retire to their attic beds in full view of the audience. Two and one half minutes later, looking years younger, the same boys had to appear coming in from the garden. How was this to be done? It was neither practical nor economical to have doubles cast as the younger boys, and certainly the boys could not get out of their beds in view of the audience in any normal manner. The final solution was individual elevators hidden under each cot in the attic room. Once the boys were snugly in bed with blankets pulled over their shoulders, the unseen elevators were lowered to stage level where the actors, hidden behind scenery, escaped to the wings in time to make a hasty costume change and appear on cue in the garden.

After the big chore of completed blueprint specifications, light plots, full-scale building details, and drawings for properties has been finished, I have the fun of painting the color sketches for the production (which at this phase of the job is being constructed in scenic carpenter shops). I make these drawings in tempera color at the scale of one-half inch to the foot. That means that my apartment backdrop painting for *Death of a Salesman* was twenty-two and one-half inches wide and fifteen inches high. In actual practice it is virtually impossible to have the time to actually paint on the final drop. Highly skilled master scenic artists square off my painting and make extraordinarily faithful reproductions on the full-scale backdrop. They do not make facsimiles because a nervous brush stroke a quarter of an inch in length should not be literally enlarged to six inches on the backdrop but should be interpreted in the kind of technique which has the necessary carrying power to theatrical scale. I use tempera color because it is a type of tempera which the scenic artist must use on the backdrop and, although my color is more finely ground, it makes the scenic artist's job somewhat easier than giving him a painting in oil or pastel to interpret in a foreign medium.

The color sketches for a production such as *Death of a Salesman* include not only the backdrops, gauzes and scenery pieces, but also color samples for properties, ground cloths to cover the stage and even dye samples for the bed sheets in the boys' attic room. Pure white on the stage is avoided if possible because to the audience's eye, under stage lighting, it becomes competition to the actor's face. What appears to be a pretty white tablecloth is actually dyed about the color of a brown paper grocery bag. When viewed for the first time the painted setting as it is being assembled on the stage may look horribly inadequate—even to the technician of long

169

experience. But once the magic of stage lights is brought into play, what a moment before was thinly painted tempera landscape on a coarse and wrinkled canvas becomes something full of illusion and dramatic power.

At best the theatre designer is always working under great pressure. It is not alone the time deadline, but the fact that the various elements of his design are executed in half a dozen shops around town. Not until the dress rehearsal can he look for the first time on the completed stage picture. He has no second chance or margin for error. Once the design is approved by author, director and producer, that is the one which will stare the designer and the future audience in the face—good, bad, or indifferent. The theatre designer is also surrounded by fellow-workers who are driving at concert-pitch—some of them hysterically, all of them excitedly, and certainly all aiming at giving life to the play. The theatre is no place for the designer who is an egomaniac. The most the designer can hope to achieve is the brilliant success of being a single sturdy spoke in a well-set wheel. The playwright is the cartwright and the play itself—not the stage design—is the the hub.

I am passionately fond of reading plays, an avid playgoer, a keenly excited and fascinated participant at the dress rehearsal (even after twenty-five years of professional theatre designing). But strangely enough, nothing gives me more pleasure than the precious hours I spend doing my color sketches for the theatre. The easel painter in me, who died before reaching maturity, would probably not have found the deep source of creative stimulus and satisfaction which the theatre holds—in a sense, I eat my cake and have it too.

SCENERY IN THIS PLAY?

by

Jo Mielziner

Jo Mielziner wrote this explanation of how he redesigned the scenic production of Abe Lincoln in Illinois *for the Playwrights' Company in 1939, long before arena-style theatre achieved the popularity it has acquired since World War II. Mr. Mielziner was planning his production for a proscenium-type theatre, but if his concise and illuminating analysis of how he reduced his scenic elements to the barest essentials is read keeping in mind the scenic demands and limitations of arena-style production, one discovers that Mr. Mielziner has written an excellent analysis of the problems of scenery for arena theatre. The aesthetic principles Jo Mielziner applied to the problem of redesigning* Abe Lincoln *are directly applicable to scenic design for arena-style production. Mr. Mielziner's discussion is reprinted from the* NEW YORK TIMES *(October 22, 1939, X, 1). In slightly altered form it was reprinted in* PLAYERS MAGAZINE, *Volume 37 (January, 1961) pp. 8off.*

A couple of years ago [1938] when that brilliant production, *Our Town,* was running on Broadway, there was much controversy regarding plays without settings. People were reported asking at the box office "Is there any scenery in this play?"

The real question, the question worth asking is: "Is there any theatre in the scenery?"

For there is no such thing as presenting a play without scenery. The moment a company of actors begin speaking their lines, even on an empty stage under a work light, there is a setting, though perhaps not a very effective one. The stage platform elevating the players above the audience is theatric in itself. The concentrating work light also adds a focal and dramatic element to the scene.

There is nothing new in the attempt to simplify the setting for a play. It dates back to the first formal drama. But there is always something new in a fresh attack on an old problem. I believe that the designer in the modern theatre (and I go back to Adolphe Appia and Gordon Craig) has always been eager to attack his job in a fresher and more imaginative manner. And the audience, for its part, is quick to welcome an unconventional production, provided it is theatrically effective.

The reason such attempts are rare is due to the fear of playwrights and producers of offending the audience's sense of reality, and to their lack of faith in the appeal of imagination and suggestive settings. Even in Hollywood, however, where belief in the literal-mindedness of the public is prac-

173

tically unquestioned cannon, the average camera man and director knows and uses to advantage such simplifications as the close-up, which eliminates all detail and focuses attention on the actors. If a lens is ever invented that will allow the entire contents of a room to be viewed under the comely chin of Charles Boyer and Irene Dunne, in a close-up, I'm afraid there will be a rush to use it. There is always the old urge to overstate facts which are only important if they are implied once.

What I call Implied Scenery is for me the most effective. It is a rare and happy day when I have the chance to caress a good play with just the right touch, and I am therefore grateful to the courage and faith of the Playwrights' Company for the chance to try a scenic production of *Abe Lincoln in Illinois* which now is in its second year in New York.

In my original designs for the play, which then was at the Plymouth, I reduced the settings to a sort of concentrated realism, with the purpose of accenting the most telling objects in each scene.

In moving the play to the larger Adelphi theatre, the Playwrights' Company presented me with this problem: to design a simple, fast-moving, easily handled production of this twelve-scene play, sacrificing nothing of its dramatic effectiveness, yet scaling the operating costs within range of the wonderful ideal of a popular dollar-top theatre.

I began by listing the endless non-essentials (and it was an endless list) which had surrounded the actors in each of the twelve scenes originally, and then proceeded to pare down the list.

Take for example, the scene in which young Lincoln visits his future bride, Mary Todd, in the formal parlor of the Ninian Edwards home. At first the scene depicted a mid-Victorian home in all—or nearly all—its fussy elegance of drapes and doodads. When I had finished my censorship of the list of items, there remained as essentials:

174

A. Beautiful, character-revealing lighting.

B. The one period sofa and the two chairs actually used for the actors to sit on.

C. A story-telling mantel-shelf and iron stove, to communicate the mood and character of that particular family at the particular period.

Left out were the walls, the doors, the window, the draperies, pictures, unneeded furniture and extra trimming. And when the scene came to be rehearsed at the Adelphi, it was found that the lack of a door did not prevent Mr. Gaines as Lincoln from making an effective entrance—its absence actually punctuated Sherwood's beautiful lines.

An emphasis of a different kind is provided in the second scene, where the pessimistic old veteran of the Revolution, Ben Mattling, is trying to dissuade Abe Lincoln from going into politics. In its original setting, the walls of the Rutledge Tavern were decorated with engravings of former Presidents of the United States, and in his diatribe against the degradation of democratic dogma, old Ben would point to each in turn as he spoke the lines, "Look at Washington. Look at Jefferson. And John Adams. Where are they today? Dead." The line was always good for a laugh. But in the present production there are no pictures of the Presidents. Old Ben speaks the line without pointing. And yet the laugh on his final indignant "Dead" is far louder than it used to be at the Plymouth.

Why?

Because a non-essential has been removed. When Ben used actually to point to the portraits, there was a slight distraction. Instead of focusing entirely on the actor and his words, the audience used to follow his pointing cane. Perhaps some of them wondered if the pictures on the wall were really of Washington, Jefferson and Adams. At any rate, there used to be a certain division of interest, whereas today the audience reaction to the scene is far quicker and heartier as a result of eliminating a non-essential.

The final scene, in which Lincoln speaks his farewell to Illinois, has now been set with only one so-called "piece of scenery"—the rear platform of the train—and only a few feet of that.

Note that although the amount of detail has been very much reduced, what there is left is still realistic—still in period. Had I designed a stylized or impressionistic train platform, it would have not been appropriate to Sherwood's script. In fact, it would have been an impertinent intrusion of a point of view foreign to the play.

With the elimination of a good deal of the physical scenery, a correspondingly greater amount must be achieved in other ways—for example, by light. In the third scene, when Lincoln tells of the death of Ann Rutledge, the setting called for him to shuffle despondently up a flight of stairs to bed at the curtain. It was one of the most effective moments in the play, and it presented a real problem in the simplification, since of course, there were no stairs. The scene was restaged, so that instead of Lincoln making the exit, it is Bowling and Nancy Green who go out, carrying the lamp and dimming the light on the stage. Lincoln sinks exhausted on his couch, and after his friends have gone he raises his head. A blue light has been so placed that as his face is lifted, his head and shoulders are outlined by a thin blue line against the blackness for a moment. Then he bows forward again and merges with the darkness as the curtain descends. I believe—and in fact I have been told—this effect is no less moving than the original curtain.

The pertinent question for the public to ask therefore, is not "Is there any scenery in this play?"—for the moment you have actors on an elevated platform, framed in a proscenium, with telling lights focused upon them, you have the essentials

176

of a setting. What they really want to know is whether the setting is dramatically effective and evocative of the play's main theme. Any producer who can give the right answer to the query "Is there theatre in the scenery?" will find a responsive public.

MUSICAL COMEDY DESIGN

by
Howard Bay

In musical comedy design, Howard Bay declares, the solution to the technical problems is of prime importance. The hanging plot becomes the designer's Bible, as it welds the scenery in the air, on the floor and on the platform stages, plots the working of the show, insures the maskings, distributes the lighting instruments and balances the acting areas. Originally written for this anthology, Mr. Bay's witty yet penetrating article first appeared in THEATRE ARTS, Volume 43 (April, 1959), pp. 56ff. under the title "Scene Design for Musical Comedy."

In the Twenties when all those heavy books on the Art of Scenic Design were compiled, there was no visible excuse for admitting design for musicals into the company of respectable scenic investiture. The musical comedies were brimful of acreage of painted foliage and architectural vistas transplanted from Covent Garden, the La Scala, and the Vienna Opera House. When Joseph Urban imported his atelier for the wholesale manufacture of scenery, the traditional was flavored with the Austrian Secessionist movement and it all was simplified and smoothed out by Urban's authority.

The break came with the decidedly clever revues at the start of the Thirties. With one brash gesture, Albert Johnson outfitted *The Band Wagon* in topical attire. The loose washes and calligraphic line of Raoul Dufy became overnight the one and only proper pictorial manner for live shows with music. A glance at the current offerings display surprisingly little deviation in style after all these years; it has weathered the seasons by virtue of that free, dashed-off look. Only two variations are persistent: the painty, nostalgic, Valentine frou-frou initiated by Lemuel Ayres in *Bloomer Girl* and myself in *Up in Central Park*—and today with my *Music Man*. The other side is the end product of trial and error cadging from the ballet. The spasmatic errors are attempts to use or adapt easel painters whose too rigid and too positive compositional structures war with the performers. Surviving in the standard repertory of commercial practice are borrowings from the second string gallery artists: like

179

the fuzzier, illustrative Berman, Piper, Tchilechev, and Clavé. A sharper, more posteresque treatment runs through Oliver Smith's *On the Town*, my *Flahooley* and the Eckharts' *Golden Apple*—these with an affinity for contemporary display and graphic art. Or the designer launches out to be gorgeous as in my *Show Boat* revival as we faced the challenge of the rose-tinted memories of the original production. Mention should be made of the craze for toothpick skeletons. We all turn out this openwork cartoon framing placed against a colored void, and it is judged daringly imaginative. Why skeleton scaffolding is imaginative *per se* is a puzzlement. "Imaginative" is a shopworn word and should not be draped on a skindeep pictorial form but reserved for idea solutions of scenic problems. For instance, in the dear, dead days when I seemed to do all the shows with "girls" in the titles, my primary objective was an overall clean and neat appearance that balanced the rough and untidy doings onstage. Or in *Music Man* with conscious restraint rejecting clever, eye-catching tricks that would disrupt the throwback Americana pastoral. Now the brazen salesman outsider bounces against a smooth, homespun milieu.

The surface aesthetic conventions are not the heart of musical design—nor are the necessary gimmicks such as the wagon stages, the turntables, the treadmills, or the jack-knives. The spirit, the feel, and the timing and rhythm are basic and are created by the designer and his fellow artisans: the director, the writers, the choreographer, the musical director and the producer. A musical is in a state of flux and does not congeal into an entity until opening night in New York. This is in decisive contrast to the straight play, where the director and the designer are interpretive handmaidens steering a finished unity, the script, to an undistorted public presentation. Only in detailing the process of fabricating a musical can the designer's craft be revealed. That these working innards have received scant attention is perplexing insofar as the musical production is America's contribution to theatrical form.

I will attempt herewith to jot down a tab version of the preparation of a show. The bringing into being of a musical is a large and mercurial undertaking. 'Tis a miracle that as many shows have vaulted over the conservative drag on the new and different and have advanced this exuberant brand of theatre. The innate conservatism stems from the hefty investment at stake. The backers are assured that the monies are entrusted to tried and true hands—preferably the hands that knocked out last night's hit. Not only is the set designer spending near $50,000 and the costume designer over $50,000, but the pressure of the schedule forces a departmentalized autonomy. Respect is paid to the designer who is technically experienced in mastering the script changes and re-shuffling that inevitably face the out-of-town try-out.

The staff is hired after suitable haggling and all read what is playfully called a "rough" script. The first get together is in the nature of a polite shakedown wherein the composer plays the score and everyone finds one number about which to be enthusiastic.

From the script and its promised renovations, from the flavor of the music, from the director's approach, the designer gathers up the scraps and seeks seclusion. Research is amassed —primarily for the feel of period and locale, rather than for detail authenticity. The script is broken down into scene types: the big production numbers, the intimate book or sketch items, the numbers "in one" or shallow book fragments, and transitional trivia called "crossover bits." It is a safe wager that at this point little of this binder material has been written. I vividly recall one successful opus called *One Touch of Venus* when nobody would face the need for those scenes in "one" until it became clear out-of-town.

Now staff conferences become work sessions. The choreographer blocks out the pattern of key numbers, the book

181

director makes known his physical requirements in the way of entrances, elevations, special props. The designer is armed with a preliminary hanging plot. This is his Bible, as it welds the scenery in the air, on the floor and on platforms; plots the working of the show; insures that the maskings mask; distributes the lighting units; and balances acting areas. The last is a seesaw with the dance director requesting unimpeded floor space to the backwall for each and every number, versus the book director with equal logic demanding that all dialogue scenes be pitched down into the footlights. The use of travellers and other close-ins, and the invention of most scene-shifting devices grew out of this contradiction that two things occupy the same space. The bygone way was simply to close-in, and in the time required to change the scenery up-stage, manufacture a diversion downfront or play a segment of the narrative on this shallow strip. With the passing of the revues and of the specialties, more fluid and integrated solutions came into being. Travellers becoming gauzes, with or without silhouette appliqué, make for a softer rhythm of dim-out and dim-in than the brutal guillotine of opaque fabric blotting out the view, as for example, my stadium exterior into the fight ring of *Carmen Jones* and the jungle transparency of *Magdalena*. Theatrical conventions die a lingering death, but for many seasons now audiences accept and revel in open scene changes right in front of their eyes. This not only revived the treadmill—which often is constricting and prohibitive helpwise—but widened the use of the overall platformed stage. Grooved at will to receive guides, units can travel in any direction on the platform stage, manually operated or winched as in *West Side Story*. The double turntable, as used in *My Fair Lady*, remains the fast-est way to get from one full box set to another.

Creative collaboration before drawings, choreography, stage business are frozen is the time when the unique spirit of a show comes to pass. The director may have a scenic concept, the designer may trace out a production number, the dance director may take a static blob of plot exposition and turn it into a musical highlight, the lyricist and the composer may telescope two involved episodes into one bright patter piece. Fussy doo-dads and extra naturalistic garbage are struck. Laborious subplots get lost and that seemingly effortless rhythm comes in the window. Whatever the necessary weight or complexity, musical comedy must above all appear light and spontaneous and airily mobile. Not speed but change of pace, not unrelieved lavishness but change of scale—iris down from a full stage of people and furnishings to a solo in a pinspot, without the surroundings turning glum or the transition obtrusive. A designer should know as well as an Abbott, a Logan or a Da Costa knows that one doesn't automatically splurge on the best number. "There's No Business Like Show Business" (from *Annie Get Your Gun*) was delivered by the four principles just standing out there "in one," backed by a plain traveller. This is close to the core of musical theatre. The aforementioned directors, for instance, plus producers who actually deserve that bandied about label "showmen," possess a common denominator: a tenacious concentration on the big values, the general line of a story pushing forward in the main entertainment values. Exhibitionalist tangents and personalities and indulgent vignettes can shatter the frame and constipate the flow of action. Lesser minds cherish that lovely show-stopper in the second act but Rogers and Hammerstein will scrap a hit number that derails the monolithic drive. That elegant, lengthy ballet or that mammoth scene of scintillating small talk may garner critical notices but the show has been left standing.

Meanwhile, back on the drawing board, the color sketches, the working drawings, the electrical layout, the drapery and upholstery swatches and specifications are all polished off and dispatched to the respective shops. The color chart is a joint effort of the set and the costume designer. A progressive

Musical Comedy Design

palette is built as consciously as the score is arranged and orchestrated. Shop supervision varies not one whit from the same chores on a straight play. There is just more of it and rehearsal changes bring forth production changes.

The out-of-town opening is everyone's first glimpse of all the elements in one place. Scenic planning and detailed shop prefabrication is obviously efficient and economical. However, more important is the fact that the quicker the show is in performance running shape, the quicker the weaknesses are exposed. The leisure for pre-Broadway doctoring is a snare and a delusion with the eight audiences weekly and the striking, moving and set-up between jumps. To sandwich in the time to write, time to arrange, time to rehearse the book, dance, orchestra; time to rehearse company, orchesta, costumes and stage paraphernalia all together; time for the the publicity pictures—and time to figure out what to do. On the road musicals often have the strange faculty of getting worse rather than better. Two prime reasons: (1) the basic format is defective and frantic scrambling and strained humor render the frailty more transparent; (2) the man in charge is not ruthless and decisive, but is vulnerable to the battalions of wives, agents and assorted sharpies that pounce. Manhattan's bistros must be drained of their steady clientele at the height of the try-out season.

A stout heart, an even disposition, and not too quick a wit, are stock equipment, for the successful designer out-of-town. It will be crystal clear immediately whether or not the hanging plot he slaved over is sufficiently flexible to allow a big scene to be shifted to Act I between two equally big scenes, and a brand new number with a spiral staircase planted in its place—before the Saturday matinee, of course. The dire happenings are hilarious in retrospect, but the moral to be gleaned is that there is no substitute for the backlog of artistic and technical miscellany the musical designer must have imbedded in his brain ready to meet any contingency.

184

As Mike Todd used to say, "You can't go to research." A premium is placed on the elasticity of the lighting plot also. Enough lamps hung with multi-directional coverage so changes can be confined to the switchboards with a minimum of time dissipated on re-focussing. Unlike electrics in the drama, in a musical, the arc follow spots supplant the majority of "specials" or lamps focussed on a specific area for a specific action. A show's sparkle isn't a result of a blaze of wattage aimed at the stage, but arises from the color contrast of strong back lighting and cross lighting cutting through the general illumination, haloing the people and hazing the background. All told, lighting is not the occult art one reads about, but the pertinent combination of a few standard hook-ups based on a sure knowledge of what each unit, plus gelatin, hung from a particular location, will do. On one occasion I was plagued by the definite feeling that the producer was disappointed when the lighting was finished and right so simply. He had been broken in by a light specialist who stopped the dress rehearsal, shouted, electricians swarmed onstage with ladders and changed two gelatins. At this point the generalization is apropos that the actual making of a Broadway product is not a matter of gruelling rehearsals into the grey dawn, containers of coffee, and gay, mad doings. In reality it is the sympathetic mixture of hard working and occasionally inspired craftsmen. Besides, a full band and a stageful of stagehands cost a king's ransom after midnight has struck.

The opening on the Great White Way and It's-in-the-Lap-of-the-Gods-Now has been sufficiently publicized in story and film. The designer is concerned that the cues run smoothly, and if it is a hit, how is he going to cut down for the road company that full rigged sailing vessel the author went and wrote into the fabric of the production.

The songs of *Carousel, Finian's Rainbow* and *Guys and Dolls* will march on; but even reproductions of musical settings are pale and inert reminders of something that has

185

passed away. Words laid end to end fall short of graphically opposing lavish but dragging scenery against the proper scenic production that blithely lifts the words and music along. The chatter about creating an unobtrusive environment, underlining the thematic spine, stabbing this or that with a shaft of pure light, is all very well when holding forth on high drama; but it is a little silly and beside the point when busying up a breakaway bed for Bobby Clark or draughting a fitting entrance for "Miss Natural Resources." The thought for the day is, however, that when folks say they want to see a show, they mean a song and dance show. For conversational purposes back at the club one may work in a matinee of That New Serious Play, but the magic, color and spontaneity that history tells us denotes theatre is here and now the American musical. And the harried designer and his little box of water colors add to the general gaiety. And gaiety is the difference for the designer between laboring on a musical and on a straight drama. Unless one is consigned to Lillian Hellman or an equivalent where everything one creates has a purpose, the amassing of flats, antimacassars and ashtrays can become quite a drag. Musicals can grandly dispense with the kitchen sink—because the audience has one at home.

Trend prophesying is a ticklish pastime. Today the entire field of aesthetics is up for grabs. The demolition of post-Renaissance spatial concepts in the visual arts is a topic that hasn't even been mentioned at Sardi's. It is a nice question too, insofar as the proscenium theatre was invented as the classic model of Renaissance space. Perhaps musicals appear smugly backward, yet the sumptuous, empty, rhinestone and plush offerings have vanished never to return. The brittle, little, little revues with their smirking sketches, their paper-thin satire, their torch singer anchored to that crazy lamp post are long gone. Although it is safe to state that nostalgia and feminine allure are here to stay, it is possible that the

186

packaging will lift some thoughts from the Orient. The single
blanket style for a show may split wide open and the elements
fashioned in totally dissimilar styles matched to their individual roles. An air of improvisation might sneak back
through the stage door as dancers come on with the beautiful
object they need to dance with, dance, and depart. The piano
player puts down his glass and picks up the ballad theme as
the tired moon is unwrapped from its old newspapers and
hung up—by Bert Lahr, naturally. Once upon a time theorists
discoursed on presentational staging but the concrete samples
were skimpy and didactic and the whole subject got lost.
Perhaps that germ will come back in a musical guise—and it
will not be precious because the customers won't stand for it.
To quote Todd once again, "It's a holiday and they get their
money's worth."

MUSICAL COMEDY DESIGN FOR STAGE AND SCREEN

by

Oliver Smith

In his comparison of musical comedy design for the stage and motion pictures, which was written especially for this anthology, Oliver Smith indicts the American scene designer as being behind the times. The contemporary architects, he believes, are far in advance of the scene designers in their dramatic use of space, form and color. Most current design, he declares, is still eighteenth-century in concept, designed for a picture box theatre. The great contemporary architects, he concludes, will force scene designers into new imaginative and challenging dimensions.

The American musical is the most complex of all theatre art forms, combining in a fluid yet compressed manner, vaudeville, opera, drama and ballet. Design for the musical stage demands a sympathetic understanding and passion for these forms.

Robert Edmond Jones once said, "Keep in your souls some images of magnificence." This statement applies not only to the designer, but to the audience as well, for it is the designer's job to arouse, to surprise, to startle and delight. And the audience must demand it, to be able to find in the musical theatre a visual escape from the rigidity and absurd hideousness of commercial art which today dominates our magazines and newspapers, our television, and even our architecture.

Musical design is more complex than dramatic design, there is more to it because it is a larger body of work. The typical musical show has from five to twenty scenes, all of which must change instantaneously. Nothing is more devastating during a performance than a long scenic wait in a show that has been racing or waltzing along, only to shudder to a halt while stagehands laboriously and noisily clatter about. Each scene must function within the fabric of the show, adding delight to its own special moment, yet retaining a single point of view and contributing to a single accumulative effect. All scenes must be interrelated so that no one scene is out of context visually with the next. The careful planning of each scene establishes the overall rhythm of a show, thus giving it a visual *élan*.

Musical Comedy Design for Stage and Screen

The modern musical show is a hybrid visually; it is often a liaison between the contemporary painting world and the world of architecture. In 1944 when I began designing musicals, they had long been dominated by the ingenious use of architecture. Subsequently, the emphasis became concentrated on the "painted" set. This was due to the economics of the theatre, the scarcity of building materials during wartime restrictions, and the indifference of the spectators to the dry and generally unimaginative architecture that usually confronts them at a musical. For the next ten years the musical stage was dominated by painters and artists who created a series of paintings. Some designers, such as Lemuel Ayers, Raoul Pene du Bois, Jo Mielziner, Boris Aronson and myself, were more concerned with color, light and a freedom from any rigid architectural scheme. What evolved stylistically, was a certain emphasis on fantasy, airiness and fluidity not seen before on the American stage. Choreographers contributed a profound influence on musical design through their work in ballet, and later for the theatre. Agnes de Mille, Jerome Robbins, Jack Cole and Michael Kidd, all of whom became expert over-all directors, not only popularized ballet in America and developed our native dance traditions, but they introduced dancing as an integral part of all musicals, using it to further plot and story and not merely as a divertissement. This affected stage design, since it demanded large uncluttered stage areas, evoking poetic, humorous or dynamic moods. The content of their works were serious and many times highly dramatic, which in turn demanded seriousness instead of frivolity in design.

The designer of the modern musical today is both architect and painter. He must create a three dimensional painting. The use and selection of color is a major requirement. Formerly, musicals were rather realistic in treatment, with a realistic use of color. Today musical design reflects the sophistication of modern painting. To design for today's musical theatre, I believe the following qualifications are necessary:

1. A talent for architectural design, a sense of use and dynamics of space and movement of objects in space.

2. The ability to paint, preferably in several styles, both abstract, romantic and realistic.

3. A tireless energy and adaptability to change, especially to the whimsical and naive taste of stage directors, many of whom are uninformed about architecture and painting, if not indifferent to it.

4. Administrative ability, the ability to organize and supervise all of the visual elements of a musical. A show involves literally hundreds of workers, builders, painters, electricians, stagehands, producers and stage managers. To meet the varied demands of these various departments means not only an organizational mind but requires the practical use of psychology as well.

5. A passion for the work itself. Without this not only is the work too exhausting, it is financially unrewarding.

The modern musical might be compared to a rather long freight train. If one department fails, it is like a car jumping the track and the whole train is derailed. To design a musical, therefore, requires an eager and friendly collaboration with all participants, it is not a place for temperamental or artistic misanthropes. Each musical is a complete microcosm and each facet of it inter-relates with the others.

For the designer, each musical begins with the conference period, which may consist of an intensely stimulating discussion of the material of the show, or a battle of egocentric wills between the various areas, or an endless soliloquy on the part of the producer who may resemble either King Lear or a nervous rabbit. This conference period is usually a rather agonizing affair. The wise designer relaxes and accepts various ideas through a kind of osmosis rather than any direct stimuli. It takes far too long for the various attitudes and probing to appear, but it is something that definitely must be endured. Unless he is astonishingly resilient and equally egocentric, the designer is apt to emerge from these conferences in a state of catatonic shock.

Having endured the conference period, the design now proceeds to that delicious moment of artistic isolation, which is the greatest reward—or the greatest agony—of all designers. During these relatively brief moments the designer is happily creating the visual shell which will either enhance or mutilate a show. He may design the show many times, and certainly it will undergo numerous changes, unless he is a man not only of giant will power but also of considerable physical restraint.

The moment when the design is revealed for the first time is a moment of terrible exposure, like emerging from the artistic cocoon. Then follows a period of vague apprehension in which the glossy-eyed director and producer make vague comments ranging from "What is it?" or "You've done it again!" to "You have outdone yourself this time." The most difficult situation of this period occurs when the designer finds himself caught between the director who wants to be a producer and a producer who thinks he can direct. Both are convinced they can do the other's job better.

Then follows a series of nightmares. The show is sent out for bids, they are disastrously high and the designer is accused of ruining the entire enterprise by his extravagance. There is that awful moment when the cast confronts the monster you created, when it looks "different," when a scene planned to shift in fifteen seconds suddenly takes an eternity of five minutes, when the lights do or do not work, when the fuses blow and there is no light at all, when travellers stick or rattle nervously, when it appears that this monster has been deliberately designed to ruin the producer's pocket book and trap the actors in a mangled web of cables, moving platforms and flying drops.

192

If the designer is strong-willed, patient, and able to adopt a philosophical humor about the unreality of it all, it is possible for him to live through the final opening of the show in New York and then commence the same furious cycle all over again. He is neither enchanted, nor disenchanted, he endures this serpentine, exhausting march of events because in the end it is the only way he can express himself. When the curtain goes up, he is also on the stage; for better or worse, he is hopelessly stage struck.

Designing for the movies is a totally different problem. Movie musicals are usually divided into two sections; the main story which involves the young or old hopefuls who wish to break into show business, who "fall in love, fall out of love, fall back in love." (Actually, there is an enormous emphasis upon the word love, although none of it actually exists anywhere in the film). The "show" is usually supposed to take place in an average theatre, but in scale the productions are more like that of giant wedding cakes that could barely squeeze through the Panama Canal. These shows within shows, have settings that are usually imitations of, and sometimes direct steals from Broadway productions. Generally, they are trite clichés, without wit or any lofty beauty. They are inclined to resemble Niagara Falls illuminated at night by pop colored lights. In fact, the water theme is very prevalent in Hollywood, movie moguls consider it erotic, and somehow stimulating to the box office. Although this was more true before the advent of television where today's musicals seem just as bad, because of the enormous cost and risk involved in producing a film musical today they are beginning to be more carefully prepared and produced. One of the problems of designing a stage musical is to withstand the terrible pressure of designing and executing a show in eight weeks; in a movie the problem is to maintain interest for perhaps twenty-five weeks and then to

193

see the favorite sequences cut completely from the film in a decision that takes exactly ten seconds.

Designing for a movie is an extremely detailed job, and means designing a setting from every conceivable angle, so that if the cameraman chooses, he can photograph it from a radius of 360 degrees. This means the composition and color has to be beautiful from all directions, like a piece of sculpture. While this is a fascinating problem, it increases greatly the labor of the designer.

The motion picture musical of the future I believe will be more thoroughly stylized; there will not be the old traditional transitions from the main story to the inevitable show within a show (when such a device is used), but a carefully calculated use of color and form, acting as an inevitable visual bridge, so one is unaware of a change from story into musical numbers into dance. In the successful and polished Broadway musical this smooth blend of elements is considered essential for success, and great effort is expended to achieve this seemingly effortless effect. In movies it is still inclined to be extremely abrupt and clumsy by comparison, despite the slickness of photography. Although the use of revolving stages, treadmills, sliding platforms and travellers are extremely effective on the stage for propelling scenery about, on the screen they are relatively ineffective as the camera does all this for the designer. Yet, the use and restraint with which the camera is used is an important part of the movie designer's setting, especially with any large screen process. Any pan shot or boom shot tends to be exaggerated because everything is enlarged considerably. While this produces a three-dimensional effect, it also violently increases audience participation in movement related to objects. An excessive use of these shots produces dizziness or a kind of sea-sickness on the part of the audience which is not at all helpful in viewing a designer's work. Experience proves that the mobility of the camera should be related generally to human possibilities and not to some supernatural cricket who can crawl through keyholes and at the same time fly over actors' heads or crawl along the floor. Such camera angles are exaggerated and call undue attention to the "cleverness" of the camera itself, which should always exist without seeming to.

One of the most disheartening things about designing settings for the movies is that so little of them finally appear on the screen. The majority of the cameramen are so steeped in the successful tradition of twenty-five years of work they are loathe to experiment, and while they consider themselves arbiters of taste in pictures, they are curiously disinterested in painting or the affiliated arts; they are sophisticated technicians, they are not artists.

I have had the good fortune, in recent years, to work on four outstanding movies, all distinctly different in their directorial and production approach. They all represent what I would call superior Hollywood musicals. They were *The Band Wagon, Oklahoma!, Guys and Dolls* and *Porgy and Bess.*

The Band Wagon, produced by Arthur Freed, a most intelligent and artistically aware man, was created especially for pictures and not derived from a previous show, although it did employ the original music and lyrics from *The Band Wagon* by Arthur Schwartz and Howard Dietz. The story was a conventional one, the creation of a musical, but with originality and excitement added to the script by Betty Comden and Adolph Green of Broadway fame. The choreography of Michael Kidd was also fresh and invigorating and the entire production was directed by Vincent Minelli, one of America's important musical comedy stage designers of the thirties and now one of the most skillful and sensitive directors in Hollywood. Working on this picture was very similar to working on a Broadway musical and a most felicitous way of starting to work in pictures. Although, all

195

the departments of a movie musical are inter-related as in a musical on Broadway, the artistic result is often inclined to be considerably more conservative. Only when the entire staff is of equal artistic and imaginative excellence, as they were on *The Band Wagon,* is the result apt to be interesting visually.

In *The Band Wagon,* it was necessary to design a series of realistic interiors, including railroad stations, shooting galleries, deluxe apartments, not so luxe apartments and backstage tableaux and then in direct contrast a series of ballet and musical numbers. At the time this show was being produced, every Hollywood musical had to have a "big" number. In this picture it was a story ballet, a satire on contemporary lurid detective thrillers. Although the picture was in technicolor I decided to design the big "flashy" number practically in black and white with certain carefully chosen violent color accents. It was stark, simple and highly successful as a background for Mr. Astaire's wonderful dancing.

The three other pictures I have worked on were similar in that they used either Todd-A-O or Cinerama, wide screens, and were all based on previous successful shows: *Oklahoma!, Guys and Dolls* and *Porgy and Bess,* which I believe is the first American Opera ever put on the screen.

Oklahoma! was a picture related to the land. Much of it was shot on location. As designer I worked very closely with Mr. Zimmerman, the director, and the camerman, in selecting the angles, usually very carefully composed, since Zimmerman has a superb visual sense; dry, economic and sparse. His desire was for clear, uncluttered compositions. Here the wide screen lent itself sympathetically to the natural horizontal compositions of the land. However, in *Guys and Dolls,* which was urban in feeling, this wide composition was extremely difficult to compose for. The dream ballet in *Oklahoma!* was reminiscent of an earlier work which I de-

196

signed for Agnes de Mille's *Rodeo*. It was curious to complete a cycle of design started eleven years earlier in the seemingly remote world of ballet, which is now affecting motion picture design as it has already influenced stage design.

Like *Oklahoma!*, *Guys and Dolls* was a complete visual departure from the original Broadway production. Since it encompassed all of New York, and was shot on one stage, it was necessary to design New York in a very stylized manner. The result was a combination of highly realistic elements, combined with backgrounds employing photographic collage, abstract painting, and realistic architecture. These elements were so blended it was difficult to tell where one began and the other stopped.

"Cat Fish Row," the main set in *Porgy and Bess*, is neoromantic in feeling, and tries to capture a nostalgia of an era passed, more beautiful and more resplendent than the present. In no way did I attempt an archeological representation of Charleston, but rather, I used the Flemish painters Pieter De Hooch, and Vermeer and the eighteenth-century Venetians, Canaletto and Guardi as inspirations. I tried to imagine how they would have painted Charleston if they had been there at the time Porgy roamed the streets in his goat cart. In contrast to the violent colors and the hard and slashing forms of New York in *Guys and Dolls,* in the Charleston setting, all was soft, delicate and muted, for in *Porgy,* I wanted the background to be in direct contrast to the harsh, disonnant score. In *Guys and Dolls,* visually, it paralleled the composer's work.

One of the rewards of working for the movies is the knowledge that for better or for worse, your work will be preserved on film; that millions of people will see it, in contrast to designing for the theatre, where it may be seen a very short time and if eventful, it only becomes a picturesque legend.

197

Musical Comedy Design for Stage and Screen

The future of scene design, I believe, depends upon the future of theatre architecture. Constantly, contemporary stage designers are trying to break down the barriers of the conventional proscenium stage. The fusion of architecture, painting and sculptoring, which is the future stage setting, be it musical comedy, ballet or cinematic design, is only possible when the space that surrounds the setting is not controlled completely by the price of real estate. Until this utopian time appears, however, we who strive to interpret the world of dreams and extend the audiences' imagination ever to further extremes, must cope with space limitations which have existed for the past thirty or forty years. The challenge of creating depth, perspective and form in a limitless space, is, of course, the pleasure of design. Perhaps if the space were too large, or the facilities too generous, the stage settings would become similar to monuments in a lonely park. I do believe the contemporary architects are far in advance of the scenic designers in their dramatic use of space, color and form. Most current theatre design is still mostly eighteenth century in concept; it is designed for a picture box theatre. The great contemporary architects will force scenic design into an imaginative and challenging dimension.

How is this to be done? I'm not quite sure that I know as there are no absolute rules for design, far less scenic designing. However, if I may be permitted to make a few observations, I should like to point out that:

All rules are made to be broken.

Quality in art is intuitive; taste may be acquired. In exciting design, taste, like formalized rules must be forgotten.

Scenic design is a sequence of emotional impressions which must contrast one against the other; a selection of large spaces contrasted with minute space; of brilliant colors contrasted with muted ones. All is contrast, juxtaposition. It is the dexterity and daring of the juggling of these elements which create quality in design. An excess of any one element

198

—space, color or dynamic tension—makes for monotony and an absence of visual drama.

Design is principally the elimination of everything which is not absolutely necessary. A beautiful set should be a skeleton, allowing air for the other participants of the theatre to breathe in. Clutter may be picturesque, but leave the ivy for the botanical gardens.

The working scheme, the floor plans of the show, are the first order of business. A designer works in several dimensions simultaneously, so that while he is drawing a floor plan he is already seeing the diminishing perspectives, the colors, the selection of ornamentation. Only in this way does the dynamic scenic design appear, whether it be for stage or screen.

SOME NOTES ON DESIGNING FOR OPERA

by

Rolf Gérard

Designing for opera, according to Rolf Gérard, is a three-way collaboration between director, conductor and scenic designer in which the music alone must dictate the general feeling and characteristics of the stage design. These notes were written especially for this anthology. A resumé of Mr. Gérard's notes was printed in PLAYERS MAGAZINE, Volume 36 (March, 1960) pp. 130-32.

Wherein lies the difference between designing for opera and designing for the theatre? Opera is a combination of music and theatre, a dramatic or romantic story unfolded in musical terms. Its actual language is music, its text is not spoken but sung. It is the designer's job to interpret the music in visual terms. This means that he has to listen to the score and understand it. By this I mean he has to be able to listen to the music and to be inspired by it in order to design for it successfully.

The opera libretto asks for the necessities of the design. It designates the place and the period of the action and gives us details of the action itself, such as entrances, exits, requirements of space, furniture and properties, but it does not suggest to us anything of how these problems are to be solved artistically. Only the music can tell us that. Only the music can give us the general feeling and characteristics of the design; tell us whether the design should be heroic or romantic, vast or intimate, or, flamboyant or muted in color. How often do we have the painful experience of finding all the scenic requirements assembled on the opera stage with no relation whatsoever to the music and therefore completely out of place. Quite clearly, the music of the opera is the guiding element for everybody connected with it. The music's color, texture and rhythm—terms that can as well be applied to painting—these are the factors which determine the opera's character. To these we look for guidance.

Although great operas have been composed with an unconvincing story and great stories have been made into rela-

201

tively undistinguished operas, the music will always decide whether the opera is good or bad as it literally occupies the same place language does in the theatre. This means that even though everything else about the opera is poor, the opera can be a masterpiece on the strength of its music alone, just as some of Shakespeare's plays are masterpieces by the sheer beauty of language alone regardless of a poorly constructed story.

Can the designer thus be guided by anything but the music? The answer is yes, but very rarely. Only if the text is equal to the music. In this case we come across that rare phenomenon of an "ideal" opera, where the composer's music and the poet's words speak exactly the same language. Strauss's *Der Rosenkavalier* and *Arabella,* for example, are such phenomena. When designing these operas I do not know what guided me more, Strauss's music or Hofmannsthal's words, so indivisible are they. But alas, the most ideal combination of music and poetry is also affected by another phenomenon, the translation of the words into another language. While the music continues to speak in its universal tones, the idiom of the language changes and thus the two are forcibly driven apart. This is what usually happens but it is a sacrifice well worth accepting in order to fully understand what is going on. Isn't it worth trading something we can not fully grasp no matter how perfect, for something less perfect which we can understand and enjoy completely? This is why opera should be sung in the language of the country in which it is being performed. Nothing will help its popularity more.

Thus, we see that the designer must search deeply into the music for its *own* meaning and explanation. In addition, he must listen to the text not only in translation but also in the opera's original language in order to get both its full meaning and feeling. This is particularly important if the libretto bears the stamp of genius like those of the aforementioned *Rosenkavalier* and *Arabella,* or *Eugen Onegin,*

202

Pushkin's poem set to music by Tchaikovsky. While working on *Onegin* for the Metropolitan Opera Company, I listened to its recording and had Pushkin's poem read to me in Russian many times. Naturally, this sounded quite different and there is no doubt but that I got additional information and enthusiasm about the characters. This was particularly valuable to me in regard to the decisions that had to be made about costumes; their colors, wigs, make-up and so on.

When I started working on the English version of *Cosi fan Tutte* I knew de Ponte's Italian text very well and this definitely helped me, because it embodies the style of eighteenth-century elegance and intrigue, particularly its many *parlandos,* and it fits Mozart's music perfectly. I got valuable information about style from the text as well as from the music. The two together convinced me that nothing about *Cosi* mattered as much as its lightness and transparency and that visually the law of gravity had to be defied somehow. So I concentrated all my efforts on solving the many technical problems involved in such "atypical" scenery.

Examples of the designer's thinking and planning of opera settings are as varied as the opera repertoire itself and until now I have been writing as though the designer worked alone with his work like a painter with his canvas, the composer with his music, or, as Dimitri Mitropoulos once told me, the opera conductor with his orchestra before the curtain rises. But even more than theatre, opera is a combined effort. There is a tremendous amount of give and take in it. And what is the designer's position in it all?

Between his first conception of a problem and its final solution, there are many other people and their ideas to be considered. Of these, the closest to the designer, unquestionably, is the director who exerts a deep and decisive influence upon the whole production. It is impossible to design unless one is in complete agreement with him. In an ideal combination, ideas for direction are often given by designers and ideas for design by the director. I have been lucky in this respect and I have learned a great deal from some of the most important directors of our time. I have also had many occasions for enlightened comparisons between directors, too, as, for example, when designing two different productions of *Cosi fan Tutte,* one directed by Alfred Lunt in New York and the other by Carl Elbert at Glyndebourne. It is beyond the scope of this article to demonstrate how these two brilliant men attacked the same problems and solved them, each in his own way. Suffice to say, I got a tremendous benefit from the experiences. Directors I have worked for such as Margaret Webster, Herbert Graf, Alfred Lunt, Joseph L. Mankiewicz, Tyrone Guthrie, Peter Brook, Cyril Ritchard and Garson Kanin have all left their individual imprints not only on their productions but on their designers as well.

The same can be said about the conductors. Their influence upon the designer is almost equally important as that of the director. The musical and visual conception have to go together and it is the conductor who actually leads the performance. This he can accomplish so much better when the stage picture agrees with his own feelings. It is the conductor also, who decides on intervals and cuts in the musical score. Thus, many four act operas have been played in three and even two acts. These decisions affect the scene changes and therefore the very possibilities of design. It is ideal when the director, conductor and the designer can work together very closely from the start and exchange their ideas at the inception of the production. Such conductors as Busch, Gui, Stiedry, Monteux, Mitropoulos, Reiner, Ormandy, Cleva, Morel and Kempe have exerted great influence on my designing, both artistically and technically.

I shall not dwell on the many other problems affecting the designer for they are mostly technical, such as electrics, touring, storing and so on, except to say that they are much

204

Rolf Gérard

greater in opera than they are in theatre. And last but not least, there are the bare facts of budget and box-office. Hence, the great need for opera workshops where all kinds of experiments and discoveries can be made. And who wouldn't like to experiment on the greatest possible scale?

There are so many problems of designing for opera that still need to be solved. To cite but a few examples: We have not as yet arrived at a very satisfactory solution to designing Wagnerian opera. In the long line from Adolphe Appia to Weiland Wagner many important contributions have been made, notably by Gordon Craig, Robert Edmond Jones, Lee Simonson and some of the more important ballet designers. But we still have to find a way that fits the many associations of nature in Wagner's music without going back to naturalism. The ideal solution might well be between the noble simplicity recently achieved in Bayreuth by a general cleansing process and the strict omission of unnecessary detail and the addition of some color or color associations like green, or just enough green light for a forest, blue for air and water, gold for the shining sun and so on. This would help dispel the austerity when it is not wanted.

And then there is Mozart. I have left Mozart to the last because he represents the most difficult problem for the opera designer because he is just *pure* music. How can one avoid being just charming when suddenly the greatest pathos is required? To go into the Mozart problem from a designer's point of view alone could fill many volumes. And what about *Don Giovanni* and the most difficult of all, *The Magic Flute?* For *Giovanni* this "drammagiocoso," one perfect solution has been found so far in nature itself when played in the open air in the Felsenreitschule in Salzburg. For *The Magic Flute*, Schinkel's classic design still represents the best solution but this means going back into the nineteenth century. Conductors are rightly afraid of the designer, regarding *The Magic Flute*, lest he might do it some damage. Yet, this is a work that has to be brilliantly staged. Many attempts have been made; one of the most important in recent years is that of the great Viennese painter, Oskar Kokoschka, in Salzburg. This opened a new perspective but Mozart and his magic flute remain as enigmatic as ever. However, this is a wonderful state of affairs for us opera designers. Imagine what wonderful things still remain to be discovered.

DESIGNING FOR THE BALLET

by

Horace Armistead

In ballet design as well as all other facets of scenic design, the designer must have enough imagination to dream the impossible, enough engineering ability to invent ways of making the impossible dreams come true, and enough understanding to present the visual image eloquently to the audience. These observations Horace Armistead wrote especially for this anthology.

As Robert Edmond Jones observed in *The Dramatic Imagination*, the designer in the theatre has to be a "person of parts." This observation can be interpreted to mean that the designer must have enough imagination to dream of the impossible, enough engineering ability to invent ways of making the impossible dreams become possible, enough insight to be able to read between the words of the playwright, and enough understanding to present the visual image eloquently to the audience. For the designer must realize the dream of his mind's eye for the eyes of the audience "out front."

How does one describe the process of dreaming? One does not. Not even Freud could do this. One might describe the methods of provoking dreams, however, for every mortal has a dream from some provocation or other, be he a bovine oaf or a fay mystic.

I suggest the prescription for dreams to be an insatiable curiosity about everything, a cultivated sensitivity to all sights and sounds; everything, everywhere. Look down the street, gaze across the Grand Canyon, peer into a barrel of fishheads. Listen to the rasping voice of a drunk, the melody of Mozart, and the beat of Brubek—and be relaxed. Let things work on you and give yourself up to their spell; flowers, children, the sea. Make yourself a storehouse and look it over often.

Now with respect to designing for the ballet, it is especially important to cultivate this sensitivity to music which is to be an integral part of the ballet. Music, as Sacheverell Sitwell says, becomes the "constructed scaffolding upon which the dancers move and are supported." For what is ballet if it is not a manifest sensation; sight and sound? The movement of the dancer supported by the counterpoint and harmony, and the compliment of the musical and visual form. Listen to the music; the whisper of the strings, the nostalgic murmur of the French horns. Perhaps there is a shimmer of woodwinds followed by arpeggios on the harp, trumpets and brass burst like blaze of light, plucked strings anticipate a light rapid entrance of a dancer. Tympani and crisp percussion lead from a deep, velvet throb to a dry sandy texture. One image follows another and form, color, light and shade appear in succession. The components of the piece pass before the mind's eye. Details of design begin to emerge. After several repetitions of the entire score the overall shape, color, and texture can be placed in true focus.

A smooth, melodic phrase of music can create nostalgia —moonlight—soft, misty green, and silver. A crisp, brilliant phrase of sharp contrasts can create feelings of conflict or happy exaltation. Fear, tragedy and despair, all of these emotions can be aroused by music and have their forms and colors. We must let these things come to us and whatever forms we employ they must not be expressed in so secret a language as to make it impossible for others to understand. We must convey the right emotion even if we cannot put an exact name to that emotion. If it could all be put into words, the whole ballet is pointless and it would be better perhaps, to write an article or a poem.

Perhaps the one thing that separates the ballet from the drama or the opera is that in ballet three arts—Music, Dance, and Design (there being no text or libretto)—must so fuse that they become inseparable, creating one whole experience—an experience which no other means could so perfectly convey. In these matters, words cease to have their normal meanings.

210

The designer must be a workman also; able to deal with mundane things: sticks and stones, rags and bones, and even hanks of hair. He must learn everything possible about the factual, tangible world; animal, vegetable, and mineral, particularly vegetable and mineral. He should become familiar with man's constructions—the Acropolis and the house *he* lives in—, the cloth men have worn and the things men have used. This study is never ending. And for the theatre man there is another area of study which must become specific, namely, the area of the stage. The designer must have knowledge of all it contains and all it might contain, the machinery with which it has worked, and even how it may be made to work.

Somewhere in the process of accumulating all this insight and knowledge one is asked to design scenery for a ballet. The *modus operandi* will be different with each circumstance, but one thing is certain if it is to be a good theatre piece, the designer will have to be a collaborator and never a solo performer. Scenery is designed to enhance not obscure the ballet. The ballet is not for the exclusive display of "decor."

Someone—the choreographer, most likely—has read an historical incident which prompts an idea, or there is a modern poem or a social abuse, or an ancient myth, and all of this calls for some kind of music to be found or written. Or perhaps, someone finds a Scarlatti piece which is asking for the most beautiful ballet in the whole world.

Many hours of conversation will ensue between the producer, choreographer, composer and designer, and if their words, thoughts, and ideas are in unison, and if the right dancers can be given enough rehearsal time, and if every necessary expense is provided for, and if everyone involved knows his job—well, one can understand why Cocteau says that a work of art is an accident. I say it is a kind of miracle, which means the rewards are boundless.

211

Designing for the Ballet

The designer listens to the music for a specific ballet many times and in so doing allows the scene to appear in his mind's eye. This picture may start with a shape or a color, or some rhythm of forms, or it may be a vast piece of fabric the like of which no one has ever seen. The designer makes rapid sketches, visits the ballet rehearsals, has conferences with the choreographer, and makes more sketches. There will be more talks, more rehearsals, and many more sketches, until everyone, or at least the choreographer, producer and the designer say, "that's it."

In substance, the process for designing costumes for ballet works exactly as it does for the scenery, keeping in mind, however, that the scenery must be sympathetic to the costumes.

Now nothing remains but to get the job done. By and large, the procedure for transferring the designer's ideas of the setting into reality is the same used for other forms of stage design. The designer lays out the floor plans and hanging plots, draws up the perspective color sketches and the working drawings. He makes sure there is sufficient space for the dancers, offstage and through the exits as well as onstage. Likewise he allows ample space for the lighting instruments which must illuminate the dancers and the areas to be seen by the audience. And if there are scene changes in the ballet, he plans them to be sure they do not exceed the time of the musical bridge allowed for the shift, be that two seconds or ten minutes.

And by the time the work is all done, the designer hopes that everything will look a great deal better than it seemed to look when he caught the last glimpse of it as it was being loaded out of the shops onto the trucks enroute to the theatre. Once the scenery is in the theatre, providing the designer is confident that the production carpenter and electrician know where every piece of scenery and every instrument belongs, the designer should keep from underfoot until that

212

time of the day when a technical or light rehearsal has been scheduled. From now on to the premier everyone involved in the production is frequently too nervous to eat or sleep; it seems as though any kind of a disaster is sure to happen. But surprisingly enough, the curtain goes up (and often on time) and it is sometime later before one really knows what one has accomplished.

SCENERY AND COSTUME DESIGN FOR BALLET

by

Cecil Beaton

The designer of ballet, Cecil Beaton believes, is like a nation under the most stringent war-time regulations; he is obliged to keep his vision stark and essential without sacrificing any of the poetry and magic. Mr. Beaton originally expressed these views in the NEW YORK TIMES (July 29, 1956), X, 11.

Ballet design is a great challenge to any artist's talent for simplicity and economy. Since dance companies (like circus troupes) are by nature nomadic, scenery and costumes must of necessity be reduced to a minimum. Decor consists, for the most part, of a few uncomplicated but striking backdrops. Costumes, too, are boldly uninvolved. Most modern ballets being acrobatic, any excessive flounce or frill can easily be a hindrance. In effect, the designer of ballet, is like a nation under the most stringent war-time regulations: he is obliged to keep his vision stark and essential. At the same time, there can be no sacrifice of poetry and magic, for ballet virtually demands a free imagination, unencumbered by those naturalistic exigencies which are the bane of play designers.

Given these militant restrictions, it is astonishing how the quality of an artist's work can be gauged from the result. In the hands of a first-rate craftsman, a paucity of means can still create the richest effect, even on a spectator at the back of the gallery.

In any survey of remarkable ballet decoration during the past few decades, Picasso's *Tricorne* would head the list as a supreme achievement in design. Though the initial shock value of this work has perhaps diminished with the years, it never fails of impact. The master's sweep and boldness are apparent in every detail, and audiences can still bask in the glow of those unusual, lyrical color combinations —emerald green, white, brick red, black and pale blue.

Derain is another artist whose telling use of paint makes

215

a backdrop as esthetically rich as one of his framed canvases. But more than that, his innate theatre sense prevents the result from being merely static, as an enlarged easel painting might be. A keen observer will realize the subtle tonal quality of Derain's coloring. Brilliant was the blending of the pale yellow, canary and primrose in *Mademoiselle Angot;* or the mixing of gray and gray-green in the same ballet. With *Boutique Fantasque,* this artist asserted fantastic clay colors, combined with Pompeiian red and Rickett's blue.

Serious painters cannot fail to produce honest and interesting decors, though even the finest artists can make the mistake of putting an enlarged painting on the stage, through ignorance of the necessary dynamics of stage volume or failure to utilize the illusory possibilities of wings and borders. In his day, Diaghilev seemed to have a special knack for inspiring painters to do brilliant work for the ballet. Since then, we have often had decor excellent in merit but static in conception.

In latter years, it was Christian Berard, more than any other artist, whose work in both theatre and ballet remained consistently stunning. Curiously, Berard had a penchant for introducing the morbid atmosphere of death into even his gayest ballets—an idiosyncrasy that may have stemmed from his family's funeral homes. One of Berard's many contributions to the theatrical scene was his rehabilitation of certain colors. He restored crimson to its former grandeur and vindicated certain cheap, synthetic-dye colors—lozenge mauves and pinks, acid greens.

Not all scene designers can be geniuses or great painters, but many tricks of stage magic can be as consciously learned as the technique of other arts. Given the task of "filling a stage," there are divers approaches open to the designer. His scenery need not be intricate in its conception; bold expanses are often more effective than filligree and mere decoration. Of major importance are light and color, as well as the advisability of having contrasting textures in the choice of materials for both setting and costumes.

Color sense is not merely the result of long experience, but can also reflect a very personal quality. Still, there are a few general cautions which even experts have ignored to their sorrow. Uniformity of color, for instance, is seldom effective; without other colors there is little contrast, and tonal values fade. Stage colors need not necessarily be vivid; gray can often be used to good advantage as a juxtapositional backbone for other hues, since it gives them a heightened quality.

Noguchi, in his ballet designs, brings a sculptor's sense of volume to the stage. All the tricks of the plastician are brought to bear as he creates legerdemain through the imaginative use of Chinese silk, flat painted surfaces and abstract modern shapes. He has, indeed, asserted the charm of using significant props in the manner of Chinese theatre.

The Japanese are past masters in the knowledge of that most important of theatrical effects—how to astonish. Kabuki dancers set a stage with the most dazzling modicum of means—a Mondrianesque screen, a lighted lantern, a mat or particular splash of color are enough. In their costumes, these dancers employ color combinations that the West would fear to handle. They even have the remarkable gift of being able to use "ugly" colors to a great advantage, combining them in a way as to create delightful harmonies. Dull lavender-pink, lettuce-green, pale orange and pale ultramarine mix artlessly under the Eastern touch. Similarly, their combinations of unexpected materials are baffling to our more conventional eyes. The Japanese know the value of cheap materials intermingled with rich ones, and will think nothing of using, for example, a very ordinary pomegranate-printed crepe in conjunction with the finest gold brocade.

These visual creations of East and West are not merely

an apotheosis of the dance itself, but rank among its finest works of theatrical magic. Ballet is one of the few uncontaminated arts we have left, and its designers rightly cherish a medium that affords them the greatest possible latitude for pure expression.

DESIGNING *THE HEIRESS* FOR THE MOVIES

by

Harry Horner

At the conclusion of this excellent account of Harry Horner's methods of creating his Academy Award winning design for the motion picture version of the Henry James novel, WASHINGTON SQUARE, Mr. Horner makes some incisive observations on the state and quality of present-day scenic design in Hollywood. Motion picture design, Mr. Horner finds, is stagnating from the sterility of obligatory realism; these observations were added for the benefit of this section on the facets of design. The original article appeared in THE HOLLYWOOD QUARTERLY, Volume 5 (January, 1950), pp. 1-7.

It rarely happens that the designer of a motion picture production has the opportunity of making his designs an integral part of the dramatic effect of the picture, but this opportunity was given to me in the production designs for the film *The Heiress*.

Many faithful Broadway theatregoers will remember the play, the story of Dr. Sloper, residing at No. 16, Washington Square North, in New York in the 1850's, and the tragedy of his daughter Catherine. Every reader of Henry James's novels will certainly remember the story, *Washington Square*, from which this play was taken.

In one of our discussions William Wyler, the director of *The Heiress* (and of such other great character studies as *The Best Years of Our Lives* and *Wuthering Heights*), said to me, "Almost the entire picture plays in one house. It will depend a great deal upon the designs and the arrangements of the rooms in this house, upon the style in which the story is told—in other words, upon the conception of the designer —how convincing the characters will become, and therefore how successful the motion picture, *The Heiress*, will be."

How does the designer translate the style and conception of a story into a practical motion picture setting? It was not enough to be authentic in period and locale; deeper analyses of the lives of the characters in the play were necessary. It was essential to know as much about their backgrounds as if the designer had grown up with them, lived and visited with them, and even hired their servants for them. To search for the smallest characteristic habits became part of the crea-

221

tive function of design. Would the doctor, after arriving home from his professional calls, go immediately into his parlor and sit in his favorite chair to rest and smoke and read, or would he more probably join his daughter and other members of his family? A question like that determined the position of the parlor in relation to the house, and determined also the position of the chair in which he would sit in relation to the parlor. Would Catherine, the daughter, take her breakfast with her father, or would she eat separately, perhaps in her room upstairs? Those are examples of the many and challenging questions which influenced and shaped the creation of the drawing board.

The fact that there was only one important set, namely, the house on Washington Square, made it necessary that the house should have a personality of its own which, in different ways, would affect those inhabitants with whom the story deals and also would impress the characters whose visit to the house plays so vital a part in the drama.

It was a challenge—to inject the house with a personality of its own. Very often, houses that have a memory of one kind or another attached to them are able to dominate the inhabitants and mould them with a definite force of their own. To Dr. Sloper the house on Washington Square bore the memory of his wife; to Catherine it represented the enclosure which became torture; for Catherine's lover the house became almost a lure, a very nearly human temptation, the possession of which he desired more than he desired Catherine.

How to design this house, how to keep it authentic and still make it come alive with its own soul and with the soul of its inhabitants, became the main task of the designer.

As a counterweight against any overcharacterization, I remember Mr. Wyler's warning not to give the secrets of the story away in the designs. "The story may be a serious one," he said, "but this should not show in the designs of the house, since the structure could not know in advance what its inhabitants would do."

So I started with the first and easiest task, which was necessary as a basis for the design, namely, to familiarize myself with the style of architecture and the living habits of New York in 1850 in general, and of Washington Square North in particular.

Armed with sketchbooks and a camera, I roamed the streets of what is now downtown New York. As the spirit of another era slowly took hold of me, Washington Square became an "uptown" district. The skyscrapers disappeared and I realized that with just a little imagination it is even now possible to find in this modern city many treasures of century-old architecture.

I rang doorbells of those lovely houses with their handsome old stoops in order to acquaint myself with the interiors which have been the landmarks of Washington Square since 1830, when the first families moved "uptown."

As I planned the design for the park, to be filled with romantic trees, I realized that I had to tone down this conception, for early prints showed that Washington Square was a parade ground in those years, with the old Victorian castle-like New York University on one side, and that it consisted of a large lawn with very few trees and very few benches. After I had searched many weeks in the picture collections of all the libraries, and had benefited by the kind help of all the historical societies in New York, a clear picture of life in a city of those past years crystallized in my mind.

Wandering through this early city, I hit upon such lovely museum pieces as the Tredwell house, an example of the typical residence of a rich merchant. I wandered through backyards of houses and saw those gardens and dwellings along the "Mews" which once represented the stables of the elegant places on Washington Square. Here I picked up

223

a detail from an iron fence which would express the wealth of Dr. Sloper, and there a stairway which would help to dramatize Catherine's last climb up the stairs.

Those details were helpful, but ultimately the basic character of the house came from analysing the past of our doctor. Although the main action of the story is laid in 1850, with a short episode five years later, I traced back the doctor's life from the indications in the play and in the novel so that this house would have the atmosphere of having been lived in for years.

Dr. Sloper, according to my notes, was married to a wealthy New York girl about 1835, and the house was built while they were on their honeymoon in Paris. It was probably designed by him in the current popular style, the Greek Revival, with its high columns inside and double mahogany sliding doors connecting the rooms. It even contained the doctor's office, with direct access from the street.

When the doctor and his bride returned from France, they furnished the house with delicate pieces in exquisite taste—Duncan Phyfe pieces, and others which they brought with them from Europe. A French spinet occupied a special place, and the whole house had an atmosphere of loveliness.

Then his wife died, and as the doctor's practice improved he enlarged the house. He kept the old part untouched, giving it the feeling of a shrine. He moved the spinet into the back parlor near his favorite chair; and he added, in the now modern Victorian period, a small wing containing a winter garden and a study.

After having gleaned what I could of what Dr. Sloper must have done to the house, I proceeded to design it. It was to become not a house of one period, but of many—it must give the feeling of having gone through several styles, thus making that first phase of his life which existed only in his memory stand out and become visible to us.

The ground plan had to conform with the restrictions of

224

those enclosed, narrow building lots which characterize Washington Square North; entrance in front with a narrow long hall, and garden and stable at the back. This gave reality and feeling of enclosure within a city block.

But within this plan many vital elements must be incorporated. There had to be room for a dramatic staircase which was to play an important part in the story. One of the old houses of downtown New York gave me an idea for a staircase which was laid out so that from one vantage point three flights of stairs could be seen—with the father's bedroom on the second floor and the girl's bedroom and guest room on the third floor. There had to be room for an interesting arrangement of hall, dining room, front parlor, back parlor, study, and so on. All this we built in the studio, with the sliding doors placed so that certain vistas into rooms became dramatically important. The father's chair in the back parlor, for instance, dominated the house, and a direct view to the entrance hall was possible.

The garden and stables were planned with flowers and had to work in different seasons. Trees with foliage and summer flowers were replaced by bare trees, or by the foliage of spring—all with the careful consideration of the characteristic vegetation in New York. The grass had patches of bad growth even in the summer, and anyone who appreciates the difficulty of growing nice grass in New York will know that we were authentic.

Then there was the planning of the period of 1855—five years later. Again careful research into the characters' personalities gave the clue for changes in the house.

The father had died, and now that only women inhabited the house, the elegance and strictness disappeared, and a feeling of less discriminating taste was noticeable. The curtains became softer, more Victorian; certain pieces of furniture were changed, slip covers had been put on others, and we hoped to give the impression that the women in the house were drifting slowly toward a status of unalterable spinster-hood.

The park changed too—fortunately I found that the years around 1850 were full of changes in New York. Gas was introduced on Washington Square; so our audience sees the change from the early kerosene lamps to the laying of pipes for the new gaslight. And of course, the old "Washington Square Parade Ground" was now really called "Washington Square Park."

One of the most costly problems was to find adequate furniture to match the description of exquisite taste and wealth, both of which were attributes of Dr. Sloper. Our expert on furniture, Emile Kurie, went to New York and bought fine antique furniture, including the spinet, fine paintings, and ornaments, knowing that under the examining camera close-up the standard prop furniture would not convince anyone of the great wealth of the heiress.

Thus the whole house was built, the life and habits of the characters were carefully considered, hundreds of sketches were made to indicate the most effective camera setups, and the director liked and approved it all.

But there was yet an obstacle before those sets could be called ready. This obstacle, so different from those of real life or of the stage, was the camera itself, with the sound boom. Proportions of the room had to be carefully thought out so that they would photograph: not too high, or too much ceiling would be lost outside the range of the lens; and not too low, of course, or there would be lost the typical architectural proportions of elegance and period. And, what was more important, all those walls and ceilings had to be constructed so that they could come apart—they had to be made "wild," as the technical expression goes—to make elbow room for the cameras.

After having seen the house standing on the stage, almost habitable with its main floor, garden, and stables, and the staircase leading up to the second and third floors, it was pitiful to see it torn down again, limb by limb, a windowed wall here, a corridor ceiling there, so that a shot could be taken from behind a column, or so that the sensitive sound boom could reach into a narrow passage without picking up too much echo. It is typical of a movie set that the further the shooting of the picture is advanced, the more the walls of the set are pulled away; but no audience will ever know how little of the house was left, how little of many months of work remained standing when that final scene was taken.

No audience will ever see that last scene the way we saw it, or will ever have to use as much imagination as the actress had to, in order to make herself believe that she was left alone in a big house. This is what they would have seen when Olivia de Haviland played her last scene, the scene in which Catherine ascends the staircase as her lover knocks in vain on the entrance door of the lonely house: Where that lonely and silent house was supposed to be, there was a big boom with the camera on it, there was the camera crew giving orders, there was the man who lifted the high boom arm up to the third floor, and in the midst of all the turmoil was Olivia de Havilland as Catherine, masterfully ascending the steps of an abstract staircase which was completely detached from all the remaining architecture and stood—Daliesque—in the middle of a swirling and active group of men who were trying to direct, to photograph, to light, and to sound-control the scene of a dark and lonely house, deserted and silent.

* * *

After every design I've ever created for the motion pictures, a strange feeling of "unfulfillment" remained, a feeling which I never have when I am designing for the stage, even though the work on some of the films was absorbing and important to me.

227

What is the reason for this feeling of "unfulfillment," this striking difference between designing for films and designing for the stage?

That abstract stairway described above, on which the heroine slowly ascends as more and more of the walls of the house are peeled away as the shooting of the film progresses, illustrates vividly the basic difference which exists between stage design and motion picture design. On the stage all work is directed toward and culminates in the opening night performance. At that moment, when the expression of the artists involved makes contact with the audience as the curtain rises, the goal of completion and the realization of all the visions connected with the play are at their fullest. And all the artists; the writers, director, actors and designer work toward this goal.

In the films, this moment does not exist. In fact on the last day of shooting, the walls are all pulled apart, the actors not necessary in the last scenes have drifted away, and all that remains is a sense of matters unfinished which robs everyone who was involved at the beginning of their sense of participation and the joy of creation.

The motion picture artist, whether a designer or a director, creates the complete idea of his conception first and then he is forced to pull it apart into its components, like the pieces of a jig-saw puzzle. He never sees it as a complete unity again throughout the entire working period. Never, can he, like a painter, stand back to survey its total impact at different moments of progress. For this reason he must be able to remember clearly at all times what his original intentions were. This of course, is difficult and there is always the danger that the original freshness may disappear and be replaced by a studied or belabored effect. The original conception can be easily forgotten and the details become more important than the whole.

The temptation to overemphasize the importance of detail

228

can be dangerous to the design of a motion picture. In historical or period pictures one often finds that small items of decoration overload a setting so much that the total unity of the design is harmed more than helped. I remember seeing a Biblical film in which there were so many small items of seeming authenticity that the film as a whole had no unity. The characters were surrounded by thousands of props but none of them had the grandeur of Biblical simplicity. The whole film looked more like a collection of museum pieces than a story of great and heroic people. The overaccumulation of "design" distracted and spoiled the development of the story.

A play designed for the stage might resort to "unauthentic" and imaginative elements of design and yet it might achieve a greater faithfulness of inner reality than the most elaborately designed film production.

The problem mentioned above is created by the accepted idea that films have to be realistic. The motion picture audience knows that a camera can only photograph a "real" thing. Therefore, all stories must necessarily be told in *realistic* terms. That this is not true can be proven by the fact that some of the early German films used unrealistic backgrounds and much more imaginative design than we ever dare to use today. Even the Italian films famous for their realism are more successful in creating desired moods by their selectivity. The piling up of too many details in a motion picture is like piling too many colors into a painting.

Of course, the designer of stage settings faces a different challenge and thus his imagination is kept more constantly active. He is free to create his own level of reality. He starts by creating the machinery for the changes of scenery. This alone gives him a tool of dramatic accent which does not exist in motion pictures. The dramatic effect of a turntable for instance, to lead the audience from one scene to another, creates a spell non-existent in motion pictures. The level of reality might vary according to the judgement of the designer. With the proper use of a few stylized shapes and constructive elements, he can create the mood of an entire house. A few outlines and the proper lighting is completely acceptable to the stage audience in today's live theatre.

The designer of films, on the other hand, is forced to use the elements of realism as his starting point of design. No producer today would consider anything else than a more or less realistic interpretation of a scene. An unrealistic or imaginative conception is branded in Hollywood as "ARTY." Unfortunately, this often robs the motion picture designer of a wide area of imaginative interpretation. To envisage the house in *The Heiress*, for example, on a motion picture screen only in terms of its dramatically essential elements, namely, the staircase and the door fading off into shadows is unacceptable in film. Yet television for economic reasons has resorted to just such effects with much imaginative staging. It would be an important step forward in motion picture design if the designer were allowed to free himself from the sterility of obligatory realism. It would free many pictures, particularly those of a historical nature, of their sterility.

The average motion picture audience (and I am only speaking about American audiences at this moment), is used to a literal setting that has to look like an illustration for a breakfast cereal. The many recent historical and Biblical motion pictures illustrate my complaint. With all their research, all too often they lack the dignity of the story they serve. If the locale is to be Rome, then every authentic Roman ornament is piled into the design and every historically correct color employed in the scene—so much so that often the essential simplicity of the scene is lost. I am still waiting to see a motion picture of a Biblical story designed with the beautiful imagination and restraint of a Rembrandt design for a similar subject, or with the crispness

230

of the Biblical figures of a Breughel. These artists felt free to dress their Biblical giants, their prodigal sons and their various kings in the folds of their own emotional comprehension, never losing for one moment, a sense of the Bible. Yet, the motion picture Bible is crowded with the stilted and self-conscious costumes and ornamentation which are the by-products of research departments and libraries who use again and again the same source pictures which they borrow from one another over and over.

It occurs to me now, that it might have been very feasible to create the setting for *The Heiress* in a more simplified way. By carefully examining what the dramatic necessities for the picture were, possibly an interesting mood might have been created by merely designing the dramatic staircase without the surrounding walls; possibly just the entrance to the house, looming up at the bottom of the stairs, surrounding these elements with the lights and shadows to suit the different scenes. But these are mental configurations which would have to be examined carefully for their full effectiveness and their limitations.

And to all of this, I see my readers and critics shake their heads in disagreement. No, they say, such an abstraction would not be enough to fill the needs of this film. And yet —what a fascinating road of film making might be started by examining the aesthetic values of design in this direction. And those whom memory serves, will have to admit that this would not really be a new start, but a continuation in the direction that such interesting films as *The Cabinet of Dr. Caligari* and the French *Jean D'Arc* by Dreyer, started many years ago.

SCENERY IS FOR SEEING

by
S. Syrjala

The special aesthetic problems of scenic design for television are clearly defined with penetrating insight by S. Syrjala. The difference between television and theatrical design, as Syrjala sees it, is the difference between designing for direct and indirect vision. In television one designs for an instrument which will be guided to see and transmit in its own terms while in the theatre one sees directly. This comparison was written especially for this anthology.

Design, being visual, can only find response in vision. This is not as simple as it seems, for most of us are casual in distinguishing between two forms of seeing, each of which is in substance actual yet separate.

Whenever our eyes are open, we see directly. This is the actuality of seeing. Even though photography is used as if it transcribed actuality, it is indirect seeing, in the same manner and extent that a painting is the vision of another, presented for our direct visual understanding. A mirror is perhaps the most realistic means of seeing, for a means has been employed to enable our vision to see beyond its own range.

A photographer places a camera before an object, choosing an angle, selecting a lens for results he knows will be achieved with the combination of his lenses and the sensitivities of an emulsion, or, in the case of television, an electronic system. All of this is so encumbered with the wish and selection of another that it can under no circumstance be a transcription of our own seeing. It is no more than a conveyed image which may or may not succeed in telling what someone would like to have us see. It is indirect seeing which we tend to accept as actuality, for reasons based only upon an assumption that photography is as literal as it seems.

Although scenery is scenery no matter how it is constructed, it does not follow that the same concepts of design are applicable to both the direct-seeing theatre and the indirect-seeing screen. For direct vision as in the theatre, one designs for the actuality of vision. For indirect vision in cinema and

233

television, one designs for an instrument which will be guided to see and transmit within its own terms. Indirect vision has two separate visual planes; the screen itself and that which has been transmitted to the screen. The essential screen plane is of course, the product of the other.

Although the screen plane is in the realm of design and picture-making, the designer seldom has a direct voice in its organization. There are many hands stirring that pot, each tossing in its own brand of herbs. Quite often the end result is committee creation which leaves the designer sulking because his effort has not been seen as it was intended to be seen.

It is common to see visitors in a film or television studio gasp at the beauty of settings which they see directly. It is not uncommon afterwards for them to commiserate with the designer for the lack of "seeing" which the director and technicians imposed on the screen. That commiseration arises from the misconception that indirect images should compare with direct seeing out of context. While it is true that some directors and cameramen lack imaginative pictorial organization and that technicians tend to be hidebound by conventions or rules of procedure, more often the fault lies with the designer who mistakes the camera for nothing more than a magnifying lens to provide the ultimate spectator a better view of his creation.

While the designer is only one of many people concerned with the organization of the directly seen picture plane, in designing that which is to be seen by the interloper lens, his importance is great, if his understanding is sufficient for him to control the final results at his point of conception.

From where I am writing, I look across a room towards windows which overlook a river, and far upstream there is a bridge. I may create the room as my vision plane if I make it my main concentration, and the river with its bank of apartment houses and the bridge in the distance are sensed

234

S. Syrjala

only in peripheral awareness. Yet, with hardly a thought, my concentration can leave the room so that it is only a foreground awareness while I choose either the apartment houses, the river or the distant bridge as my main concentration. My concentration may flit from one vision plane to another, leaving all others to exist only in awareness. This concentration can be so sharp that on a clear day, I may contemplate the movement of cars and trucks crossing the bridge five miles upstream while the room I am in remains no more than a framing placement for my awareness. My concentration makes it possible for me to focus and select any vision plane I choose. I am in a room and beyond it. My vision plane has moved back and forth with the rapidity of my concentration or awareness—as if my eyes had tentacles which groped and felt the space and the shape of things.

That is the nature of direct and actual vision. For its substance one designs settings for a live performance. We create the guiding organization for capturing visual concentration. Actuality of visual experience at a live performance is all-encompassing. The proscenium is not a boundary for vision and the stage platform is a readily accepted convention. In any case, we go to hear a play as importantly as to see it. Scenery is an adjective to the fact. The very platform nature of the performance and the matter-of-fact acceptance of the conventions of the platform are contributing factors to the ease with which the performance of a play without scenery is readily accepted. The author's words build images in our minds unfettered by imposed ornamentation. Without ears we miss the major portion of a stage performance. We are mainly in the presence of the vocal word.

The screen story though is mainly picture. Illustrative or abstract, a deaf mute can read it. It cannot exist without picture organization. In front of the viewer we have placed a screen, limiting vision. The eye tentacles reaching out find only a flat surface of indefinite space. A world for vision must be created upon it with all the elements seeing needs for concentration. The impenetrable screen has taken the focus from the viewers, and if we are to keep them in their seats we must conjure on the void of flatness a sense of space delineation and concentration. We cannot hold attention for long or repeatedly with shadowgraphs and magic lantern kaleidoscopes. Remember how our direct vision found space in the change of concentration from room to river or to the bridge. Concentration was our means of realization. Without that concentration our vision would be unorganized, a meaningless jumble of shapes in unrelated space; at best, patterns with or without organization at an uncertain plane without dimension.

The human eye is wide angle vision with the ability of telephoto-like concentration on a fragment while retaining peripheral awareness. Concentrating on a small object it retains the realization and reference to place. This is particularly evident at a live performance where even a single face is the concentration in the vastness of a great arena. This is not within the capabilities of the lens. Lenses are each separate in their qualities and limited to their area of focus and concentration. Even the wide angle lenses are devoid of peripheral qualities beyond their focus. Peripheral awareness must be created, not circumferentially as in direct vision, but within the focus of a given shot, or by cutting back and forth from overall to concentration.

A screen story photographing entirely with closeups would result in a drama of intense unrelieved emotions in an abstractly generalized place. Analytical and psychological in context, as exemplified by the silent motion picture, *The Passion of Joan,* wherein place was only suggested by fragments of architecture and texture seen between or around the constant flow of closeups. Conversely, if one created a screen story in which most of the shots were long and wide,

236

as is greatly done in non-psychological westerns or was the only technique known in early film making—such as *The Great Train Robbery*, the story would be all impersonal action. The human eye sensing the flat screen cannot single out the emotions of an individual; for action is the dominant statement.

Perhaps this partly explains the dullness of film or video productions photographed like performances from a fixed audience-like point of view. Superficially the new billboard-like screen with its bigger than ever faces and sweeping peripheral material might help to correct this, if it still weren't necessary to bring the concentration even tighter and to carry the vision plane from concontration to concentration.

Although the screen camera photographs settings and employs actors for whom play-like dialogue is written, the result is not a photographed play. A story, not a play, is being told with pictures. The screen which we see does not perform, unless we define the projecting machine as performing. The screen is telling and showing. The many natural conventions of a stage performance are ludicrously out of context on the screen, unless we are telling about a performance. The syntax of the screen consists of pictures, pictures, back and forth, narrating.

Many times I have found designing a real chore, sharing despair with a director as we tried to find *pictures* in a script by a lazy adaptor or a play or novel who did no more than cull pertinent dialogue. The simple, but expedient breaking of scenes into cuts, dissolves and fades with a glib selection of dialogue does not make a screen picture narrative.

Designing for the narrating camera which tells what it sees on a screen, is at odds with design for the stage if for no other reason than as we have discovered, the design is not seen directly or in its entirety by a viewer in a fixed position.

Though at times a grand view of the setting does occur on the screen, it is more often seen in bits and pieces be-

237

tween and around the foreground actors who seem to be within touching distance of the spectator. These fragmentary views of the setting must satisfy the peripheral vision's search for place and identity. As the setting shares a meagre portion of a total screen picture dominated by the foreground actors, place must be realized in depth rather than in surface expanse. This is in direct contradiction to the stage wherein the actors occupy the smaller vision area and the set surrounds them expansively.

On this stage platform the setting is in an actual sense flat, for the fundamental movement of declaiming actors is lateral. The picture screen finds its best expression in placement which moves forward or recedes. At a stage performance we follow that which happens on a platform from the determined position of our tickets. In contrast the screen image places us in the focal length of the photographing lens which may change frequently from shot to shot. Thus we gain the sense of being *within*—we are in a room, we are out-of-doors. We do not look at the set from a grandstand —we move into it and become a part of it. We are alternately within kissing closeness of the blonde or rifle range away— yet always, we are there. Even though the tired springs of the seat we sit on are still in our awareness, if the image is true we will be there with the image. We have become an invisible and impersonal interloper in the very presence of the characters who have become our concentration. It is no longer the flat plane of the actors on a platform whose performance is to be marveled at from our bleacher position. We are there, wandering around, seeing from all points of view, over one character's shoulder or breath-close to his face we see the antagonist or protagonist, then through cross shooting we reverse our position for a reverse understanding.

Often an insignificant foreground object contains a greater statement than the set in the background, delineating place and mood, constantly defining space by the diminishing size of receding planes. Instead of designing across the platform in a kind of mural organization, we stagger elements in depth. We slash and perforate the picture plane for a realization of spatial dimension. Our designing for the transmitting lens is not that of a painter making a picture to be installed behind the actors, but much more that of the architect planning not a façade but an organic space element or structure for one to move within, around, and through.

Unfortunately at times, particularly in live television production, the designer's efforts are erased by photography which mistakenly removes itself from the structure, exposing its naked studio self by revealing the set in its native studio habitat. Then we no longer exist in a place but in a studio which contains a set. This divorcing of an image from its own context is equally disturbing in settings of abstraction, phantasy or realism, for the world of the screen is still that of the magic lantern.

Although our design must have that concept of the whole in space, we do encounter the anomaly that the fragment must make as positive a statement as the whole. If this is lacking, a result occurs which for the lack of an established definition I choose to call *no pictures*. Often it comes about through a too literal acceptance of a director's, author's or budget directive that only a flat is needed behind an actor for a brief shot. It has been an easy incentive for an evasion of the fundamentals of screen design.

Even though an actor or two are prominently in the frame, that between or around them conveys nothing. The scenery or space surrounding them is a gravity-less void. At this point, a director will scream, "Get a picture on that wall. Hang some smilax," as if a picture or a sprig of smilax were the cure-all. This *no picture* quality may also come about in a large set when a director or cameraman will choose to shoot a scene close to an area which the designer had conceived as a part of the whole of a longer shot that would

239

be self-explanatory in that relationship. To guard against this devastating contingency there is a tendency for designers to overdress their sets to the point where no area is left unembroidered with pictures, patterns, or textures. As this procedure of safety can become hackneyed or attention diverting it is more to the point to think in terms of space creation.

At this stage it is of concern to recall another's experience with the screen image. It is the experience of perhaps the greatest designer for the theatre. I can only summarize and in great part deduce what actually happened to Robert Edmond Jones when for a while he went to Hollywood to design for the color camera. It is an easy guess to know that his only consolation on returning home was that he had been paid well for his efforts. I am likewise sure that he was bewildered with the results of his creating. In truth he created *no pictures.* Jones was not a bits and pieces assembler of patterns and details. His highly elective taste and precisely flawless sense of form relations found their expression in simplicity of statement. Sumptuously he underdressed. Richly, great expanses were naked of all but space and beautiful light, rich only in the context of balanced forms. His world was the stage in which the whole expanse surrounding and bathing the actors was the vision and statement. It must have been grotesque to see the camera selecting bits and pieces and making them meaningless out of context. Thus we return to the phenomenon that the fragment must contain as positive a concept as the whole.

Unity becomes a problem on the screen in proportions unknown to the stage set designer dealing with a setting seen in its entirety. Sharp variations of patterns in separate areas can be quite logical when seen as a whole concept. When seen in bits and pieces by alternating cameras cross cutting from one shot to another, a disagreement of identity may result which can be both disconcerting and jarring. This optical confusion will bring forth from the average technician, an utterly cautious person, demands for such extreme consistency as to create a screen image of constant one-note dullness. It is in this area that a designer with proper understanding of the problem can relieve the screen of technical tedium and caution.

It has been this viewer's occasional pleasure to see rhythmic alternations of tonalities, forms and patterns in opposition creating dramatic tensions, even the surprise of comedy. To achieve this is not difficult when working with film where intelligent shooting and understanding in the cutting room can be synchronized with patience. Live television contains many problems for achieving those nuances. The elements of timing and chance are sufficiently beyond direct control that few will risk it. This choice is in the hands of a director and technicians hindered by limited rehearsal time. The designer can only be grateful when by accident it happens as he hoped it would. A far easier accomplishment comes in creating dramatic movement and mood development when plotting the sets and their sequences. As the moving screen image is a montage of pictures related and interrelated one can create in the design patterns a correlated development building towards a dramatic height. All this is possible if the script is substantial. Needless to say when productions are started with an unrealized script, as they often are on the belt production line of our commercial producing, revisions can be of such drastic consequence as to make a shambles of the designer's intentions. That consternation is not limited to the concept of the whole. I am sure that I am not alone in knowing the defeat when the basic plan of an individual set designed for specific movement patterns must be adapted to movement having no relationships with the original concept. It must now be obvious that a designer should be well stocked with rabbits' feet, and at all times have one as handy as the pencil and brush, for who knows which at a given moment is needed most.

Yet it isn't all despair, unless one has a large unconsolable ego, frustrated by weak lungs and a limited vocabulary. With such a handicap even the directly seen living theatre can be a hazard for ego satisfaction. Our concern at the moment transcends the disappointments involved in creative work to an understanding of the penultimate values which do create the ultimate magic of images made with light and its absence.

The object, person or set being photographed does not establish the style unless the "lens" creates a point of view. Realism, abstraction, expressionism, etc., are the products of the "lens." They are not an offering to it, asking to be photographed. Recall the abstract, expressionist or other non-realistic scenery in a screen image photographed transcriptionally, leaving the scenery nakedly itself without quality other than decoration or something queer.

From the dimness of my memory of the primitive classic, *The Cabinet of Dr. Caligari,* I remember the fault of photographing expressionistic scenery, make-up and gesture. It was the documentation of an expressionistic performance. It was not the creation of an expressionistic screen technique at the ultimate level wherein expressionism was inherent in the light and shadow of the magic lantern. Several years ago, I did see a short film, *Jazz Dance,* by Roger Tilton, taken in its entirety at a dance hall in New York seemingly during an evening's session. All the material photographed was actual, yet on the screen it remains as a vivid example of expressionism. The style and form were inherent in the point of view of the lens.

Style and form are the inner structure of any creative effort. Their perfection in realization is the quality which gives a work of art universality of understanding. The screen image, having been assembled by a motley crew, often betrays its parliamentary origin.

Occasionally the motley crew happily are of a single pur-

242

pose. More often a single dominant force will seize the reins and drive with self-determination. In either instance, a point of view will probably exist. If the substance of the statement is of importance, that which is guided to the screen will vibrate on it with style and meaning.

SOME DIFFERENCES BETWEEN SCENERY FOR TELEVISION, OPERA AND LEGITIMATE THEATRE

by

Frederick Fox

In this paper, which was presented to the National Society of Interior Decorators in New York City in April, 1958, Frederick Fox discusses briefly some of the differences facing the designer who creates scenery for television, opera and legitimate theatre. Chief among these differences, Mr. Fox finds, is the matter of scale. Television is a medium of reduction, legitimate theatre near normal but everything is scaled up in opera. Grand opera, according to Frederick Fox, is grand.

We are all designers here, concerned primarily with the same thing—the aesthetic arrangement of space. The interior designer creates a true reality for everyday living while the scene designer tries to create a representation of reality as dictated by the script and the medium he is working in.

I wish to discuss briefly some of the differences facing the scenic designer in producing scenery for television, legitimate theatre and the opera. First let us look at these three media from an audience point of view, which is also my point of view as a scene designer. Television is a single camera eye, theatre is a multi-point, close range picture frame view and opera is a long-ranged, big picture view. Bearing these three basic visual differences in mind, let us examine them one at a time, turning to television first because it is the most prevalent. As a medium it has a few great advantages which are fascinating to a designer. Because of the single viewpoint of the camera eye, the designer (and the director, too) can select any angle and any portion of a setting he wants you to see, at the time he wants you to see it. This selectivity is both rewarding and exciting since visually you are leading the audience by the nose. When we did the TV spectacular, *Babes in Toyland,* for example, we opened in front of a huge gateway and led the audience through the parting doors into an endless fantasia. I say endless advisedly, because it brings us to a second advantage, the lack of a third dimension, which becomes a great asset in television. A flight of stairs leading into infinity, for example, can be painted to appear as real as if they were actually built. In the theatre, however,

245

these painted steps would look like steps painted on a backdrop, but the television camera will show them as reality. In television a small space can be made to look like infinity.

Scale is as flexible as the imagination because the lack of dimension makes the human being the only standard measurement. You are all familiar with the results of this no man's land of scale, such as the camera tricks employed in *Alice in Wonderland,* and all those used in the science-fiction films. In the theatre this kind of trickery does not work because instead of becoming reality, it becomes fantasy. In the theatre we can see the relative sizes of objects. We may enjoy the trickery but we do not believe it.

Television satisfies a certain craving for reality in our scenic concepts. Because it is a photographic medium we can set up scenery ahead of time, and we minutely decorate interiors with real pictures and expensive furnishings. We can build up walls in relief which do not shake upon the opening and closing of doors. We can even make detailed fragments of scenes that become little gems for that one perfect shot.

Television is a medium of reduction. It is photographed life-size and piped out onto twenty-one inch screens. If it is demanding in its details for close-ups, it is positively benevolent on the long shots; for on these we designers can get away with much in the name of reality. That magnificent inlaid marble floor you saw on the television screen last night, or that beautiful aubusson rug, for example, were painted in anything but the exact detail you would find in marble or aubusson. Rococo ornament painted over a doorway can appear very real on the twenty-one inch screen, while a stray nailhead would look like a railroad spike on the motion picture screen of the Roxy theatre.

Scenery is scenery, and as such it will always be with us. It is the stuff that backs the dreams we are creating, sometimes beautiful, sometimes ugly. It can convince an audience of reality or it can transport them into fantasy. It is wood, canvas and paint—paint, canvas and wood because they are the cheapest materials a producer can think of. As designers we can think of a lot of other materials; metals, plastics, silks, etc., but then a manager asks, "What do you need that for? Why, Howard Bay did a set—the greatest I've ever seen—and he only used a piece of cardboard, a hunk of rope and a rented cyc." Further discussion on this point is superfluous.

One thing that we have come to realize is that television scenery is not very mobile. In the theatre, it has to be, if for no other reason than to be able to move it out of the theatre after its first and final appearance.

The theatre program informs the spectator of the locale; "Second floor parlor of the Mercier family, 21 Rue Capuchin, Paris, 1890." And the instant the curtain goes up, the audience must accept the scene before it can give its undivided attention to the dialogue and action of the playwright. Is it the second floor? Is it 1890? Do the Merciers have as much money as the furnishings represent? Is the ground plan of the parlor architecturally correct? All of these things must be instantly believable. In the theatre the scene designer is on his own. He has no motion picture or television camera shot of the outside of the Merciers' house, dollying across Rue Capuchin to the second floor where we cut to the interior to rely upon. His reality is created purely by design, color and selective furnishings.

I mentioned earlier that the theatre is a multi-point of view medium. The designer is faced with the "eyes all over" problem—the spectators who sit way down front in the end seats, fifth row center or in the balcony—and he has to take all these seats into consideration and compose his setting so that everyone in the theatre has an unobstructed view of the action at all times.

The width of the stage and the height of the balcony are determining factors in design. Since the producer does not always know what theatre the show is going into at the time the set is designed, we adopt a standard for interiors of fourteen feet high and a stage opening of thirty-two feet. As you can see, this creates problems. Visualize that cozy colonial living room, low beamed ceiling, wood paneled fireplace and charming wallpaper, fourteen feet high and thirty-two feet wide. Scale cleverly employed can alleviate this problem. The reduction of the height of the set in the rear, the enlarging of the wall paper design, the selection of oversized properties, increasing the door heights from the standard six feet eight inches to seven feet six inches, and the shading of the scenery with paint from dark at the top to light at the bottom, can produce acceptance of this scale and even admiration from an audience.

The tools of the trade are many. The selection of fabrics and color is important also, in creating the mood the designer seeks. Comedy generally suggests bright, light colors, gay fabrics and furniture of pleasing shapes. On the other hand, heavy fabrics such as velvets and brocades in dark rich colors, together with massive, even pretentious furniture achieve wonders for tragediennes like Judith Anderson.

Opera is similar to the theatre insofar as it is a live medium within a picture frame, but there the similarity ends. With few exceptions, there is nothing intimate about the opera. Grand opera is grand. Because of the necessity of blending voices and orchestra, the distance between the first row of the opera audience and the stage is equal to the distance to the last row of seats in the average legitimate theatre. But not only is the aesthetic distance greater, the subjects are bigger, the passions greater. Opera is traditionally designed for huge audiences and the scenic effects must be done on a proportionally grand scale. When I designed *Andrea Chénier* for the Met, I thought that I had accomplished tremendous things in parading a whole army across a bridge under which a tumbrel was drawn carrying con-

248

demned prisoners to the guillotine, until I saw *Mephistoph-eles* produced at the Caracalla in Rome. Here, at the finale for the second act, they set the whole place on fire. Real fire.

An opera company employs normally about one hundred persons who are on a weekly salary and managements from the days of Verdi have insisted that composers keep these people busy. Consequently large mobs must be considered in the designer's lay-out for a scene, for most assuredly, all one hundred will pour out onstage for the finale, and unless the designer has provided room for them, the music critics will complain the next morning in the *New York Times* that the stage was cluttered. At the same time, however, the intimate scenes have to work in the same areas. For example, eighty per cent of Act One of *Tosca* is composed of two duets, one between Cavaradossi and Angelotti and the other between Cavaradossi and Tosca. Finally, in the last minutes of the act everyone appears, filling up the stage. In *Andrea Chénier* we had the same situation but we were able to cope with the situation. A transparent gauze curtain was hung in front of the ballroom, softly lighted, providing an intimate atmosphere for the opening scene. In two bars of music it tableaued out, revealing a full set teeming with people in fancy costumes.

Furniture, too, has to be scaled up to size in the opera. The Met has its own property shop that is constantly making all sorts of big furniture and bric-a-brac that would be impossible to purchase elsewhere.

Opera, like ballet, is an artist's paradise. The designer is dealing with vast areas. The lighting equipment is comparatively simple and all effects are dependent upon painting.

And to conclude, let us compare some relative sizes. Television interiors usually run between eight and ten feet high. In the theatre fourteen to eighteen is considered average. In opera, however, twenty-four to thirty-six feet is minimum. These figures should indicate the amount of detail that goes

249

into the final product of each. In television we build mould-ings, six foot eight inch doorways that do not shake, frag-ments of sets beautifully decorated, all in natural scale. In the theatre we rescale doorways, fireplaces, windows and wall-paper patterns. The furniture remains natural size but we satisfy the viewer's eye by arranging it cleverly. And thirty-two feet remains the average size in the theatre, regardless whether it's a ballroom or cottage. In opera the concept changes radically. Living rooms become fifty feet wide, door-ways twelve feet high, furniture becomes enormous and sparse and numerous platforms, alcoves and balconies appear to accommodate the hordes of singers in the mob scenes.

PART FIVE—VARIATIONS

DÉCOR

by
Stark Young

Stark Young's critical appraisals of Broadway between the two world wars have contributed substantially to the growth and maturity of the contemporary American theatre. Few critics have been so concerned with all aspects of theatre art; not only the literary value of the play, the quality of the acting, or the artistry of the director or designer, but with the production as a work of art. Few critics have so consistently tried to reveal the relationship of the art of the theatre to the rest of the fine arts. Mr. Young has written voluminously on the various aspects of theatre art and this discerning essay on the function of the scenic designer clearly illustrates the lucidity and insight with which Mr. Young has always observed the theatre. "Décor" was originally published in THE THEATRE (New York, 1927), pp. 139-156, recently republished in the Hill & Wang Dramabooks series.

Electricity and mechanical progress have carried the theatre a long way from what it was when Aristotle was so easily able to say of the spectacle or décor that, though an attraction, it was the least artistic of all the parts of the theatrical art and had least to do with creation. The designer has become one of the important artists of the modern theatre.

There are people no doubt who would deny it, but we could say, I think, that, of all the arts, words come first as the medium by which the culture of the human race has most been handed on, or at least this is true of the Western races. Words may not be the deepest or purest, but they are the most immediate, universal and socially necessary medium of expression that we employ. Certainly, it is true that, whatever may be said of them in their own spheres, painting and architecture do not come first in the theatre as mediums for conveying the idea. For a single occasion the importance of the décor will of course vary with the quality of what is to be expressed, whether it comes out best in words or music or acting or visual design. In general, the play and the acting come first; they are far ahead of the décor as means of expressing the dramatic idea.

As to the realistic setting so frequent in the theatre of the last half century and often so costly in their demands, it is plain they are the natural children of the realistic drama and the "free theatres." The concern about realistic detail that troubles so much modern drama becomes the pride of such designers as aim to give us reality to the last item. These

253

realistic designers wander in the same confusion as the dramatists and the public over the relation of art to nature, and much of their effort is as inconsequent, incidental, and unimagined. It is obvious that the fundamental principle involved in realistic décor is the translation of the real material, such as a room or a scene, into the quality of the play. More often than not this translation does not happen; for lack of all those familiar stage tricks of reproduction, duplication of objects, sounds and places that excite a childish delight by being so exactly contrived, are low forms of theatre; they are not part of the dramatic movement; they stick out of themselves and thus intrude on the right dramatic content or idea.

To such unrelated reproduction, or photography, as this last we may object, since it is not art at all. To realistic décor we can have no objection when the quality it goes with is realistic—no setting could be more perfect than that the Moscow Art Theatre gave to Chekhov's *The Cherry Orchard;* it was an element in a fine theatre work in which the play, the acting, the décor and the directing all had one texture and all contributed toward a theatrical body for the informing idea. To admire realism in stage design merely because it presents some new trick or carries further some ingenious effect of actuality is only puerile. To object to it because it is out of date or not the newest thing is superficial, faddish and idle. The necessary thing in every case of course is creative imagination by which the setting becomes cousin to the play.

Words cannot convey what such settings are like, but I may cite such instances as the mob scene in Reinhardt's *Miracle,* for which Mr. Norman Bel-Geddes did the design, or Mr. Robert Edmond Jones' designs for *The Hairy Ape* or *The Great God Brown,* or some design like that of Mr. Ernest de Weerth's for a drama of the French Revolution in which the form of the guillotine is present in diverse lights and

disguises throughout every scene, suggesting in one a doorway, in another a lattice, or a wood, a courtroom, and so on.
Of this kind of décor we may say that if realism in décor
can sink to mere photographic repetition and tricky clap-
trap, this other extreme can drop to mere obvious allegory
and platitudes of stylization. In our French Revolution
drama, for example, this contrivance of the guillotine form
in every scene may have in it a source of power, it may unify
and excite our responses. But it is not in itself necessarily
any more imaginative than the more photographic representation of the doorway or wood or courtroom would be.
It may make more demand on the spectator's imagination if
you like, since he has to conjure up for himself this diversity
of places. But this extra effort on the part of the audience
does not imply extra imagination on the scenic artist's;
if that were so the man who put a drop of water in the middle
of the stage and made us guess that it presented the chamber
in which Lady Macbeth had tried to wash the blood from her
hands, would be the greatest artist in all theatre design. The
trouble with symbols and stylizations is often that, the symbol
or motif once found, is not used with imagination, so that as
soon as we have found the key to it it begins to grow flat
and unexpressive. Mere elimination of likenesses or mere
stylization need not in themselves imply anything beyond a
certain novelty, if that. This confusion over what is and what
is not imagination has made a great mess of modern theatrical
design.

To have an actor use a mask to show us what he is in
another man's eyes as contrasted with what he is to himself
when shown without the mask, may be a visual device happily
suited to the play in hand; it may be in complete unity with
the quality of the idea and the writing and to that extent
imaginative creation. But it gets no further except insofar
as the artist, at every point where the mask is used, contrives
to express through it what nothing else could express so

255

wholly. In a play where the nerves of the dramatis personae are very much awry the designer may distort the room and the furniture and even the clothes to accord with the character's state. But this invention in itself is soon exhausted, nothing in fact could be more easily hit upon than such a device and nothing could sooner lose its edge. Such a setting, if that is all it comes to, merely succeeds in getting in the dramatist's way. Nothing is more obvious than symbolism when it is poor or perfunctory. Nothing is less expressive than stylization that merely tries to avoid naturalism.

There is no right way in décor, neither the stylized nor the realistic; in every case the end is the same, which is to create something that justifies itself by expressing what nothing else could quite express. When this happens in the décor, it rises to its high place in the art of the theatre. Otherwise, if it is not bad or intrusive, it may be a humble surrounding for the characters and action, a pleasant ambient that we take for granted or scarcely see.

In the theatre of today there are numberless theories major and minor of design, from a complete elimination of setting to the utmost complexity; we have a naked stage such as Copeau used, or curtains, or the screens of Gordon Craig, or a permanent architectural background like Norman Bel-Geddes, *Arabesque,* or scenes that try to copy reality to the last degree of illusion or duplication, as in Mr. Belasco's production of *Lulu Belle,* or the scenery that looks like an enlarged painting, brush strokes and all, as in Roerich's sets for *Schnegourotzka,* or constructionist design, as in the Russian *Lysistrata* or *The Man Who Was Thursday*; all of which the files of *The Theatre Arts Monthly* afford the best record in English. In the history of theatrical décor there are many phases: the architectural setting of the Greeks; the Elizabethan stage with apron stage, inner stage, painted cloths; the elaborate baroque architecture of the seventeenth and eighteenth century on the Continent; the intimate interior of Molière's day; the scene painter's various but more or less undesigned efforts in the nineteenth century, and so on. All these varieties of design rest on the same basis and have the same purpose, which is to create a theatrical setting for a theatrical idea. New ideas and qualities demand a new character of design that will express their character. Types of ideas—the general conceptions characteristic of an epoch, for example—demand and evolve their fitting décor. Each of these types of décor illustrates the same movement through many changes until the form natural to the idea is achieved, after which the movement sets in from this form and toward a changed form for a changed content.

As has often been said, the décor depends on one man only where the rest of the production depends on many. This is most evident of course. The dramatist must rely on the actors and the director, the actor on the play and the director, and the director on them; but the designer, though his idea may at the start be tampered with by the dramatist or producer, works straight when he goes to work and uses his medium directly. In one respect only must he depend on another medium; for his costumes he depends on the actor's art in wearing them, which on our stage at least is nearly always nil. Through this one-man fact it is easy to see how we may sooner find nowadays an admirable set at the hands of a designer than an admirable scene at the hands of the playwright, actors and director combined. I have seen few plays and little acting in late years that could compare with some of Mr. Robert Edmond Jones' designs, and nothing else modern of any kind in the theatre that was equal in imagination to Mr. Norman Bel-Geddes' *Dante Model* (*The Divine Comedy*). The next generation may see better plays and worse décor, or one country may now excel in one theatre element, another in another, as happened in the seventeenth century when France led in the drama of Molière and Racine and South Europe led in the famous baroque décor. In any other

257

art the several elements vary from epoch to epoch and artist to artist in excellence. For color Titian carries painting beyond Bellini but does nothing for line; and Spenser carried English poetry far ahead of his forerunners in all but narrative construction.

Settings may strike exactly the same character as the scene they contain, as in Mr. Simonson's designs for *Les Ratés,* the play by Lenormand, in eleven episodes, produced by the Theatre Guild. These eleven settings were changed in less than a minute, developed from a few lines, objects and motifs, just as the written scenes were, and like them expressionistic in method and direct and vivid in tone, and of the same degree of imagination and technical craft.

Or the décor provided by the designer may push the play aside; he may tend to dwarf, distort or estrange the scene by the setting he provides, as Mr. Norman Bel-Geddes did in *Arabesque.* In *Arabesque* there was a scene in which the citizens of the Arabian town came in pursuit of the lover who had shamed a maiden by looking on her face unveiled. Down the steps into the court and up again and over the housetops the figures streamed, covered in darkness, each with his pierced lantern whose light ran here and there over the walls and ground. Of this scene with its searching fingers of light and shadow, its flying shapes, its nuances of color, space and motion, we can say that here was a case where words could have done nothing compared to what this device achieved, that it was visual expression carried to a complete and astonishing degree. In this case the particular play in hand was wrecked, the ruling idea of the occasion lay in the visual part of it. What was needed to balance matters was a play from the same hand as the design.

* * *

No one who considers the theatre and its nature, could fail to wonder what effect the décor has on the actors in a play, how much the mood that the designer creates may color, intensify, cramp, exalt, overshadow or project the actor's state of mind and his effect on the audience. We may take the work of Mr. Robert Edmond Jones as an example. No one could fail to wonder looking at the designs and costumes of Mr. Robert Edmond Jones, what effect such an investiture of genius could have on the actors in the play. These actors are the immediate protagonists at hand in the drama out of life that the dramatist has given them to present. But in the vaster theatre within which the actors, the designer and the dramatist together move, the protagonists are the souls of the actors, the soul of the dramatist and the designer's soul. Within these settings that the designer provides, the business of the costumes is to reveal and ennoble the actor's part, as his business is to fill them; together mutually they define and illuminate each other. And if the actor and the dramatist is poorer than is good for the designer, it is the business not to design down to them, as it were, but to express what may have been, even beyond the dramatist's own conscious purpose or the actor's capacity, the nobler and living origins from which, however far off they may be, their impulse and idea have sprung.

This is the lift and fecundity, these are the conceptions at work, that we have seen in Mr. Jones' productions, in the magnificent *Birthday of the Infanta,* in *Hamlet* and elsewhere. We may take his Banquet Scene in *Macbeth.* That scene—with its fierce, ghastly colors, its light and dark, its figures of king and queen and banqueters—not merely bold and obvious like so many designs of its type, among the Germans especially—is, for covered and insuppressible passion, quite unequaled among stage drawings, so far as I know them; it has in it the memory of some horror when the worshipers peered into the reeking viscera of some primitive sacrifice, it is full of voices within us as old as the race, and yet it is held to the ideal mood of great drama.

259

Décor

To a soul, Plotinus says, in one of those passages of his that shine on the center of our thought, is allotted its own fortunes, not at haphazard but always under a Reason, as the actors of our stage get their masks and other costumes. With the designer for the theatre it is the same. As this soul's fortunes are to it, to the designer is allotted his fortune, the drama that he is to clothe, what background of the visible world it shall be given, what garments, furniture and light. He, like this soul in Plotinus and like this actor, adapts himself to the fortunes assigned to him, ranges himself rightly to the drama that he must invest, and to the whole principle of the piece. He too must speak out what business is given to him, exhibiting at the same time all that a soul can express of its own quality, as a singer in a song. But like this soul and like this actor, the designer holds a peculiar dignity. All three of them act in a vaster place than any stage, and have it in themselves "to be masters of all this world."

The designs of a fine artist in the décor of the theatre assume the fortunes that the dramatist has allotted to him, and express them, carrying radiantly the necessary essence of the idea. They further and reveal the meaning of the characters and the event, and convey the shock of their vitality; they sing the drama's song. But they sing the singer, too. He himself creates within the part assigned him.

REPRESENTATIONAL OR PRESENTATIONAL THEATRE

by

Alexander Bakshy

In this discussion on representational and presentational theatre, from the essay, "The Aesthetics of Theatre" (THE THEATRE UNBOUND, London, 1923, pp. 92-107), Alexander Bakshy suggests, with historical precedent, a return to the true form of theatrical art wherein the "image of life" is frankly presented on stage before an audience in a theatre consciously enjoying a performance.

We have now reached the stage where we are faced with the question: What is the art of the theatre? Or, in other words, how can a dramatic spectacle of imagination, of imaginative life partake of the nature of art? Let us consider first what forms a dramatic spectacle can assume. The main forms are two. The spectacle can be treated as a true image of life existing outside, and quite independent of the theatre, which form may be called *representational*, or it can be treated as an image of life existing in the theatre and finds its expression in the forms of the theatre, which other form may be called *presentational*.

The representational form can be used for portraying life in its various aspects such as the naturalistic, the conventional, and the symbolic aspects. But, whatever the aspect of life, its reproduction in the theatre is always based on creating the illusion that it represents a world entirely different from that in which the audience is while in the theatre. The methods of creating such an illusion vary according to the character of the play, that is, they are themselves either naturalistic, or conventional, or symbolical. But their common characteristic is that, except when they try to carry the illusion so far as to transform the auditorium with its audience into a part of their imaginary world, they usually confine themselves to the stage behind the proscenium arch. In this way, the picture represented obtains a life of its own, while the spectator is either ignored entirely, or is, when he lends imagination to the building of the picture, induced to collaborate with the actor and renounce his position as an independent observer.

The European theatre of the last forty years or so has been so preoccupied with the struggle for predominance which naturalism, conventionalism, and symbolism have been waging with one another that the public has come to regard them as expressing the only fundamental divisions in the art of the theatre. Yet, if we probe somewhat deeper, we find that all the three methods mentioned rest on the same, namely, representational basis. To take the naturalistic method first, we see that the attempt to give an exact replica of life as it exists outside of the theatre can have but one effect, namely, the creation of an illusion that the picture of life on the stage is something entirely self-complete and independent. It is realised, of course, that the very fact of showing something to the audience who must be in a position to see, to hear, and to understand it, imposes certain limitations on the development of plot, on acting, and on mounting. But, though certain concessions to the conditions of the theatre are made they are made grudgingly, and the follower of naturalism tries his best to free himself from such limitations.

Unwilling or unable to condense the story into a few connected acts, he will give loosely related scenes, using "atmosphere" as a means of binding them together. In acting, he will ignore the need of making the speeches audible, and will place the actors with their backs to the audience. In mounting, he will try to disregard the proscenium opening and will place a row of chairs or a fireplace . . . the so-called "fourth wall," . . . along the footlights. There is no limit to the ingenuity of the naturalistic producer bent on making the stage look like anything but a stage. The finest theatres and the commonest, vie in this with one another. The Moscow Art Theatre poured rain on its actors. And Drury Lane in one of its recent productions did the very same thing.

But let us turn to the other two methods. The terms "conventional" and "symbolical" have no fixed meaning and are often used as interchangeable. When applied to the theatre, however, "conventional" usually refers to the mounting, and "symbolical" to the reference or subject matter. It would be more correct to define the first as a method of picturing life from a more or less preconceived standpoint, which informs the convention used, and colours the picture in an arbitrary, mostly non-realistic tone. On the Continent the stage application of this method has received the name of "stylization." On the other hand "symbolism" represents an effort to grasp the essence of things. Sometimes the essence grasped is merely an extract of outward characteristics, being no more than mere simplification. Sometimes it is allegory. Sometimes it takes a flight to the supernatural realms and parades before us as a barely clothed spirit. Sometimes again it looks just like ordinary mundane things, but it reveals itself through the inner significance with which those things are instinct. Dostoyevsky's novels, for instance, are more symbolic in this sense than many a literary work delving into supernatural experiences and mystic symbols. However, on the stage, "symbolism" means mostly a tendency toward allegory and the mystic interpretation of life.

As an illustration of the conventional method in the theatre, one may quote the productions of Mr. Granville-Barker. Plays describing common things in uncommon ways, or uncommon things in common ways, were produced as beautiful visions materialised on the stage in the form of tableaux. More than the dramatist and more than the actor, the musician and the painter were the mainsprings of such productions. The object was to create an imaginative picture of life. At the same time, it was realised that this could be achieved only by arousing the creative imagination of the audience itself. Hence, one may say that the "conventional" method recognized the audience as an element of the theatre and was, therefore, an advance on the naturalistic method.

265

Nevertheless, like the latter, it was employed to produce the same effect, namely, an illusion of life complete in itself and existing beyond the theatre. The audience was induced to forget that it was in the theatre, and the stage was transformed into a picture which had no connection with its real form or function. In so far, therefore, the conventional method was purely representational. And with equal force this applies to the symbolical method, of which one finds the most characteristic examples in the designs and actual productions of Mr. Gordon Craig. By picturing life in symbolic forms, both as regards its subject matter and its materializations on the stage, you do not make the performance less representational. The object remains that of creating an illusion of a separate world, and the stage and the auditorium are necessarily treated as something that has to be disguised or overcome.

Now, is the representational form of spectacle art or not? I think it is art, but only a forced, impure, and incomplete one. It is art because a vision of some world, provided it is significant in itself, can be experienced by the spectator as an independent reality, which is essentially a characteristic of an aesthetic experience. This form of spectacle, however, must be considered forced, because, in order to produce such a vision, it has to suppress and disguise all that distinguishes the theatre as a theatre. It eliminates the auditorium by keeping it dark. It disguises the stage by deceiving the spectator into a belief that it is something else. It suppresses the actor by showing him, not as a creator, or even interpreter, but as an incarnation of a character in which no trace of the actor's individuality is left.

My reason for calling this form impure is that it harnesses into the service of the theatre other arts, such as painting for instance, the proper province of which is entirely outside of the theatre. Why is the painter called in at all? To give support to the actor? But this can only be done at the expense

266

of the actor, who loses his predominance on the stage. And even then, as the aesthetic appeal of painting and acting are entirely different, the result is only a mixture of unrelated impressions. The idea that the theatre is a synthetic art is a fallacy. To different arts we apply different standards, and no real success can be obtained in trying to force some sort of unity upon such a static art as painting and such a dynamic art as dramatic action. If you secure this unity you do so only by sacrificing the standards of each art involved, and you will never achieve a unity.

Finally, I call the representational form of the theatre incomplete because its appeal is based on the significance of the world portrayed and ignores the inherent significance of the medium of the theatre with the help of which the former is conveyed to the spectator.

These criticisms indicate the conditions a dramatic spectacle should fulfill to earn its title to be called "artistic."

The reaction against naturalism in art and in the theatre brought us conventionalism and symbolism. But we already see that all three of them are merely variations of the same illusionistic principle. There is a growing demand and a growing realization of the fact that the theatre has a nature that is peculiarly its own, though the practice of today has been to disguise it as much as possible. Among the pioneers of the new movement, William Poel, by his inspired re-creation of Mediaeval and Elizabethan stage, and Gordon Craig, through his sheer love of theatre as a medium, though primarily in search of symbolical forms of representation, were the first to suggest the new conception. Other artists of the theatre, like Meyerhold in Russia and Jacques Copeau in France, still further developed the principle of theatrical presentation in a number of remarkable productions. Thus, at present, the ground has been sufficiently prepared to enable one to encompass the whole problem and clear away whatever encumbrance and inconsistencies are still clinging to it by mere force of tradition.

It is fashionable nowadays to extol the music-hall and denounce the theatre. A great deal of this can be accounted for by affectation and mental cowardice or senility, as it is so soothing to one's conceit to prop up one's lack of interest in vital soul-gripping art, with an air of superiority. At the same time, if we disregard the rubbish which is so literally thrown on the music-hall stage for the delectation of its patrons, the fact cannot be gainsaid that actors like Nelson, Keys, Little Tich, Harry Lauder, and many others, are greater and more faithful exponents of the pure art of the theatre than is any living English actor of the legitimate stage. (One is inclined to make exception in the case of Henry Ainley . . . an actor of tremendous resources and range of emotion. Unfortunately, it is very rarely nowadays that one sees him at his best.)

While, as far as conditions of aesthetic appreciation are concerned these are certainly much more favourable for the audience in the case of the music-hall than in that of the ordinary theatre. Nor does the general atmosphere of the former leave the spectator his freedom of judgment and appreciation, but even the stage mountings and acting itself seem to emphasize the fact that he is merely witnessing a show. Take this example: An orthodox music-hall comedian is acting in a scene laid on a beach. He has to wipe his boots. So he takes a piece of cloth and dips it into the sea, which is painted on the backdrop. Again he feels shaky, so he leans against the painted sky. The audience naturally laughs, and its laughter finds an easy explanation in the contrast between the real objects painted on the backdrop and the fact that they are nothing but painted canvas. But the important thing is that the music-hall is not afraid to emphasize the purely theatrical, make-believe, unreal nature of the performance; whereas, on stage, the legitimate stage, the painted sea is a sea and not a

268

sign of a sea, much less a backdrop, and the audience seeing the actor dipping a towel into the painted water is expected to believe that the towel has actually been made wet.

The illustration just cited brings us to the very crux of our problem. Should the play appear as something existing outside the theatre? Or as a make-believe world, which derives its reality not from its powers of deceiving the spectator but from its frank recognition that it is nothing but make-believe? Likewise, should the actors impersonate real characters, and incarnate beings of symbolical significance? Or should they present them through the prism of their own individuality and acting-craft?

It has already been suggested that the representational form of dramatic spectacle, by trying to create an illusion of life outside the theatre, produces art that is forced, impure, and incomplete. On the contrary, the presentational form draws from the very source of pure theatrical art in laying stress on the fact that the image of life it "presents" exists in the theatre and is expressed in the forms of the theatre.

To begin with, however, what kind of imaginary life can exist in the theatre? It might seem that once you destroy the self-completeness and independence of the imaginary world you might destroy its imaginative existence altogether. But is that really so? Is it necessary in order to believe in a king on the stage to forget that he is an actor at the same time? And do we ever believe that the fighting on the stage is real fighting? Or that the character struggling in agony is really dying? If so, if this is so, why should it be more impossible to act a scene of life in the theatre without trying to disguise the fact that it is in the theatre? The art of make-believe will still be there, but it will be just what it is: a make-believe which does not pretend to be anything else. In other words, it will be a presentation of life determined by the peculiar nature of the theatre itself.

This nature can be reduced to four elements—the audience, the stage, the play, and most of all, the actor.

The spectator, who comes to the theatre in search of art, is obviously entitled to demand that his power or aesthetic appreciation should not be interfered with. Not only, therefore, should he oppose all attempts to turn him into an actor, but he should be equally determined to claim his spectator's "place in the sun." In this class division and class war, he will reject the co-partnership plan of the conventional-symbolical theatre, but will fight for a full recognition of his trade union. Perhaps the metaphor should not be stretched too far, as the relationship between the spectator and the actor is more in the nature of the relationship between the consumer and the producer than between the workman and capitalist. But, whether as a member of a trade union or a consumer's society, the spectator is certainly entitled to be recognized as a spectator, and not to be either entirely ignored, or coaxed into a surrender of his independence and his critical faculties.

Equally straightforward should be the treatment of all the other elements of the theatre. The stage as a part of the theatre building, serves as a pedestal on which the plastic structure of the enacted play is raised. What justification is there for disguising the pedestal and creating the impression that the real foundation of the play is not in the theatre building but somewhere outside its walls? Is the stage so base, so destitute of all that goes into the making of art, as to require a veil to hide its nakedness? And has not the contrary been proven true by the whole history of the theatre from the days of ancient Greece, throughout the Middle Ages, the Renaissance, and down to the end of the 17th century? Not only was there no attempt in those days to disguise the stage, but its presence was actually emphasized and made the means of building the dramatic spectacle.

To say that this was due to the lack of technical resources

270

would be simply betraying an ignorance of spirit which animated the old theatre. The Romans, who were the first to attempt a division between the auditorium and the stage by making the latter architecturally more self-complete than it was in the Greek theatre, and the Italians of the 17th century who invented the proscenium arch, introduced these changes not because they were in possession of greater technical resources, but because they found the old stage inadequate for their new, illusionistic aims. Conversely, a recognition of aims other than illusionistic disposes of the necessity of disguising the fact that the stage is actually inside the theatre building and that it is there for the express purpose of enabling the actors to perform the play.

The presentational method which sets itself the aim of creating the dramatic spectacle through the pure medium of the theatre, therefore, demands that the stage should be constructed in a way that would make clear both its position as a part of the theatre building, and its function as an essential element of the spectacle. It is conceivable, and history proves this by numerous examples, that the principle here stated can be embodied in diverse architectural forms. The Greek stage, the Mediaeval processional, the Japanese Noh stage, though unmistakably presentational in their position and function, present considerable differences in point of actual construction. The important thing, however, is the principle, and if, in modern design, this finds an adequate material expression, it matters little whether the old models have been adhered to or not.

Next to the proscenium arch, the principal means of creating an illusionistic picture on the stage is the mounting. Naturally, all such forms of mounting, whether they be elaborate or simplified, as tend to disguise the stage are ruled out of the presentational method.

The principle from which it proceeds is that the setting must be in harmony with the stage actually used. It would,

271

for instance, be absurd to have an architectural setting on the Japanese stage and a pictorial one on the Greek stage. In the stone-built theatres of Europe, the presentational stage must clearly have a marked architectural form, and the minimum of mounting this stage would admit must equally be made subordinate to the same principle. But it must also be borne in mind that, unlike the picture-frame stage, the presentational stage itself forms an element of mounting. An illustration will make this point clear. Let it be supposed that the actual stage is built in the form of a three-decked and roofless platform, hedged half-way around by a permanent architectural screen and standing some distance from the back of the hall. Curtains or screens might be used on this stage to hide one or another part of it as the case might require. For an interior scene it would be sufficient to set up a special screen on one of the lower terraces. But should this scene imply the presence of people outside, as, for instance, when a character speaks through a window to a crowd in a street . . . the upper terrace of the stage might be actually filled with the crowd which would thus be seen at the same time and at one with the persons in the interior. In this way, the relative position of the characters would be "presented" by a mere division of the stage, while the spectators would be induced to see the scene, not as they would have were they themselves taking part in it, but as they ought to see it, in their position of spectators in the theatre.

No matter how far the play on the stage may depart from the correlation and sequence of facts and things in the world portrayed it will be theatrically justified so long as it succeeds in translating that world into terms of stage presentation.

The same principle would apply to acting. Instead of living on the stage or pretending to live on the stage, the actor would simply masquerade his part, "serve it up" to the audience, regardless of the possibility that thereby he might in-

272

fringe the psychological unity of the part taken as a whole. The only unity with which this actor would be concerned would be that built up in the imagination of the spectators. It will be seen from this that for the presentational theatrical acting, the questions of "asides," "soliloquies," "addresses to the public,"—these time-honored and so bitterly assailed conventions of the stage, does not really arise. They are justified by the mere fact of answering, in so far as they do answer, the demands of the presentational method.

It would be a mistake, however, to think that the latter is confined only to the traditional stage plots and types. Many of these things have ceased to be universal, fundamentally human, and have become merely historical curios of the theatre, mere faint and colourless theatrical echoes of a life which no longer exists. Were the theatrical make-up here advocated merely equivalent to the theatrical conception of life as developed and fixed by stage tradition, it would be of little account for the future of art in the theatre. The theatre must throb with the life that surges and whirls in the consciousness of mankind. It must be vital in its message and forceful in its appeal. And it is for this reason, if for no other, that it should express itself in its own language, and should cultivate its purity and freedom. Naked theatrical make-believe is just that natural language of the theatre. It stands for no specific conception of life, being merely a method of expression, but it has its own laws, and those must be obeyed. Thus only will honest, pure, and virile art be restored to the theatre.

THE CONQUEST OF STAGE SPACE

by

Mordecai Gorelik

"The art of stage setting . . . is turning from the techniques of illusion and static mood toward the technique of an immediate ritual in theatre; an immediate, not reminiscent type of staging. . . . Aside from the task of making a setting both reminiscent and theatrical immediate at the same time, modern designers face more and more often the problem of having to show several scenes simultaneously. All this is leading to a new dynamic artistic concept which departs completely from the box setting and produces a new type of setting." Written almost a decade before World War II, Mordecai Gorelik's perceptive predictions become all the more amazing because Mr. Gorelik's observations on scenic art in "The Conquest of Stage Space" (which appeared in THEATRE ARTS MONTHLY in March, 1934, pp. 213-218), reads like an appraisal of recent developments in scenic design if one substitutes plays such as Hatful of Rain, Summer and Smoke, Voice of the Turtle, Blue Denim, All Summer Long *and* Death of a Salesman *for those Mr. Gorelik mentions in his first long list. Only the final paragraph was rewritten for this anthology.*

There is a popular supposition that styles in art follow each other as reactions, as if artists as well as patrons, becoming surfeited with style, turn perversely to another form opposite in character. This theory does not take into account the deeper fact that all styles correspond to the society out of which they grow. As societies change, their art forms change. These changes may come about almost imperceptibly, or they may make their appearance with a sudden crystallization.

Thus in the art of the stage setting, the transition from Belasco naturalism to, let us say, Robert Edmond Jones romanticism, was a comparatively smooth one which involved no change in what theatre historians have so aptly described as "the stage of the fourth wall," "the peep-box stage," or "the picture-frame stage." A type of staging was required which gave a concentrated, boxed-in illusion of a real locale; the eighteenth-century system of side wings and backdrop slowly gave place to the increasingly architectural box setting of the nineteenth and early twentieth centuries. Looking into the peep-box of the proscenium the spectator now saw a picture which was reminiscent as possibly of some locale in the outer world.

In the case of Belasco this authenticity was sought by means of authentic detail. But later designers found that the mere accumulation of such detail did not always reproduce the living spirit of time and place. They found, indeed, that they could oftener attain their end by elimination of detail; their artistic problem was to see through the meticulous authenticity of a locale into the essential character of the locale.

275

The Conquest of Stage Space

The reminiscent type of setting was a logical part of the theatre which developed in the preceding century and which is now giving way to a newer form. It must be remembered that this theatre, with which we have all grown up, has not been the essential form of the theatre since the beginning of time. The theatre has not always been a peep-box lit by electricity, situated indoors and having a curtained, picture-frame proscenium which emphasizes the detachment of the audience from the play. This particular theatre-form and stage-form evolved along with a definite social and cultural trend brought on by the decay of feudal society, the development of large-scale industry, and the consequent major role of the middle class with its ideal of naturalism and individualism.

The great development of middle-class culture has been its extraordinary analytic research into the human soul, a research attended by discoveries of the springs of character, reconstruction of emotional moods, and exploration into the recesses of mysticism. The theatre of the middle class demanded from the beginning a method of production which would allow theatre audiences to relax and watch with detachment the unfolding of a human analysis in the lighted box before them—an analysis which referred not to the actual presences and movements on the stage, but rather *through* them, reminiscently, to some people or events outside the theatre in a suburban flat, in an Italian palace of the Renaissance, or in far-off China. And it was the business of the scene designer to evoke as movingly as possible the ghost of the locale. (I use the past tense only because I have in mind the newer approach; this style is still with us.)

In the past decade, at first imperceptibly and now quite noticeably, scene design has been entering a new phase, illustrated by such constructions as Norman Bel Geddes' *Lysistrata*, Jo Mielziner's *Street Scene*, Aline Bernstein's *Romeo and Juliet*, Lee Simonson's *Tidings Brought to Mary*, Robert

276

Edmond Jones's *Macbeth,* Cleon Throckmorton's *Peace on Earth,* Raymond Sovey's *She Loves Me Not,* and my own *Men in White.* I leave aside Donald Oenslager's *Pinwheel,* Woodman Thompson's *God Loves Us* and my own *Loudspeaker*—all consciously but superficially based on constructivism.

An examination of these and similar types of settings discloses that their common feature is, either intentionally or inadvertently, *an immediate, not a reminiscent type of staging.* Yet none of them represents a distinct break with the older type. The fact of immediacy does not preclude a reminiscent quality, but rather passes beyond the fact of historic reconstruction into a quality of immediate value—of the stage setting not only for the historic mood it describes, but for its separate architectural, plastic or mechanical effect within the theatre building. Thus, while the setting for *Street Scene* is at first glance almost in the style of Belasco, it shortly becomes evident that the apartment house façade is first of all a theatrical convention which permits the play to be staged in a new and arresting way. The longer the setting remains on the stage (in this case it remains throughout the play), the less the audience identifies it as an actual place. Instead the audience sees and accepts it as a sheer theatrical device. Similarly, Jones's *Macbeth,* while evoking a mystical conception, uses abstract forms chosen for their intrinsic theatrical effect.

It now becomes clear that the art of stage setting, enriched by its experience with the reminiscent, introspective form, is turning from the technique of illusion and of static mood, toward the technique of *an immediate ritual in theatre.* It seeks to create a current, not a remembered, emotion in the spectator, making him react objectively to the play of action, color and light which is taking place before his eyes. It is proper to say that the new settings seek a *cubism* of experience, translating into stage terms the phenomena of the

277

outer-world, just as the cubist and post-cubist painter translates the world into a pattern of paint on canvas. This throws some light on what may be described as the slogan of Gordon Craig: "Toward a theatrical theatre." To be sure, Craig advanced this slogan on a purely aesthetic basis which did not explain itself and which sometimes led him to absurd conclusions. But his intuition was correct: the modern theatre as it passes out of its introverted, "atmopsheric" period, moves toward the basic stage form of theatrical ceremony.

What does this mean in its social context? It means that the period of individualism, of introspective analysis, individual psychology and mysticism, is coming to a close along with the historic period of private initiative in industry. The psychology of every man for himself, of individual greatness, "rugged individualism," is changing into a conception of social obligation, communal effort and a sense of fellowship with one's neighbors. It is no coincidence that so many recent plays concern themselves less with individuals than with large human enterprises and with the common bond of the individual human beings in these enterprises. Among the many such plays may be named: *Street Scene; The Last Mile; Five Star Final; Broadway; Grand Hotel; We, The People; Sailor, Beware; False Dreams, Farewell* and *Men in White.*

This is far from mere theory. Aside from the task of making a setting both reminiscent and theatrical immediate at the same time, the modern designer faces more and more often the problem of how to show two or more scenes simultaneously taking place. One stage is no longer enough on which to present the many facets of a modern dramatic situation: where formerly dramatists wrote plays in three leisurely acts, modern authors pile scene upon scene, and do not hesitate to call for five or more scenes at once.

For the designer the task becomes that of finding half-a-dozen stages where only one was before. This is at first a matter of ingenuity, and plenty of that has been employed in devising rapid shifts, stages on numerous levels, revolving, elevator, truck, treadwheel and jack-knife stages. But these mechanical bases eventually lead to a dynamic artistic concept which in turn makes a complete departure from the box setting, and produces new type settings almost without precedent.

It is interesting that the new scenic formula is unhesitatingly accepted by all types of theatregoers. To the layman the new type of setting which would have appeared peculiar years ago, is now as theatrically real as any other. Clearly, the average conception of what is "real" in the theatre depends on the prevailing culture and temper of the times; what is real in one generation may not at all be real to the next.

EPIC SCENE DESIGN

by
Mordecai Gorelik

*It has been said that Epic theatre presents the only new
aesthetic approach to theatre since the appearance of the
realistic movement. One of its staunchest advocates for many
years is Mordecai Gorelik who has written on all aspects of
Epic theatre. Originally written for this anthology, Mr.
Gorelik's essay was published in THEATRE ARTS,
Volume 43 (October, 1959) pp. 75ff.*

The controversial nature of the Epic stage form, as developed in Berlin in the 1920's, is nowhere more evident today than in its scene design. With his staging of Alfons Paquet's *Flags* in 1924, the director Erwin Piscator had inaugurated the use of film sequences on stage, a method which was to characterize many of his productions. An example was his staging of Ernst Toller's *Hoppla, We Live!* (1927), a play about a man who comes out of a lunatic asylum for the first time in nine years, gets a look at the world and decides to hurry back to the asylum. However, before he can get there, he is caught up in the violence of contemporary history and escapes from an insane world only by hanging himself. As a prologue, Piscator provided a newsreel review of the past nine years of world events. The rest of the action alternated between scenes on stage and film episodes. Two movie screens were used, one behind the other, the front one being, on occasion, transparent.

For *Rasputin,* in the same year, Piscator used three film projectors and two thousand meters of film. The stage setting resembled a segment of a globe that opened in sections and turned on a revolving platform. The globe itself formed one projection screen, another screen hung above it, while at one side of the stage, a narrow filmic "calendar" kept marginal notes on the multitude of events of World War I. At times captions were superimposed on the film as it ran along. Thus, over a shot of the battle of the Somme, there appeared the words, "Loss—a half-million dead; gain—three hundred square kilometers."

The Good Soldier Schweik was also produced in 1927, which recounts the adventures of a sly peasant soldier, a Czech conscript who endured all the horrors of World War I, including its hopelessly snarled red tape. Under Piscator's direction, two treadmills, placed parallel to the footlights, formed the depth of the stage and brought scraps of settings on and off. Behind the treadmills, a translucent projection screen was provided for the anti-militarist animated cartoons of George Grosz and for movie sequences showing the road which Schweik traveled on his famous march to Budweis. In addition, full-size cut-out cartoons of freight cars and soldiers passed by on the treadmills.

Leo Lania's *Competition* (1928), also staged by Piscator, told what happens when an oil well is discovered and two international oil concerns begin a ruthless competition. The play opens on a bare stage. Three travelers lie down to sleep. They discover oil, hammer a crude stake into the stage floor. Now begins the sale of parts of the stage. Large signs go up as the rival companies fence off with barbed wire. The drillers arrive, followed by loads of lumber for the derricks which are erected then and there. Finally, the stage is crowded with oil derricks.

Piscator's experiments were matched, in the same era, by those of the dramatist-director Bertolt Brecht. Brecht's *Threepenny Opera* had, as a permanent background, a pipe-organ outlined in electric lights. A small orchestra occupied the middle of the stage. The *Opera* employed free-standing pieces of scenery, including iron-barred prison cages and a long stairway on casters. Unlike Piscator, Brecht never resorted to films on the stage, but like Piscator, he did make use of projection screens, usually placed on either side of the stage, or above the actors' heads. Explanatory titles and illustrations were shown on these screens. Thus, the stable in Soho, London, for the wedding scene of the *Threepenny Opera*, had the projected title: "Deep in the heart of Soho, the bandit

Macheath celebrates his marriage to Polly Peachum, daughter of the King of Beggars."

In the New York production of Brecht's *Mother* (1935), a small revolving stage stood just left of stage center and was partitioned through the middle with wooden panels a little more than head high. A projection screen hung above it. At stage right were two grand pianos. The stage was illuminated by visible spotlights hanging in the proscenium opening. Illustrations and information were flashed on the screen; a photo of the factory where the workers were employed, a portrait of the owner of the factory, a list of food prices in Mother's untutored hand. The Hollywood, California, production of Brecht's *Galileo* (1947) also contained projections; these consisted of illustrations taken from Galileo's book, *I Dialoghi*. Introductory titles for each of the scenes were thrown on a half-curtain that was used to mask scene shifts.

The half-curtains strung on wires across the stage became a feature of Brecht's staging, much as the film sequences typified Piscator. They served again for Brecht's *Mother Courage and Her Children,* a play which may well be remembered as Brecht's finest work and very likely as one of the great dramas of this century. *Mother Courage* was produced in Zurich in 1941 and in East Berlin in 1949. It is still in the repertory of the Berliner Ensemble, a company devoted to the production of Brecht's plays and plays of the Epic style. Its story is that of the market woman, Anna Fierling, who follows the armies of King Charles X of Sweden during the Thirty Years' War, losing her three children in the course of many adventures. As directed by Brecht and Erich Engel, this production contains no settings in the ordinary sense, only stage properties. Of these, the most important is Mother Courage's market wagon, which rolls on from year to year and country to country, maintaining its place against the movement of a huge revolving stage. There is no background except a bare plaster cyclorama, but when a more enclosed

283

quality is needed, curtains or rough cloth are hung from visible battens upstage. The many locales of the action are indicated by means of names woven out of tree branches and let down from the fly-gallery above. The lighting is entirely uncolored. For the song numbers the actors took a "singing position" downstage and at the same time there is lowered from the flies a special property made up of battle drums, flags, trumpets, and three or four illuminated glass globes. As the war drags on, this "prop" becomes dusty and battle-stained and the glass globes are broken and left unlit.

New York recently saw an example of Epic design in the settings for Duerrenmatt's *The Visit* (1958). These consisted in part of a backdrop painted with deliberate crudity to indicate a small town, before which appeared mere scraps of scenery—the façade of a small railway station, the counter of a grocery store, the balcony of a hotel. Cut-out lettering, let down from above, named each locale specifically.

In collaboration with Heinrich Kilger, Teo Otto, the designer of *The Visit,* also did the settings for *Mother Courage.* Other European artists who have worked in the Epic style besides the Swiss Otto, include, most notably, Caspar Neher, designer of the original *Threepenny Opera* and a number of other Brechtian dramas including *The Rise and Fall of the City of Mahagonny* (1929), *Galileo* (Berlin, 1957), the Brechtian *Antigone* (Chur, Switzerland, 1948), *Herr Puntila and His Handyman Matti* (Berlin, 1949), *The Tutor* (Berlin, 1950), and *Mother* (Berlin, 1951). Since the founding of the Berliner Ensemble, several new designers have been initiated into the Epic method, principally Karl von Appen, who contributed settings for Brecht's *The Good Woman of Setzuan* (1957) and *The Caucasian Chalk Circle* (1954), Farquhar's *Drums and Trumpets,* (*The Recruiting Officer,* 1955), Vishnevski's *The Optimistic Tragedy* (1958), and Synge's *The Playboy of the Western World* (1956).

To my knowledge the first original Epic settings by an American were my own, for the New York production of Brecht's *Mother*, already described. I have been given little further opportunity to work in Epic style on Broadway. However, my designs for the off-Broadway *Volpone* were in the Epic tradition, as were my settings for Gazzo's *A Hatful of Rain* (1955). In the latter production, a tenement flat in Manhattan was indicated by means of screenlike walls and a kitchen on a raked platform; an iron ladder and a fire escape led up from each side of the stage, and a skylight hung independently over a hallway area. My designs for *They Shall Not Die* by John Wexley, were an Epic project in 1934 never realized on the stage.

During the era of Federal Theatre, the Living Newspaper unit, in dramatizing topical events and statistics, made use of fragmentary settings, projections, and film sequences, borrowing freely from the pioneer work of Piscator. Especially noteworthy was the work of Hjalmar Hermanson for *Triple A Plowed Under* (1936) and Howard Bay's *One Third of a Nation* (1938).

During his American period at the Dramatic Workshop (the school which he founded in New York), Piscator carried out a number of productions of unusual interest scenically. The settings for Pogodin's *Aristocrats* (1945) consisted mainly of changing projections on a group of screens. Klabund's *The Circle of Chalk* (1941) had an arrangement of Venetian blinds. Robert Penn Warren's *All the King's Men* (1948) made use of a spiral staircase flanked by projection screens and supplemented by mobile platforms. Piscator has since put on a new series of experimental productions in Western Germany and elsewhere in Europe. His staging of Miller's *The Crucible* (1954), Faulkner's *Requiem for a Nun* (1955) and Tolstoy's *War and Peace* (1955) featured translucent platforms jutting into the center of the auditorium and lighted from below. In the case of *War and Peace,* the stage

285

floor had sectional maps of Europe projected on it from underneath.

Scene design in the professional theatre in the United States today is mainly in the tradition of selective Naturalism, varied by Theatricalism in its more imaginative work. But some tendencies toward Epic may be noted. These recent trends may be related to the work of Brecht and Piscator only by coincidence, but whether coincidental or not, they are noteworthy. Thus it is now common practice for American musi-comedies to use fragments of settings working arbitrarily in space in front of more permanent backdrops. A parallel to the method of Piscator's *Competition* may be seen in the design by Peter Larkin for the construction of a teahouse on stage in *The Teahouse of the August Moon* (1953). Boris Aronson's setting for *J.B.* (1959), while Theatricalist in conception, utilized furniture and properties with Epic precision. Even more Epic in quality were Jo Mielziner's settings for *Cat On A Hot Tin Roof* (1955) and *Sweet Bird of Youth* (1959). Working with the boldly imaginative director Elia Kazan, Mielziner began in these plays to push beyond Theatricalism. His designs remained romantic and had a confusing residue of Theatricalist make-believe (as in the use of invisible doors and the invisible pull-cords of the Venetian blinds); but he proceeded nevertheless to the free use of properties and furniture in space, and to the reduction of environment to a "report" (projections of porch, columns and fireworks in *Cat* and projections of Venetian blinds, palm trees and seascapes in *Bird*). Specifically and tellingly Epic was Kazan's use of a television sequence in *Bird,* in which a demagog and his henchmen were shown in action. This scenic element was no mere novelty but a legitimate device for an Epic widening of Williams' story. Similarly, a projected sequence of this sort occurred in a now forgotten play, *Spread Eagle* by George S. Brooks and Walter B. Lister. As directed by Jed Harris in 1927, with settings by Norman Bel

286

Geddes, this unusual Broadway drama, epic in scope, included a scene of a film-showing in a movie theatre in order to illustrate the use of high-powered propaganda in drumming a nation into war.

The scenic innovations of Epic Theatre have attracted attention and are undoubtedly influencing world theatre. But they are more than novelties or bright ideas. On the contrary, they are the product of a whole new philosophy of production, part of a theatre larger in scope than the theatre of today. Piscator resorted to projected comment and film shorts in order to make up for the deficiency of his scripts, which were written in the prevailing Naturalistic or Romantic style. In an attempt to add historic perspective to these scripts he wove in movie sequences which gave some of the background of the stage events and used projected captions which started trains of thought not suggested by the dialogue. Seeking this wider view, Piscator rebelled against the concentration of the single setting; instead he tended to break up the action into a flowing movement of a great many scenes. His adaptation of Tolstoy's *War and Peace,* with its forty-five scenes, could almost serve as a film-shooting script. In view of the demands he has made upon the scene-shifting mechanism of the stage, it is not surprising that Piscator finds today's stage machinery out of date. There is no reason, he thinks, why the modern stage should not be as beautifully equipped as the modern factory. No doubt he looked forward to the automated stage.

Brecht was less interested in the use of stage machinery than Piscator, but he too objected to the "well-made" play and its Naturalistic setting. These he considered not only old-fashioned but part of a "magical" technique for tricking an audience into a cheap emotional jag. The principle of alienation underlies not only Brecht's writings but the kind of scenic production his plays require. He wishes to "alienate," to "cool off" the dramatic story, to "hold it at arm's length,"

287

so to speak. In this way he hoped to make audiences more reflective and critical, to keep them from being "entranced" by a curiously exciting, over-emotional empathy. His use of lettered comment or of projected titles summarizing the action of each scene in advance, was intended mainly to put a brake on such excitement. Any director in quest of excitement and emotion would tear his hair at these recommendations. But Brecht was not interested in "schmaltz." He called his own dramas "learning-plays," and did not hesitate to declare that pedagogy is the true purpose of drama.

Scenically, Brecht rejected not only Naturalism but the picturesque, atmospheric stage picture as well. Instead of surrounding his actors with an atmospheric reproduction of a locale he asked his scene designers to proceed by what he called "the inductive instead of the deductive" method. This meant, in practice, to begin by giving the actors the furniture and properties necessary for the action, following up with a "report on the environment." The "reports" are painted or projected tokens of locale; a photograph or framed picture of a house, town, or countryside; a drop so obviously painted that it cannot create any illusion; the name of a town in cut-out lettering hung over the stage. All in all, the Epic setting becomes so utterly functional that it cannot be distinguished from an organized group of stage properties. Even a whole house on stage retains the quality of a stage "prop."

Such an approach runs head-on into the doctrine of theatrical *synthesis* as formulated by Richard Wagner and endorsed by artists like Gordon Craig, Adolphe Appia and Robert Edmond Jones. Brecht was not disposed to soften the impact of that collision. Instead, he demanded that *autonomy* be restored to all the production elements, including the setting. The setting must not be allowed, he said, to blend "magically" with the costumes, lighting, properties, music and acting in order to create an overwhelming emotional experience. Rather, the setting, and each of the other elements of staging

288

ought to function autonomously, in the same manner as the elements of a scientific lecture-demonstration, in which the retorts and Bunsen burners are utilized as they become necessary.

The cyclorama, or sky drop, with its suggestion of infinite space, is banished from the Epic setting, which is *sachlich* or finite. Furniture, pieces of rooms, sections of walls, doors or windows—sometimes without surrounding walls—may be used to serve the action. The stage lighting, employing, usually, only naked white light, does not pretend to be sunlight, moonlight or the glow of a fireplace or lamp. Stage light may be colored in primitive fashion, however: a simple blue tone, perhaps to indicate night, or a color to distinguish an event, as amber when a song is sung, or pink to illuminate the visiting Chinese gods in *The Good Woman of Setzuan*.

While Epic design may be new in some of its aspects, it lays no claim to being unprecedented. In common with Theatricalism, it accepts the platform stage as against the picture stage, and it shares with Theatricalism the opinion that the setting must be a frank scenic construction or apparatus, not an imitation—however selective—of "life itself." But Epic design is in greater accord with the Chinese and Japanese Theatricalism than with any European Theatricalist tradition. The oriental influence upon Epic is evident in its clean-cut functionalism and its appreciation of the unadorned textures of wood, stone, metal, plaster and fibre. Epic design differs from both eastern and western Theatricalism in insisting that everything scenic that appears on the stage must be "the object itself," not an illusion of the object. Thus, a backdrop must never pretend to be anything but painted cloth; an electric bulb may be used to represent a star, but must not give the illusion of a star. Nor must anything be theatrically stylized: a Baroque door, an Empire chair, a Victorian wardrobe, must all have historic and geographic

289

documentation, even if the door stands on the open stage without a wall around it.

Epic goes beyond all previous styles in its emphasis on function. But it should be remembered that good scene design in any style knows that it must justify its presence on stage, and that the designer who does not help the actors is nothing but an interloper. In *My Life In Art* Stanislavsky declared that he would rather have one good armchair on stage than all the backdrops painted for his theatre by the best artists in Russia. He was exaggerating, of course, but the remark is to the point. It should be added that Epic design is by no means casual, disorderly or poverty-stricken. It requires at least as much organization and care as any previous method, and can be equally rich and colorful. Almost always, it is more dynamic than its predecessors.

For those who become intrigued with the scenic novelties of Epic Theatre, a word of warning may be necessary. Epic is an honest attempt to bring some of the principles of science into the theatre. It is not intended to be a snobbish exercise for "brilliant" designers or directors nor a new plaything for technicians who are keen on "experiment." A designer does not automatically become gifted and modern if he makes use of projections or half-curtains on a wire; indeed there is always the possibility that a designer with a genuine feeling for Naturalism or Theatricalism may be out of his element with Epic. The half-curtain, the movie sequence, the projected titles, happen to be the personal trademarks of Brecht and Piscator. They are not a guarantee that we are witnessing an Epic production. They are what Brecht himself called *primitive* Epic design—first steps toward a technique that may someday embody, in scenic form, the principles of a classic, scientifically-minded theatre of the future.

No one can foresee what Epic design will look like eventually. Since it departs radically from current practices, and since it has a genuine philosophic basis, it opens a whole new field of scenic invention. Most striking is its scientific bent. I once indicated, for a town square in Brecht's *Round Heads and Peaked Heads,* a collection of shopkeepers' signs hung over the center of the stage. "The Gorelik effect," Brecht called it, after he had used it and found it effective. He proposed very seriously to begin cataloging scenic effects of proven worth as contributions to a classic future form of stage setting. The very notion of such a catalogue will, no doubt, horrify many talented designers, but there may be others, equally talented, who will not feel that there is an impassable barrier between art and science. Indeed, they may find that the reverse is true: the spirit of science may yet enable scenic art to reach new levels of imagination.

SCENE DESIGN: AN EVALUATION

by

Howard Bay

In this appraisal of scene design and the position of the scene designer in the professional theatre since World War II, Howard Bay reveals that as a result of queer and twisted economics on Broadway today, the artist is forced to contend with an attitude of lavishness and wastefulness that has no rational or practical approach to theatrical art. Incongruously, Mr. Bay laments, this approach has developed a conservative attitude on the part of the producers which is currently responsible for the lack of innovation and experimentation in American scene design. This evaluation appeared in THEATRE ARTS (March, 1953, pp. 66-69) in a slightly longer version under the title "Settings . . . by Howard Bay." The conclusion was revised for this anthology.

Scenery hasn't rated much discussion since the 1920's when American stage design was supposed to have had its poetic birth. That was where I came in and I still bear the scars. The minds of all young designers of that era were warped and twisted with Expressionism, Constructivism, Illusionism and such tall talk.

By the thirties, the expansive projects for *Hamlet* simmered down to one commercial style: a few tasteful objects of furniture properly spaced against a fuzzy, Constable-Turner type watercolor—a monochrome of sepia or soft blue, what George Jean Nathan referred to as "Beekman Place refinement." It was labeled "selective realism." It still is. It isn't a trend anymore, it is just a fact of life.

With the depression of the early thirties came the Federal Theatre; and no such rough and ready hypodermic has even grazed the theatre since. New and untraditional problems faced the designers. I was pitched into the most dramaturgically unconventional division, the Living Newspaper. The novelty of not considering the existence of graceful furnishings—only the direct delivery of ideas by any handy means—projections, films, cartoons, blow-up props, vaudeville, olios. The four-story set of *One Third of a Nation* was built mainly out of gifts from the Tenement Demolition Department; the pipe framework of the stage tenement was rented for $75 a week. And yet the production generated an excitement that can only be matched today with continuous music and countless girls.

Designers are also type-cast. It looked for a time as if I

293

might spend the rest of my life manufacturing slums or similar grim locales. The word went around Times Square that if you really wanted to depress an audience (for whatever high-minded reason), Howard Bay was the man for the sets. I created an abandoned factory, corroded like Swiss cheese, for *Marching Song* and a snaky mass of gas meters in a Daliesque pattern for *Brooklyn, U.S.A.*

Others were caught up in this trend. Norman Bel Geddes made the rotting wharves for *Dead End;* Harry Horner created the perspiring bedlam of a laundry for *The World We Make;* Boris Aronson contrived the crawly Turkish bath for *The Gentle People* and Herman Rosse the seamy backsides of billboards for *The Great Magoo.*

This intense, often lyrical, hyper-realism matched the plays for which it was designed; but such plays began to lose their vogue when World War II began. You still see one once in a while and the sets to match, Horace Armistead's design for *The Medium* being the latter-day standout.

The sharp edges of design were softened and rounded off, and designers—in keeping with the plays—returned to a more pictorial concentration. Fragments in space such as Jo Mielziner's *Dream Girl,* George Jenkins' *I Remember Mama,* my own *Eve of St. Mark* and *The Patriots*—all of these were more polished and self-contained, extending the genre that began in the twenties with Lee Simonson's *Goat Song.*

Often the design of a scene became only a chair and a table and a shaft of light; and it reflected the episodic, often cinematic, writing of a few playwrights of the forties.

But trends come and go, and today you are likely to find the normal interior—an attempt by designers to wring out the maximum mood from an accumulation of a few painted flats, furniture, drapes and an assortment of the right knick-knacks. The scenic designer less than the movie art director falls into the rut of neutral architecture and the fetish for research; the tradition of stage design is angled towards a particular environment created for the spirit of a specific script. Only the challenge of a drama with stature can derail the penchant for dressing the stage with pretty rooms filled with tasteful antiques. The difference is illustrated by the stage and film versions of *The Little Foxes*. The film was embellished with a grand, consistently Southern mansion that would have served nicely for *Gone With The Wind*. In the theatre setting, I mixed a less elegant ensemble, combining not only the standard Southern inheritance but the *nouveau riche* aping of the latest from the Northern drawing rooms. It wasn't as lovely as its movie cousin but it added an insight into that Hubbard clan. But that's one of the better sort of trends and not at all the dominant one. The dominant one is bad and is related to a queer and twisted economics. It has nothing to do with anything except somebody's determination to have an overdressed stage and to hell with the play. And that reflects changed attitudes toward the whole business of producing a show. Years ago, the producing manager was a showman whose detailed backstage knowledge was carefully brought to bear on every item of production. And that made good sense: it was a way of assuring that the showman's business could have a reasonable chance of continuing from show to show and from season to season.

Naturally, a showman had advantages then that he wouldn't have nowadays. He had a healthy road business, and the people who worked for him couldn't be lured away by the promise of television monies.

During World War II a new kind of showman began to emerge—loaded with war money. This new "showman" was actually a producer-promoter who had neither the experience nor the desire to keep costs down. The sheer size of the show had the wastefulness with which the money was used—how many kickbacks were made and how many nests were lined that had little or nothing to do with the good of show business or its healthy development.

295

Scene Design: An Evaluation

The war and the easy money have long since been left behind, but the *attitude* remains, and many producer-promoters remain. Let's face it: musicals aside, the hits of 1953 are compounded of sensationalists, so-called "off-beat" elements—with stars. If the script is weak, two stars are thrown in, along with a flossy production. And yet the first complaint, and the loudest, made in the theatre today is that production costs are too high. So they are, but no one makes any real attempt to fix the blame or look for remedies.

The complainers are the old-line managers who put on as good a play as they always did but can't explain why there is no public. They blame the high costs, in which of course the public has to share by paying to see the play. And they blame anybody who comes into their heads as responsible for the high costs. But underneath all this is still the attitude of the producer-promoter that lavishness is the thing, that wastefulness doesn't matter. The result is that no rational and practical approach to the cost of a show is made at all.

Actually, a healthy saving on the physical production costs can be insured by careful planning and by feeding the work to the execution shops in the slack periods. But this is ruled out because the theatre is geared to a one-show economy. The last-minute scramble for backers of one show leaves no leeway for bargaining. Goodly savings would inevitably flow from a producers' jointly owned warehouse of costly bulk such as platforms, portals and the like. Designers have no urge to dissipate funds on neutral yardage of masking or step units but would rather use the money on items unique to a given production.

Beyond the obvious relief through careful planning, plus imaginative ideas, plus simplification of backstage running operations, a more elusive problem lies: Designers push out front their own trademark brand of commercial artist's self-advertising. Superfluous display and exhibitionism stem from the elementary fact that for all the loose talk in the abstract about the virtues of unobtrusive scenery and "imagination," the notices and the prizes fall on the show-off pieces. The designer is willy-nilly an entry in the race for credits. We all cram scrapbooks with appreciations of engineering marvels; but I for one would rather hear a little more about the incisive economy of the set and lighting for *The Shrike,* for instance, which I designed. The Pulitzer prize play was written as a multi-scened script and any amount of wagons and gauzes could have tricked up the stage; and only the author, the director and the designer would know why the concentration and rhythm of the drama was dissipated by the costly gimmicks.

I have the sneaky feeling that despite all our ingenuity and technical polish American scenic design is coasting. Our busy craft cannot pause to take note of the lack of any true innovations for over a decade. The easy retort is that current dramaturgy is not ploughing any virgin ground and we scenic artisans are simply dutiful interpretive handmaidens. So be it, but there are other factors: the most obvious stemming from the timidity of managers in buying the safe product—a comfy replica of countless other settings. Beyond this brake on experiment is the curious isolation of our craft from the contemporary arts generally. The visual revolution that has pulverized and dispersed the solid, permanent object has shaken painting and sculpture right out of the tradition. We makers of scenery stand on the sidelines and find no point of contact with an artistic attitude that sweeps away our firm stage floor and our very naturalistic actors anchored to that floor. We do lift scraps of surface style now and then— mainly the transparency and the fragment-symbol-for-the- whole-object—but basically we are back there with the beginnings of Impressionism. Embroidering variations of nostalgia is our bread and butter, but this anachronistic

297

suspension in the middle of the twentieth century will be broken only when we find ways and means of getting with it. We must find our methods of handling modern visual thinking that will complement and not destroy the human figure. In short, surround them with a present day environment.

SCENE DESIGN AND THEATRE

by

Eugene Berman

Mr. Berman wrote this introduction for this anthology.

The following article was written in Milan in 1956 while I was working on the production of Cosi fan Tutte *for the Piccola Scala in response to a request by my friends, the architects Guido Frette and Carlo Emilio Rava, to express my views on stage design for the Italian architectural magazine PROSPETTIVE (No. 12, 1956, pp. 67-80). In translating this letter-article from Italian to English three years later, I felt a certain amount of editing was desirable for the inclusion in an American anthology on scene design. Certain passages that had a specific interest for Italian readers could be eliminated or shortened while others dealing with scene design in America should be expanded for the benefit of the American readers.*

Another reason for editing the original article was my decision to retire from active stage designing after completing the production of Don Giovanni *for the Metropolitan in November of 1957. The views of a retired artist must necessarily acquire a deeper sense of perspective and*

300

Eugene Berman

a greater finality of judgment. I also felt that in some ways I could now speak more frankly and freely on certain matters and without too much preoccupation of the sensitivities of former friends, colleagues and competitors in the profession. Finally, I wish to state that the views expressed here, which constitute a summing up of my past experiences, ideas and conclusions, are still my credo after twenty years of active work in the theatre. This article, coupled with the one I wrote for the SATURDAY REVIEW OF LITERATURE at the time of my work on Don Giovanni *(which is also reprinted here) constitutes a sort of artistic testament on my part, to which I believe, nothing else needs presently to be added.*

E. B.

Rome, May, 1959.

My dear Frette:[1]

I respond to your request for an article on my ideas on the theatre with a letter.

My task will be made much easier that way—one can skip and jump from one idea to another without a preconceived plan or order, exactly as when we were having those nice meetings in Milan at the time I was working at La Scala and we had so many questions and answers to throw at each other. So let's pretend this is another of our animated debates and I am imagining the things you would like to talk about.

The theatre has always fascinated me. As a very young boy I saw magnificent spectacles at the Imperial theatre in my native St. Petersburg and on travel abroad and later, when I left Russia in 1919 to follow my family to Paris and live there from 1919 to 1940 I hardly missed any of the new crea-

---

[1] Guido Frette, Italian architect, author, and expert critic on stage design, lives in Milan. Formerly editor of the section on stage design for the magazine, *Prospettive,* he currently is editing the same department for the Italian magazine, *Sipario.*

301

tions of the famous Ballet Russe of Diaghilev until his death and the disbanding of his company in 1928. Add to this many dramatic productions seen in Russia, France and Germany in childhood and early youth (the Alexandrainsky Drama Theatre in St. Petersburg, Stanislavsky, Meyerhold, Reinhardt, Brecht, Dullin, Jouvet, the Comédie Française, etc.) and as much opera as I could take in in the various places of residence or travel and you will see that the amount of beautiful and exciting theatre I did see in my formative years was truly imposing and inspiring. And what was all important to an aspiring young painter in most of these spectacles was the novelty and artistic quality of the stage design.

In Russia and in Europe the best stage designers of the period were of a new type . . . a revolution was taking place everywhere and the old fashioned professional stage specialists were being replaced by young, ardent, avant-garde painters. Especially in the field of ballet this revolution bore spectacular results in the years 1910-1914. After World War I the revolution instigated by Diaghilev continued and the new Russian designers (such as Bakst, Benois, Golovine, Roerich, etc.) were in turn discarded by the famous impresario and we saw settings and costumes designed by Picasso, Braque, Matisse, Rouault, Derain, Utrillo, Miro, Ernst, de Chirico, Larionov and others. So it was only natural that with my early interest in the theatre and its music and seeing these fabulous spectacles created by the artistic elite of Russia and of Western Europe with the brilliant contributions of all the best and most advanced painters elsewhere, I would consider stage design as a most desirable and fascinating part of my calling as a painter and eagerly prepared myself to become one day one of the new designers for the stage. And quite a few of my young comrades of that period, like Tchelitchev and Berard, to name only the most outstanding of our group, had the same desire and ambition.

But if a strong impulse to become simultaneously a painter

302

and a stage designer was given by the spectacular and new productions of the Diaghilev Ballet and some others, the greatest influence upon my development as a stage designer was exercised on me by a completely different source—by the architectural works of Palladio and his Teatro Olimpico in Vicenza.

For a young man who had his earliest artistic training in Russia in contact with Russian architects and theatre designers, this was almost inevitable. Palladio was not only well-known to all of them, through his books on architecture, his illustrations, engravings and other documents, actually he never ceased to be a dominating influence on Russian architectural education and thinking. For anyone planning a trip to Italy, Vicenza, the town of the great master, was one of the high spots of such a voyage, while in Paris and most of the rest of Western Europe, Palladio was then almost unknown or forgotten. Thus, when I was able to start from Paris on my first trip to Italy in 1922, one of my very first stops was Vicenza to see the buildings of the great man and his famous Teatro Olimpico. That became the A.B.C.'s of my ideas on the theatre and the foundation of my future craft as a stage designer. It also became the foundation of Berard's treatment of space and scenic illusion. Later it influenced Dali in his stage work and many others. Hardly any of the stage designers active today in America or in Europe have not followed the Palladian trend or have failed to discover through our work the ideas and concepts of the great architect from Vicenza.

I do realize, of course, that there are other ideas, other principles, other methods of devising the space on the stage and of creating a setting for a play, a drama or a ballet. But they are not for me. I believe in a world of poetic illusion and of imaginary reality in both painting and on the stage. I believe that the combination of carefully studied and constructed perspective in depth, of painted canvas, of architectural and plastic elements when they can be of

303

greatest effect and practical use and based on a true poetic feeling and understanding of the subject to be represented, constitutes the foundation of both classic and modern stage design. Naturally, there are many possible deviations to this approach. Many successful and at times, brilliant modern productions have ignored these principles and achieved spectacular results. The Russian constructivistic theatre of the twenties and early thirties may have seen some of the most interesting experimentation of new plastic means and abstract thinking; at times approached by not unsimilar German experimentation in the field of expressionist or abstract scene designing. But that seems to have been a short-lived trend which possibly may be revived in the near future since much of modern art of today is busily taking new inspiration from earlier trends in this century.

Many earlier production designs, especially in America, have been based upon the ideas and themes devised by Gordon Craig and Adolphe Appia; all of the much publicized recent Bayreuth productions of the Wagner boys stem from these unmistakably very important sources. I must admit that I have never been really impressed or convinced by these ideas and trends. The Appia, Craig, Bel Geddes and other schemes of colossal nude platforms, of massive forbidding columns or steps have always seemed gloomy, rigid and depressing in their puritanistic primness and intellectual intolerance. I could never separate such stagework from a comparison with the dreadful Fascist and Nazi architecture of the twenties and thirties, so arrogant, clumsy and dated at the moment of its greatest popularity and expansion in Italy and Germany. That the same style, the same approach, the same dated ideas could presently be regarded as a new trend in opera design and achieve spectacular success in Bayreuth is absolutely beyond me. I can only explain this as a sign of abysmal drop in public taste and intelligence.

But let us return to the beginning: I believe that the modern stage designer should be something of a universal artist; a painter (and a real one who keeps experimenting in the field of painting and does not give it up as soon as he achieves some degree of success in the theatre), an architect, an inventor, a perspectivist, a good scholar of the history of art, a competent judge of styles and periods, an able costume designer, something of a costumier, milliner, interior decorator, or furniture designer and above all, a true man of the theatre with a poet's mind and imagination. Last, but not least, a man of practical views and methods, capable of dealing with the thousand and one material difficulties and limitations of the stage, with forbidding regulations, insufficient budgets and allowances, with problems of outside help and collaboration. He must be a tough but able diplomat. Most certainly, he must also be something of a stage director.

On this last qualification I have had numerous discussions with my Italian colleagues and friends while I was working in Milan. They frequently argued that the painter is almost always the best director of an opera and that many productions would be better staged if directed by the painter himself, a point on which there are many pros and cons. Indeed, among the successful stage or movie directors we have a few who started out as scenic designers and to whom this graduation seemed quite a natural step. Especially in the field of serious opera (meaning the musical drama) the painter can at times be considered the creator of the complete concept. The pictorial and poetic atmosphere that is seen at the rise of the curtain and through each following act or scene, the treatment of space, the placement of the singers and the masses, the whole plastic conception of each scene, its depth and various levels; all these elements can stem from the designer's imagination and his ability to create a setting in which the action will develop, good or bad, clear or confused. Well planned, well imagined or evocated, the scene will permit the stage director to play

305

on velvet, to use successfully every possibility, every advantage offered to him by the helpful combinations and situations devised by the painter-designer. In such cases, it is the painter who is the guiding spirit of the production. Such a situation, however, although quite desirable, is rather exceptional and known stage settings capable of such prowess are few.

On the other hand we know of excellent directors who have very clear and imaginative ideas of how a scene should be conceived in order to achieve a strong dramatic unity of action and are able to get the desired setting and effects from painters who lacked the infinite vision of how a scene should develop dramatically. In this case, it is obvious that the stage director is the real leader or inventor and that the painter follows. And still there are other cases, where stage direction is a completely balanced merger between director and designer who are so receptive to each other's ideas and suggestions that the staging is a piece of complete collaboration and understanding—a give and take of the best each artist has to offer. I believe this is the best that can happen to an important stage production and perhaps it is because such an encounter is so rare that so few operatic productions can be readily viewed as completely satisfying.

Even if we for a moment turn our back on operatic drama and consider comic opera and the dramatic theatre, where the contributions of the stage director obviously should be more predominant, we still will have to give the painter-designer credit and proclaim that in many outstanding contemporary productions it was the designer who contributed the lion's share to the success of the production. I need only recall the two beautifully staged productions of Molière plays, *L'Ecole des femmes* by Jouvet, and *Les Fourberies de Scapin* by Barrault. In both cases the settings and costumes were designed by the late Christian Berard whom I consider the best and most competent stage designer of our times. I am not able to swear that the initial idea and plan of each production was originated by Berard and not the fruit of an ideal meeting of two exceptionally creative and imaginative theatrical minds but in both cases, at the very rise of the curtain it was clear that the ideal locale and mood were firmly established and the final triumph already achieved. And when I recall so many other spectacles and productions by both Jouvet and Barrault—spectacles which range excellent and good to fair and acceptable, but almost never achieved that magical enchantment which was Berard's top secret weapon—then I am compelled to conclude that it was Berard who was the guiding force in the French theatre of the late twenties and the thirties, and that without his collaboration, the best effort of these two great French directors never quite achieved the beauty and integration which he managed to command so frequently in his best years. I can recall only one instance when Jouvet produced a sensationally spectacular staging without Berard, but that was when he had the collaboration of another of the greatest stage designing talents of our time—the Russian Pavel Tchelitchev —for the production of the Giraudoux play, *Ondine*.

Now let us turn to two points which seem important to me. First, the rapport between the designer and the actual sketches and their translation into scenic reality—the settings and costumes which the spectators will see behind the footlights. Many contemporary painter-designers create their sketches in great haste and fury (sometimes limiting themselves to very approximative jottings and notes), and once they have consigned these sketches to the executors—those professional scenic painters and costumiers who will carry out their ideas and their designs—very few show a great desire or urge to participate further in this final stage of translating the initial ideas into stage reality. Some designers, especially successful Broadway designers, are by this time already busy with some other new project, while others don't think it is important enough to watch and to hover over this rather tedious and drawn out part of the production. Often, the supervision of the execution is given over to assistants, who in turn may have other assistants to take charge of what they consider above their dignity of doing themselves. The result is that the true personal artistic statement (if the designer has any to begin with) can rarely survive effectively that process of delegating power and control to other people instead of facing that very grim reality that nothing that looks good in sketches and on paper is necessarily good on stage unless the artist himself has controlled every part and bit of his production and feels that this is the very best and the most exact translation into final scenic being of his often hastily and not completely defined idea.

The reason, or excuse, most often advanced by such designers is that the professional scenic painter, costumier and other collaborators and "executors" who must necessarily take over are so expert and able, that all will go well or even better, if the designer leaves everything to their capacity and judgment. No one denies, of course, that the success of a scenic production depends to a considerable extent on the ability and quality of the "executors," that is to say, of the painters who will paint the scenery, of the costumier or dressmaker who will take charge of the costumes, of the electricians who will handle the lighting, and so down the line. Good executors can make mediocre designs look good and bad ones can ruin the best ideas and sketches. And it is only proper that at the beginning of his career, the young designer should be guided and illuminated by the experience and competence of capable executors, in order to arrive eventually at a clear and precise understanding of the techniques and methods best suited to realize his ideas and of his own painting or designing techniques into stage reality. That apprenticeship is the very best school an aspiring designer could possibly have; it is only through it that his true theatrical personality can

308

be formed and evolved, and even a mature and experienced designer will gain in quality and richness of imagination through repeated similar experiences. His evolution as a creative artist can only expand with each renewed contact and struggles with the ways and means of handling every successful stage production, with improved and fresh ideas resulting from his previous work.

To renounce this invaluable experience and not wish to interest oneself in this really crucial part of theatrical work, not only seems absurd to me but positively dishonest. Imagine an architect who would limit himself to approximative sketches of the edifice he is building and not share in the preparation of the precise plans, elevations, calculations and all the other work which must be vigorously controlled before the building is erected, or the mural painter who would only make a sketch for his fresco and leave all the real work to assistants and collaborators without participating actively in what will be the true or untrue rendering of his initial ideas. Or a composer (and by that I do not mean the talented composers of Broadway musicals and songs) who could not or would not orchestrate their own scores but would call in some experienced specialist to do this most important and integral part of the work for them.

To throw down some attractive dashes of colors and produce some effective but vague sketches of settings and costumes is fairly easy and simple, but to create on stage a setting which would give life, vitality and a soul to an opera, a drama, a comedy or a ballet is altogether a different thing. Therefore it is in the translation of a good sketch into an even better and enormously constructive and effective theatrical reality that the real mystery of good stage work lies.

All the modern painters who have contributed to the substitution of the traditional and unimaginative stage design of the end of the nineteenth century and the first years of the present century by the new art full of fresh and stimulat-

309

ing ideas were profoundly interested in the theatre and came, through personal experience and involvement in every part of theatrical work, to understand it completely. Let me cite a few examples at random. When Picasso designed *Parade,* his first ballet for Diaghilev, he came to the scenic studio with a group of cubist-painter friends and with their aid he painted the famous *Parade* curtain. Thus, it became an invaluable museum piece later. He repeated the same process on the decors or curtains for other Diaghilev spectacles. Parts of his *Quadro Flamenco* decor, and other similar pieces were also painted by his own hand and have been sold, exhibited and collected as original Picasso paintings, which they are. I have seen Chagall, when he was creating the decor and costumes for Ballet Theatre's *Aleko* in Mexico City, slip secretly into the company wardrobe room and repaint costumes and masks because he was not quite satisfied with the way they had been executed and because he felt that only his personal touch would give them a true "Chagallesque" look on the stage.

I have done the same thing myself on most of the productions I designed for the opera and ballet. At times, the entire scenery, and others, the essential parts were painted by me, or touched up by my hand. It would take too much time to list here how much of my decors and curtains are essentially 100%, 85% or 50% original Bermans. Tchelitchev and Berard have done the same on a smaller scale but only because their decors were conceived in a way which demanded much less painting and detail work. When that was needed they did not hesitate to do as much as was necessary to give a mask, a costume, or a piece of scenery that inimitable personal touch which was the real signature of their work and which made it a Tchelichev or a Berard original.

In St. Petersburg, Golovine always painted all his scenery himself—every bit of it. It took him a year, sometimes several years to complete one of his productions for the Marinsky Theatre. Larionov did an enormous amount of work on the realization of his ballet decors for Diaghilev and helped with every detail of supervision in the creation of the decors of the ballets and operas designed by Natalia Gontcharova, his wife, who was his most invaluable and critical collaborator. Bakst, Benois, Derain, Braque, Miro and Gris participated actively in the creation of every part of their stage settings and costumes. When I was working for La Scala in Milan in 1956 I saw a similar attitude and concern on the part of the young Italian stage designers who worked for La Scala simultaneously with me. Piero Zuffi and Salvatore Fiume, both of whom created extremely original and and powerful decors, knew exactly what effects they wished to achieve on stage and how to obtain them. Both commanded the execution of their sets and costumes as a captain would guide and command the crew of his ship in difficult waters. I could quote many more names, many more instances of the same professional dignity and integrity on the part of all the better painters and stage designers of our time. But the idea is so clear, the truth so blatant that additional examples are not necessary to further the argument. It should not be very surprising therefore if I react rather strongly against the uses and methods practised presently by the leading American stage designers. It is not their talent and their abilities that I want to disclaim or discredit—but the accepted methods and honored Broadway practices and rules which deprive the American theatre of truly first rate artistic achievements. First of all, the existing and drastic regulations which allow only those designers who are members of the Union of Scenic Designers the right to work for the American theatre. (To join this union is an extremely difficult and rather costly proposition but there is no need to lament this fact any further here.) The result is that many excellent American and foreign painters are discouraged from or afraid to face the difficulties and penalties of attempting to try their hand at scenic design in the United States. And that, of course, is a great shame, because as we all know, the revolution of the decor in our century and all the new and fresh ideas in the theatre have come from the leading painters in Russia, France, Germany and now in Great Britain, Italy and other countries. Having made this statement, I can only add my fervent hope that in the near future conditions will change, therefore affording many more American and foreign painters the opportunity to work in the American theatre and to bring to it new ideas, a greater painting quality, and a greater link with modern art in general.

In Europe it is all part of the game, there are no barriers, no lines of segregation drawn between the purely professional scenic designers (such as Georges Wakhevitch) and the many avant-garde painters who having an occasional active interest in the theatre have proven their value in this field. In my opinion, it would be highly desirable in the United States if the avant-garde painters were allowed to design, for I believe it would create as much of an artistic change in our theatre as that which took place in Western Europe thanks to the initiative of Diaghilev and the contributions of the painters who created his decors.

I am sure that quite a few American painters could design excellent settings and quite different ones from those that we are currently seeing in Broadway productions, probably not any more clever or more efficient, but certainly of a much higher pictorial level and quality of plastic expressivity and invention. (In the domain of solving technical and practical problems of stagecraft the good Broadway designers are probably matchless.) And I can not wait to see the disappearance of the incredibly dated and unproductive cooperation between two designers for each production, one specializing only in decor and the other only in costume. With extremely rare exceptions, this is an absolutely unthinkable division of

312

work anywhere in Europe—no designer worth his salt would submit to such a division of work and admit that he could do only one part—either scenery or costumes—but not both.

I do not remember having ever seen a completely integrated stage production where these two integrated parts of the spectacle were not the brain child of a single mind. After many years of scenic activities in the United States I am still baffled and rather indignant to see that this old distinction which was common practice everywhere in the nineteenth century still successfully (or rather harmfully) survives in America. I very firmly believe that when we will have a crop of new designers on Broadway who are equally capable of doing both parts in completely balanced and integrated creation, and who will refuse to design only one of the two competing parts of a stage production, the American theatre will take a great leap forward in visual creative artistry and really come of age. Until then it is truly artistic only on rare occasions. Foreign visitors to New York, who are almost always completely overwhelmed by the quality and vitality of American plays, American staging and acting, never fail to express their keen disappointment in the visual merits and quality of design which they see on the stage. Sadly enough, I very often reluctantly find myself forced to agree with these unflattering views of the inferior decorative merits of the American theatre. But at the same time it must be truthfully reported and recognized that some of the styles and mechanics devised and created by American designers for modern American plays have been most successfully exported and copied in Europe. This means that only a heightened sense of aesthetic thinking, a higher awareness of artistic imagination and of a pictorial and plastic mastery is needed to bring American stage designing into full bloom and make it equal (if not superior) to the best that Western Europe can presently give us.

Another very grave point is the complete divorcement in

America between the theatre and the creative plastic arts. Take most of our producers, directors and all people who are selecting and directing the productions and plays on Broadway and elsewhere in America: hardly any one of these persons really knows what's going on in the rest of the intellectual and artistic world, with the possible exception of literature, because a book could after all, become the basis of a future play or movie. Even our best writers and stage directors quite often are ignorant of names and values in modern painting. Some of them may know this or that name, drop it at some opening at the Whitney or the Museum of Modern Art, and buy paintings by this or that painter for reasons of prestige or by counsel of some museum director or art dealer friend. But the fact remains that this is done the way other people occasionally buy a new piece of furniture or a rug for their living room. A producer, a writer, a director on Broadway will never say, "I need this painter as designer for this play and no one else will do." He may toy with such an idea awhile to prove to others and to himself that he has enough culture and taste to consider such a possibility but he will inevitably fall back on some well-known and experienced Broadway designer who will offer him the maximum of contrived security and the assured plaudits of the same first night audience who like to see the success of an old consecrated friend or of a new young talent already belonging to the exclusive and insular Broadway set.

In that sense, the best Broadway producers, directors and writers are the most conservative and timorous people I have known and I can only express my hope that this too may change in the near future and that the invisible but very definite cultural iron curtain which separates Broadway thinking from the rest of true American artistic life may soon begin to crumble and completely disappear.

Having completed this side trip to Broadway (because it is significant to the whole of stage designing in America) I

314

want to turn now to a second equally important aspect of stage designing—the merits of stage designs in themselves and their historical value and importance as documents for future generations, attitudes prompted by an interesting and challenging article by the aforementioned young Italian designer, Piero Zuffi (which was recently published in *Prospettive*).[2] Speaking of the stage designer as a man of the theatre, Zuffi observes that a good stage setting must be functional, not too evident, stylistically unified, anti-decorative, anti-mechanical and anti-literary[3]—to which, to a degree I can subscribe myself. But another idea of this designer, I believe, merits special attention. He writes that magnificent decor sketches and stupendous costume designs are not enough to make a beautiful stage production and then proceeds to state that the techniques of some great painters are so personal and demanding that they can easily overshadow the entire work. The true scenic designer, he believes, who is above all, a man of the theatre, although making sketches and

[2] Piero Zuffi, "Scenografio—Uomo di Teatro," *Prospettive*, No. 8 (1954), pp. 65-74. Translated into English under the title, "The Scenic Artist and the Theatre," Zuffi's essay was reprinted in Guido Frette, *Stage Design, 1909-1954*, Milan, G. G. Gorlich, 1956, pp. xxxvii-xl.

[3] Editor's Note: While most of Zuffi's characteristics of a good stage setting seem self-explanatory, perhaps the terms anti-mechanical and anti-literary need explaining. Zuffi explains anti-mechanical by saying it is not advisable to hide all the artifice of the stage, for he believes that it will take away the atmosphere of *make-believe* which is the real poetry of the theatre. However, Zuffi believes it would be even worse to put too much artifice before the eyes of the spectators, or to make them too complex or too artificial. The changes of scenery, he believes, should take place silently and smoothly in view of the audience, creating an effect similar to the dissolve technique of motion pictures. Anti-literary he explains as follows: The spectator likes visual clarity and we cannot pretend that besides the effect of interpreting a text which is itself literary, that the spectator should be further required to make an effort to interpret the scenery.

designs which, as such, may appear to be mediocre works of art, can create truly inspired theatre once these designs are realized, properly lit and used on stage.

This is a challenging but rather contradictory and confused statement to me. True enough, it is fair enough to say that some of the most original and important modern painters have made some very bad stage designs and ruined some very ambitious spectacles. However, when this did happen, it was always the work of a painter who was not truly interested in the theatre but only in creating for himself a springboard from which to glorify and publicize his own painting. In discussing a very personal style of a painter, which in some instances can be very detrimental to the spectacle, I must clarify exactly what I mean. We must recall, for example, that the very personal style of Picasso was never harmful to the productions which he designed, because he always showed a very keen sense of the theatre and because his designs were always in perfect harmony with the subject, the music and the choreography that were integral parts of the ballet he helped to create. The same thing obviously was true for most of the outstanding painters and designers referred to previously in this essay, and the simple truth in this lies in the fact that these most individual and important painters were also obviously real men of the theatre with a keen understanding of the complex problems of their tasks and not only anxious to put an exhibition of their latest paintings on the stage.

I firmly believe that a distinct personal style is an absolute necessity for everyone in the theatre, be the artist a scene designer, a stage director, a composer, a choreographer, a singer, dancer or an actor, because as a true artist he must beware of creating a style which becomes rapidly a formula, a personality which ends up in being a mere shell. He must watch also that the capacity for experimentation and evolution (in some cases revolution against one's self), of inner

316

growth and expansion should never cease. These arguments seem too obvious to need further pleas for their validity. I agree with Zuffi that some very effective theatre can, at times, be based upon very summary and even mediocre-looking decor sketches and costume plates, but in that case the credit for a visually interesting and successful production must be given to the "executor" or to the scenic director who knew how to transform poor or mediocre looking designs into effective and impressive reality onstage. It may also happen that very good designs will not really contribute to a good show, but that is another matter altogether. Good shows—good productions are rare anyway, because they require such a completely integrated and harmonious fusion of all the essential component parts which have to be equally good, taken separately or together. How many plays, how many operas and ballets that are familiar to us do achieve this happy final integration and that high level of excellency in subject matter, book, music, choreography, stagecraft and decor? Very few indeed—which should not prevent us from giving credit where it is due and to say, for instance, that the decor of Picasso for the ballet *Pulcinella* was splendid and the Stravinsky music for it equally so, although as a complete ballet it didn't quite come off and quickly disappeared from the Diaghilev repertory. It may also happen that exceedingly fine sketches are not well realized and lighted and thus fail to produce the hoped-for effect. It's all part of the difficult and complex game which is the theatre, where defeats heavily outweigh the victories. I firmly believe that the sketches and costume plates a designer makes for a production should be in themselves as beautiful and complete as the final settings and costumes which he hopes to see on the stage. Indeed, historically, we are able to judge the merits and style of the theatre of the past solely by the sketches and costume plates which have survived. The future museum with or without walls of the theatre, will consist of the best

317

designs of our time, whether in originals or reproductions. Future beholders will be much more concerned with the quality and originality of the designs than with anything else—the fact that such or other play, opera, ballet, etc. was or was not a success on stage will hardly matter for future generations. The theatre has always had a very ephemeral life. Indeed the spectacles of Diaghilev which I saw in Paris between 1920 and 1930 are already so much a legend of an almost distant past that it is necessary to go to museums, libraries and archives of the theatre to discover what made the Ballet Russe of that time so famous and to discover what kind of artistic contributions and innovations to modern stage designing were made by Bakst, Benois, Gontcharova, Larionov, Derain, Matisse, Braque, Picasso, Gris, di Chirico, Miro and others.

And what do we know of the stagecraft of the Renaissance and Baroque periods—next to nothing if we do not look at the wonderful stage designs or prints preserved in our museums, libraries or published in the many extant books on theatre design. It is because so many of these sketches are not only so beautiful but so precise and complete that we can truly imagine what the theatre of those periods was like and how truly magnificent and fantastically rich the productions designed by Inigo Jones, Torelli, Burnacini, the Bibiena family and others really were. Without these designs, without the color plates and reproductions that have been made of some of the most interesting and spectacular scenic designs, how would we know or be able to imagine what these representations and productions were like? How would young students and aspiring designers learn about styles of theatrical decoration and costuming of the past? Too many stage designs of the present era are hardly more than stenographic notations or summary jottings of ideas with most of the interpretation left to the imagination or judgement of the executors. It will be quite difficult in the future to gain a real idea of what certain contemporary stage productions really looked like. True, the rapidly increasing use of photography as a spreading means of documentation and information will achieve a great deal toward this end, but only very fragmentarily and incidentally and without giving us the real and immediate sensation of the artistic quality of a given stage production. Historically, I believe, the artist's sketches will always remain the true documents of the stagecraft of a certain period, and the more complete and beautiful in quality the sketches, the more the artist will gain in historical significance and recognition.

For this reason, for the historical validity of the theatre of our times (as for that of yesterday) I believe that the painter-designer-architect-costumier and complete man of the theatre must make the utmost complete and controlled sketches for his productions and follow and watch every detail in the execution of his original ideas in order to achieve the greatest perfection, along with the greatest beauty, utility and functionality of the spectacle he is helping to create on stage.

HAIL *DON GIOVANNI,*
FAREWELL THEATRE

by

Eugene Berman

Since 1936, Eugene Berman has graced the American stage with some of the most striking ballet and opera settings this country has ever seen. And, with the exception of a few continental ballet commissions, Mr. Berman's career as a scenic artist has been primarily American. Yet, in his "farewell" to the theatre he reveals himself uniquely and completely Continental in his aesthetic approach to theatrical art. Unique because he alone, among his American colleagues, embraces the European easel painters' attitudes toward the art of scenic design. Despairing the "production line" methods of producing scenery in America, Eugene Berman complains at the lack of understanding, time and money in America that seldom allows the true artist to execute his own settings, thus stamping them with his personal hallmark of style. Mr. Berman's l'envoi appeared in SATURDAY REVIEW OF LITERATURE, Volume XL, No. 43 (October 26, 1957), pp. 45ff.

Between September 15 and October 28, 1787
—a space of little more than six weeks—Mozart wrote out
and orchestrated his *drammagiocoso, Don Giovanni,* which
is regarded by many as the greatest work ever written for
the operatic stage.

When the curtain rises on the new production of *Don
Giovanni* at the Metropolitan Opera House on October 31,
1957, it will have been the work of a whole year for me to
design and supervise its execution. I received Rudolf Bing's
invitation to design the production last November in Rome,
where I had just taken an apartment in order to live and
paint for the next year or two. To do a production of *Don
Giovanni* was always a cherished dream of mine; this was
the time to do it or never. I gave up the thought of all other
work I was going to do, and started to sketch ideas for the
twelve or thirteen scenes of the opera.

Lest this seems an investment of time peculiar to this particular project, I may mention the production of *Cosi fan
Tutte,* which I designed in 1955 for the opening of the Piccola Scala in Milan. That job, smaller in scope because there
were fewer scene changes and the theatre (built into the
Scala complex for special performances of chamber operas
of the seventeenth and eighteenth centuries), of very limited
dimensions, still took eight months of almost uninterrupted
work.

Why is such a lavish outlay of time and energy necessary
for production designs of operas which were created by
Mozart and his librettist da Ponte in a matter of weeks, a

321

few months at the most? It would seem disproportionate, if not downright absurd to spend so much time on something which obviously could be done much more quickly and simply.

Or could it and should it be done that way?

True, Mozart was a unique genius in the realm of music and to my mind the greatest opera composer who ever lived. True, he had the most astonishing facility to write the most excellent and sublime music *alla prima* for every scene and passage—I doubt there was ever any hesitation in his mind whether an aria or a recitative could go any other way than the one he immediately elected. We know that the famous overture for *Don Giovanni*—one that immediately gives the whole mood and color of the drama—was composed by Mozart the night before the last rehearsal. It was there for eternity—nothing could be better or more appropriate than what he did in those few brief hours, and the same can be said for most of his music.

But this was the mark of his genius and possibly, too, it was the mark of the times. At certain periods, when certain forms of art are at their peak, when everything seems to be crystal clear not only to the leading exponent in a certain field, but when even second- and third-string talents achieve surprisingly good formal results, and appear to be such skillful masters of their craft, there is no doubt, no hesitation, no waste of time, no need for retouching and perfecting one's own work. Things flow easily and convincingly. There is, of course, a difference between the work of a genius and that of the follower, but both may be marked by the same ease, by the same lack of concern and grouping. Even the most creative and novel aspects of art in such periods seem singularly devoid of the effort and strain of creative labor. That is not so in our time—probably the most turbulent, chaotic, and difficult of any period in the history of the arts.

The most acute problem of almost every creative artist

is the question of direction. What to do, where to go, what means are acceptable and significant for our time, what taboos should be respected religiously and which ones is it time to break and eliminate? What is "modern" and what is not? What is truly significant for our generation or just accepted as such? What will tomorrow bring? What aspects —so significant today according to our self-styled experts and judges who mete out indiscriminately pronunciamentos, accolades, and rewards—will be accepted by later generations as truly individualistic and characteristic of our times.

These and some other facets of modern creative working mark the essential difference between the happy, almost innocent spirit of the eighteenth century and our times. Maybe only such a protean figure as Picasso, with his tremendous vitality and his enviable *joie de vivre* and *joie de créer* can escape such dilemmas and such anguish as other artists are facing today. And there is another factor too— the loss of professional ability. In many ways we know so much less, technically and professionally, because no canons, no standards, no traditions have survived in a way that is still acceptable and efficient to the modern mind. So much of what still clings to tradition and to former standards of excellence has become dead letter or has degenerated into such antiquated and corrupt forms and practices that almost anything that reminds the spectator of familiar art forms seems immediately highly suspect—and in many cases, justly so.

Almost everything today requires re-examination, re-discovery of values and new experimentation, even when the acknowledged purpose is to go back for inspiration to a formality of art forms created in previous epochs. Even in the theatre you cannot simply copy styles of painting, architecture, furnishings, and costumes of the eighteenth century, of the Renaissance, or of any other period—not if you want to give a creative interpretation of these periods in terms of

323

the modern theatre. These aspects have to be re-lived, re-experienced, re-created with the taste, critical sense, and awareness of our time, with all the frailty of our nervous system and with the tremendous baggage of information which we can muster today on any subject, any period, any locality. Never before did we have so much material to confront us, to confuse us, and to drive us to despair.

There are other reasons, too, for the slowness and complexity of my work. In Russia, in Central Europe, in France, and other European countries since the turn of the century, theatrical design has been taken out of the hands of the professional scene designers and become the property of the leading modern painters. The most significant and brilliant contribution was made by the late Diaghilev and his famous Ballet Russe. After having promoted and brought to Europe the then most novel and unorthodox theatrical design by Bakst, Golovine, Benois, Larionov, and Gontcharova, Diaghilev quickly turned from these Russian decorative schools and commissioned his designs from Picasso, Braque, Derain, Matisse, Rouault, Miro, de Chirico, and other leading modernists of the French school. The daring and originality of Diaghilev is still unsurpassed in our time, although many of his lesser and less fortunate experiments would seem tame and dated to us.

And so it went. Since Diaghilev's time (and even before) leading painters everywhere (sometimes for the better and at times for worse) have followed the lead and designed most of the outstanding productions in the theatre, ballet, and opera. In France, England, and Italy, it is so almost without exception.

From that can be appreciated the simple fact that the painter who has originally formed his personality outside of the theatre and is known not only for a particular style of his own, but also for a special quality which he puts into his paintings and which is his real trademark, wants to, *has*

324

to put the same quality, the same personal touch into backdrops thirty by fifty feet, canvases, built-pieces, costumes and props, which should all carry the distinctive mark of his mind and his hand. A production which is designed by a real painter should look as if every part of it could have been done only by him alone—just as much as a giant canvas or fresco by a master should have the quality of a small painting or sketch by his own hand, if it is to be considered as one of his best works.

And there is still another reason why the work goes slowly, complexly, for it clashes with all the rules and uses of Broadway stage designing (of stage designing in America, generally), creating many difficulties and obstacles in the way of carrying out successfully the designs of my production. Obviously, if the designer is to insist that the whole production bear not only a very high quality of finish and loving care, but also the firm imprint of his personality, he must depend not only on very expert and highly sensitive collaborators who share his interests and sympathize with his intentions, but he must depend also on a very liberal and understanding management, generous with time and money for a production which requires such a slower and more complex working system and schedule than the usual crude examples of Broadway. For them, no time, loving care, and complex work could be possibly wasted, because no complex imagination, no special subtlety, no loving care went into the original design in the first place.

In the particular case of *Don Giovanni,* the problem is intensified by the nature of the challenge posed by Mozart and da Ponte. A work of two acts, with five scenes in each, it is characterized by music of great fluidity and movement, interspersed, of course, with set pieces—arias and so forth—in which the serious side of the story is projected. Obviously it should be the function of the scenic design to further the

fluidity and movement of the music, certainly not to inter-
fere with it.

However, Mozart did not provide music to cover scenic
changes, as Debussy did in *Pelléas et Mélisande,* for example,
or Wagner arranged for his own convenience (as dramatist as
well as composer) in *Rheingold* or *Götterdämmerung.* The
ritornello or closing passage at the end of an aria like "Il mio
tesoro," is brief, barely enough to get the singers off the
stage. Not much in the way of a scenic change can be accomplished during, or even after, the end of such an aria (even
allowing for applause), without risking serious interruption
in the progress of the music.

Needless to say, it is an even more difficult problem in one
of the older theatres, such as the Metropolitan, which lacks
a turntable or revolving stage on which one setting can be
arranged while another is being played. So we have to utilize
certain unit designs (within an interior proscenium) which
remain in place through much of the performance. We utilize a "traveler" curtain (it acts just like its name) to create
a shallow space in front of the stage in which certain musical
numbers take place while the next scene is being moved in
from the sides, though the Metropolitan, again, is very limited in facilities for this kind of technique.

I saw my first *Don Giovanni* in my early twenties, in
Paris of all places. It was a production at the Opéra Com-
ique, in which the fine baritone Vanni Marcoux played the
Don. He was excellent. The scenic design, probably dating
back some fifty or sixty years and quite old fashioned, had
a kind of Venetian feeling, like an early Canaletto, and it
was surprisingly suitable. How much of *Don Giovanni,*
after all, is really Spanish? Mozart's music certainly derived
from Italian models. This production had a great deal of
charm, and I remember it with pleasure.

I cannot speak much of my own conception, save to say
that it is more related to the 1620-1650 period of Spanish

Eugene Berman

painting than anything else. There are Spanish details in
the windows, for example, or the columns, but it is not
strictly a rendering of Spanish architecture. I feel free to take
liberties within a style, especially when the music dates from
a much later period. But the conception is not without some
Italian elements, too. The costuming, especially for Zerlina,
Masetto, and the other members of the peasantry, is more
predominantly Spanish.

After a year's work, then, my *Don Giovanni* is on the
stage. The period of time is in direct contradiction to every
local procedure. The scenic studio ordinarily entrusted with
the work is apt to regard such insistence on getting better
results as quite unnecessary, something that nobody will
notice anyway, denoting a lack of confidence on the part of
the designer. Actually, the standard procedure seems to be
that the designer should turn over his sketches to a studio
for execution and that the studio will do the rest. The less
he bothers the men who execute and interpret his sketches,
the better his standing in most cases with the management
and the men. No trouble, no criticism and advice, no lag-
ging behind fixed schedules, no overtime and additional expense. If a designer can accumulate and carry out (mostly
with the help of assistants who in turn often employ assistant-
assistants) a respectable number of shows a year, he is a
Broadway genius. If he can grab 50 per cent or more of the
Broadway productions in a year, he is a top genius. After a
few years of such activities, complete with Oscars and Tonys
or other awards, he is ready for either a comfortable retire-
ment or for a career in Hollywood. Or as a Broadway director and producer. It is a purely commercial career, and no
true quality in such working methods could be possibly required and sustained at length.

And that is why my methods of designing for the theatre
in America are so unorthodox and contrary to established
rules. It is also the reason why things are getting to be in-

creasingly difficult for such methods of work, and why *Don Giovanni* is my farewell to the opera and to the theatre in general. Now I have realized my earliest theatrical ambition, with this production of *Don Giovanni*. As far as I can make up my mind now and decide the course of the future, it means taking leave of the theatre for good. Anything after *Don Giovanni* with Dr. Herbert Graf and Karl Bohm, I feel, would be anti-climax. Maybe, later on, a new theatre in New York, with new opportunities, will pose a totally different challenge.

NOTES ON CONTRIBUTORS

HORACE ARMISTEAD. Horace Armistead is eminently qualified to write on ballet design. He worked for years with George Balanchine and Lincoln Kirstein on various ballet projects. He is also a qualified designer of opera decors. Outstanding among his commissions are his settings for Carlo Menotti's operas, *The Telephone, The Medium* and *The Consul;* the Archibald-Bergerson ballet *Far Harbour* for the Ballet Society; Kurt Weill's *Regina* for the New York City Center Opera and Stravinsky's *The Rake's Progress* for the Metropolitan Opera. Mr. Armistead is currently teaching scene design at Boston University.

ALEXANDER BAKSHY. Alexander Bakshy, a Russian expatriate, wrote extensively in London on theatre aesthetics and Russian art and theatre during World War I and immediately thereafter, including *The Path of the Modern Russian Stage* (London, 1916), *Modern Russian Painters* (London, 1917) and *The Theatre Unbound* (London, 1923). His essay on representational and presentational theatre, long out of print, is considered to be a classic.

HOWARD BAY. Howard Bay made his debut as a designer on Broadway with such notable settings as *Marching Song* and *One-Third of a Nation* for Federal Theatre. Settings for *The Little Foxes, The Corn Is Green* and *Brooklyn, U.S.A.* soon typed him as an extremely talented realistic designer. During World War II, however, Bay became known as *the* man to design musical comedies, a reputation he has maintained ever since. Settings for productions such as *Carmen Jones, Up In Central Park, One Touch of Venus, Magdalena, Flahooley* and recently, *The Music Man,* make him a logical choice to write on musical comedy design for this anthology.

329

Notes on Contributors

CECIL BEATON. Best known in this country as a superb photographer (he's royal photographer to the British Crown) Cecil Beaton made his debut as a theatrical designer in 1930 when he was invited to design settings and costumes for Charles B. Cochrane's smart London revue, *Follow the Sun*. Since then he has designed for de Basil's Ballet, Sadlers Wells Ballet, New York City Center Ballet and Ballets des Champs-Élysées of Paris. As a designer of dramatic plays Mr. Beaton made his debut in America with his striking settings and costumes for *Lady Windemere's Fan*. Among many, his decors for *Quadrille* and the costumes for *My Fair Lady* are as handsome as any seen on the American stage during the past decade.

EUGENE BERMAN. An émigré White Russian, Eugene Berman lived in Paris where he studied painting during the twenties. He came to America early in the thirties. Internationally known today as an outstanding easel painter obviously influenced by the Italian Renaissance, Mr. Berman made his debut as a stage designer in Hartford, Connecticut, in 1936. Since then he designed extensively for the ballet (his designs for the American Ballet Theatre's *Romeo and Juliet* a notable example), and since World War II, for the opera. His designs for *Rigoletto, Forza del Destino, Barber of Seville* and *Don Giovanni* which have contributed so much to the renewed popularity of the Metropolitan Opera in recent years, makes his "farewell" (at least to the American theatre) all the more lamentable.

FREDERICK FOX. Even since his debut in 1937, Frederick Fox has been very well established on Broadway. The settings for *Johnny Belinda, The Two Mrs. Carrolls, Anna Lucasta, Darkness at Noon, East of Eden* and *The Reclining Figure* (to select titles at random), are indicative of his work through the years. In 1955 the Metropolitan invited him to design their new production of *Andrea Chénier*. Frederick Fox was one of the first Broadway designers to turn to television design after World War II and for many years his credits were seen weekly on the productions

330

"drags." He designed many of the early Admiral television shows and for five years Mr. Fox was Max Liberman's chief designer for the Sid Caesar Shows and the Max Liberman Saturday Night Spectacles on NBC.

ROLF GÉRARD. Ever since Rudolph Bing took over the Metropolitan Opera company and engaged in a long-ranged plan of restaging and remounting the opera repertoire, Rolf Gérard has been one of his chief designers. Since *Aïda,* his first commission in 1946, his settings and costumes, such as he created for *Cosi fan Tutte,* have continued to captivate Metropolitan operagoers season after season. A busy artist who divides his time designing between America and the Continent, Rolf Gérard spelled out the problems of operatic scene design especially for this anthology.

MORDECAI GORELIK. Mordecai Gorelik has been a designer on Broadway ever since he was apprenticed to Robert Edmond Jones in the early twenties. During the thirties he was the chief designer for The Group Theatre, providing backgrounds for such successes as *Success Story, Men In White, Sailors at Cattore, Golden Boy, Thunder Rock* and *Rocket to the Moon.* Mr. Gorelik has written much on the art of the theatre; his best known work is his history of style in theatre production, *New Theatres for Old* (New York, 1940). A strong advocate, Gorelik has written extensively on Epic Theatre.

HARRY HORNER. A native of Vienna, Harry Horner came to this country in 1937 as Max Reinhardt's assistant when Reinhardt produced *The Eternal Road* in New York. Since that time Mr. Horner has been busy designing legitimate dramas, musical comedies, operas, motion pictures and scenery for television. In addition to *Lady in the Dark,* his notable Broadway assignments included *Family Portrait, The World We Make, Christopher Blake, Hazel Flagg* and *Il Trovatore* and *The Magic Flute* for the Metropolitan. In recent years Mr. Horner has devoted much of his time to motion pictures and television.

331

Notes on Contributors

NORRIS HOUGHTON. The author of the series of interviews, "The Designer Sets the Stage," is a scene designer in his own right with the decors for Broadway hits like *A Trip To Bali* and *How To Get Tough About It* to his credit. He has served as associate editor of *Theatre Arts Monthly,* is the author of *Advance of Broadway* (New York, 1941) and *Moscow Rehearsals* (New York, 1936) and recently, one of the founders and producers of the Phoenix Theatre in New York.

ROBERT EDMOND JONES. Robert Edmond Jones was one of the founders of the new stagecraft in America. Ever since his history-making designs for *The Man Who Married a Dumb Wife* in 1915, Mr. Jones held a position of prominence in the American theatre, providing settings for some of the most important productions of the twentieth century, including *Mourning Becomes Electra, Desire Under the Elms, Ah Wilderness, Green Pastures, The Iceman Cometh,* the Arthur Hopkins-John Barrymore productions of Shakespeare, and in the last years of his career, the exquisitely lovely *Lute Song.* His book, *The Dramatic Imagination* (New York, 1941) is one of the finest of its kind in the literature of the theatre.

LEO KERZ. Leo Kerz is another designer who emigrated to this country after the second world war. Mr. Kerz made his debut as a Broadway designer providing the striking settings for the Katherine Cornell production of *Anthony and Cleopatra* in 1947. Since then he has designed for the theatre, motion pictures and television. Of late, he has turned his attention to producing.

ALINE LOUCHHEIM. Mrs. Aline Louchheim Saarinen has been an art critic and staff writer on fine arts for the Sunday *New York Times* for many years.

KENNETH MACGOWAN. Critic, director, author, producer and teacher, Kenneth Macgowan has contributed much to the contemporary American theatre. He is one of the few critics still living who witnessed the development of the new stagecraft. Macgowan has written for numerous periodicals such as *Century*

Magazine, Theatre Magazine, Theatre Arts Magazine and published *The Theatre of Tomorrow* (New York, 1921), *Continental Stagecraft* (with Robert Edmond Jones, New York, 1922), *Footlights Across America* (New York, 1929) and *A Primer of Playwriting* (New York, 1951). He has also been chairman of the Department of Theatre Arts, University of California, Los Angeles.

JO MIELZINER. Ever since his debut on Broadway in 1924 with his settings for the Theatre Guild's production of *The Guardsman,* Jo Mielziner has designed more than 225 productions for Broadway. He is one of New York's busiest designers and the list of his recent commissions reads like the record of Broadway's hits since the second world war. Although he has expressed himself often on the theatre, its art and architecture, in interview-articles like "Script to Stage: Case History of a Set," Mr. Mielziner himself has not written as extensively on theatrical art and aesthetics as some of his colleagues.

DONALD OENSLAGER. Donald Oenslager made his debut as a designer at The Neighborhood Playhouse in 1925, and since then has designed extensively for legitimate drama, musical comedy and opera. *Girl Crazy, Tristan and Isolde, Of Mice and Men, The Fabulous Invalid, Pygmalion, Otello, The Man Who Came to Dinner, Born Yesterday* and *The Ballad of Baby Doe* are indicative of his versatility. For many years too, Mr. Oenslager has taught scene design at the School of Drama, Yale University, successfully combining a professional and an academic career. Author of *Scenery, Then and Now* (New York, 1936), Mr. Oenslager has contributed to numerous periodicals on stage design.

LEE SIMONSON. Together with Robert Edmond Jones, Lee Simonson is considered one of the founders of the "new stagecraft" in America. As a founding member of the Theatre Guild and for many years one of its directors and its chief designer,

Notes on Contributors

Mr. Simonson, like Mr. Jones has created settings for many important productions including *Back to Methuselah, Marco Millions, Road to Rome, Goat Song, Idiot's Delight, He Who Gets Slapped* and *Amphitryon 38*. Recently, he redesigned *The Ring* cycle for the Metropolitan Opera. Mr. Simonson is equally well known as a writer, lecturer and theatre historian. In addition to *The Stage Is Set* (New York, 1932), Simonson has written the autobiographical *Part of a Lifetime* (New York, 1943) and *The Art of Scenic Design* (New York, 1950).

OLIVER SMITH. Oliver Smith's settings for the Agnes de Mille ballet *Rodeo* in 1942 (his debut) established him immediately as a scene designer of consequence. The decors of *Fall River Legend, Fancy Free* and *Onstage* (for ballet), *On The Town, Billion Dollar Baby* (which he helped produce), *Brigadoon, Gentlemen Prefer Blondes, My Fair Lady* (musical comedy), *In The Summer House, The Burning Glass, A Clearing in the Woods* (drama) and *Guys and Dolls, Oklahoma!, Band Wagon* and *Porgy and Bess* (recently for·the movies) are indicative of the extent and caliber of his activities.

SOINTU SYRJALA. Perhaps Syrjala is not as well-known a Broadway stage designer as some of his colleagues, although he has such hits as *The Fourposter* to his credit. Mr. Syrjala is eminently qualified to write on television design. During the six and one-half years Robert Montgomery produced the Robert Montgomery Presents dramatic show on NBC television, Mr. Syrjala served as his principal designer creating new moods and backgrounds every week.

STARK YOUNG. Critic emeritus of the *Theatre Arts Magazine, New Republic* and the *New York Times,* Stark Young has written and lectured extensively on the theatre. His published works include *The Flower of the Drama* (New York, 1923), *Glamour* (New York, 1925), *The Theatre* (New York, 1927) and *Immortal Shadows* (New York, 1948).

334